T0301692

Research Advances in Intelligent Computing

Researchers and scientists have invested a great deal of effort into developing computers and other devices to be more capable of doing a wider range of tasks. As a result, the potential of computers to do a wide range of tasks in different environments, at varying speeds, and in smaller forms is growing dramatically every day. Currently, there is a race to create robots or computers with human-level intelligence. Artificial Intelligence (AI) is the ability of a machine or software to think like a human being. The study of the human brain, specifically how humans learn, make decisions, and react when trying to solve issues, is the basis of AI. The creation of intelligent software and systems, or intelligent computing (IC), is the outcome of AI studies. An IC system can perceive, reason, learn, and use language. In IC systems, AI and other cutting-edge techniques are employed to give system intelligence. IC has been applied to almost every area of computer science, including networking, software engineering, gaming, robotics, expert systems, natural language processing, computer vision, image processing, and data science. In modern times, IC is also employed to tackle a wide range of challenging issues in numerous disciplines, such as weather forecasting, agriculture science, medicine, and economics. This book offers the most recent advancements in both IC and AI for all these reasons.

Research Advances in Intelligent Computing

Volume 2

Edited by
Anshul Verma and Pradeepika Verma

CRC Press
Taylor & Francis Group
Boca Raton London New York

CRC Press is an imprint of the
Taylor & Francis Group, an **informa** business

Designed cover image: © Shutterstock

First edition published 2025
by CRC Press
2385 NW Executive Center Drive, Suite 320, Boca Raton FL 33431

and by CRC Press
4 Park Square, Milton Park, Abingdon, Oxon, OX14 4RN

CRC Press is an imprint of Taylor & Francis Group, LLC

© 2025 selection and editorial matter, Anshul Verma and Pradeepika Verma; individual chapters, the contributors

ISBN: 9781032561165 (hbk)
ISBN: 9781032561172 (pbk)
ISBN: 9781003433941 (ebk)

DOI: 10.1201/9781003433941

Typeset in Sabon
by KnowledgeWorks Global Ltd.

Contents

About the editors

Dr. Anshul Verma received his M.Tech. and Ph.D. degrees in Computer Science & Engineering from the ABV-Indian Institute of Information Technology and Management, Gwalior, India. He has done postdoctorate work at the Indian Institute of Technology Kharagpur, India. Currently, he is serving as Assistant Professor in the Department of Computer Science, Institute of Science, Banaras Hindu University, Varanasi, India. He has also served as Faculty Member in Computer Science & Engineering Department, Motilal Nehru National Institute of Technology (MNNIT), Allahabad, and National Institute of Technology (NIT), Jamshedpur, India. His research interests include IoT, mobile ad hoc networks, distributed systems, formal verification, and mobile computing. He is serving as Editor of the *Journal of Scientific Research* of Banaras Hindu University.

Dr. Pradeepika Verma received her Ph.D. degree in Computer Science and Engineering from the Indian Institute of Technology (ISM), Dhanbad, India. She has received M.Tech degree in Computer Science and Engineering from Banasthali University, Rajasthan, India. Currently, she is working as Faculty Fellow in Technology Innovation Hub at the Indian Institute of Technology, Patna, India. She has worked as a postdoctoral fellow in the Department of Computer Science and Engineering at the Indian Institute of Technology (BHU), Varanasi, India. She has also worked as Assistant Professor in the Department of Computer Science and Engineering at Pranveer Singh Institute of Technology, Kanpur, India, and as Faculty Member in the Department of Computer Application at the Institute of Engineering and Technology, Lucknow, India. Her current research interests include natural language processing, optimization approaches, information retrieval, and mobile ad hoc networks.

List of contributors

Mitul Kumar Ahirwal is at Maulana Azad National Institute of Technology, Bhopal, Madhya Pradesh, India.

Sanika Ardekar is at Dwarkadas J. Sanghvi College of Engineering, Mumbai, Maharashtra, India.

Mishachandar B. is at Vellore Institute of Technology, Amravati, Andhra Pradesh, India.

Arunkumar Balakrishnan is at Vellore Institute of Technology, Amravati, Andhra Pradesh, India.

Riya Bihani is at Dwarkadas J. Sanghvi College of Engineering, Mumbai, Maharashtra, India.

Alexander E.I. Brownlee is at University of Stirling, Stirling, United Kingdom.

Mukkoti Maruthi Venkata Chalapathi is at Vellore Institute of Technology, Amravati, Andhra Pradesh, India.

Khushi Chavan is at Dwarkadas J. Sanghvi College of Engineering, Mumbai, Maharashtra, India.

Rajkumar Dhakar is at ICAR Indian Agricultural Research Institute, New Delhi, India.

Durai Selvaraj is at Vel Tech Rangarajan Dr. Sagunthala R&D Institute of Science and Technology, Chennai, Tamil Nadu, India.

Tanay Gandhi is at Dwarkadas J. Sanghvi College of Engineering, Mumbai, Maharashtra, India.

Sushopti D. Gawade is at Pillai College of Engineering, Mumbai, Maharashtra, India.

M. Mohamed Iqbal is at Vellore Institute of Technology, Amravati, Andhra Pradesh, India.

Yash Jhaveri is at Dwarkadas J. Sanghvi College of Engineering, Mumbai, Maharashtra, India.

Yash Joshi is at Dwarkadas J. Sanghvi College of Engineering, Mumbai, Maharashtra, India.

Brahma Naidu K. is at ICFAI Foundation for Higher Education (IFHE), Hyderabad, Telangana, India.

Adi Narayana Reddy K. is at ICFAI Foundation for Higher Education (IFHE), Hyderabad, Telangana, India.

Srinivasa Reddy K. is at Vellore Institute of Technology, Amravati, Andhra Pradesh, India

Prerna Kamani is at Jamia Hamdard, New Delhi, India

Praneeth Kanagala is at University of the Cumberlands, Williamsburg, KY.

Pratik Kanani is at Dwarkadas J. Sanghvi College of Engineering, Mumbai, Maharashtra, India.

Malvika Kanojia is at Jamia Hamdard, New Delhi, India.

Gautam Siddharth Kashyap is at Jamia Hamdard, New Delhi, India.

Aniket Kore is at Dwarkadas J. Sanghvi College of Engineering, Mumbai, Maharashtra, India.

Lalit Kumar is at Maulana Azad National Institute of Technology, Bhopal, Madhya Pradesh, India.

Karan Malik is at Arizona State University, Tempe, AZ.

Varun Mehta is at Dwarkadas J. Sanghvi College of Engineering, Mumbai, Maharashtra, India.

Nancy Nadar is at Dwarkadas J. Sanghvi College of Engineering, Mumbai, Maharashtra, India.

Manish Pandey is at Maulana Azad National Institute of Technology, Bhopal, Madhya Pradesh, India.

Abirami Parthiban is at Vellore Institute of Technology, Amravati, Andhra Pradesh, India.

Deepkumar Patel is at Dwarkadas J. Sanghvi College of Engineering, Mumbai, Maharashtra, India.

Nilesh Patil is at Dwarkadas J. Sanghvi College of Engineering, Mumbai, Maharashtra, India.

Naga Simhadri Apparao Polireddi is at IKON Tech Services LLC, Phoenix, AZ.

A. Mallikarjuna Reddy is at Anurag University, Hyderabad, Telangana, India.

Vairamuthu S. is at Vellore Institute of Technology, Amravati, Andhra Pradesh, India.

Vinay Kumar Sehgal is at ICAR Indian Agricultural Research Institute, New Delhi, India.

Devang Shah is at Dwarkadas J. Sanghvi College of Engineering, Mumbai, Maharashtra, India.

Vishakha Shelke is at Dwarkadas J. Sanghvi College of Engineering, Mumbai, Maharashtra, India.

Mithun Shivakoti is at Vellore Institute of Technology, Amravati, Andhra Pradesh, India.

Ayesha Siddiqui is at Friedrich Alexander Universität Erlangen Nürnberg, Bavaria, Germany.

Ramsha Siddiqui is at Friedrich Alexander Universität Erlangen Nürnberg, Bavaria, Germany.

Samar Wazir is at Jamia Hamdard, New Delhi, India.

Jinesh Melvin Y. I. is at Pillai College of Engineering, Mumbai, Maharashtra, India.

Preface

OVERVIEW AND GOALS

As the computers and other machines have been developed, researchers and scientists have worked very hard to increase their capacity to carry out a variety of jobs. Thus, computers' capabilities in terms of varied working areas, adaptable duties, processing speed, and smaller size are increasing exponentially every day. We are currently competing to develop machines or computers that are as intelligent as people. Making a computer or a piece of software think like a smart human being is what artificial intelligence (AI) is all about. AI is influenced by the study of the human brain, namely, how people make decisions, learn, and respond when attempting to solve any problem. The findings of this study serve as the foundation for creating intelligent systems and software or intelligent computing (IC). An IC system is capable of learning, reasoning, solving problems, perceiving, and using language. AI and other cutting-edge approaches that provide a system intelligence are used in IC systems. Virtually every branch of computer science has seen the use of intelligent computing, including networking, software engineering, gaming, natural language processing, computer vision, image processing, data science, robotics, expert systems, and security. Today, IC is also used to resolve a variety of complicated problems in many different fields, including disease prediction in medicine, crop productivity prediction in agriculture science, market growth prediction in economics, weather forecasting, etc. For all of these reasons, this book provides the most recent developments in AI as well as IC. In this perspective, the book contains the most recent research on machine learning, neural networks, deep learning, evolutionary algorithms, genetic algorithms, swarm intelligence, fuzzy systems, and other related topics.

TARGET AUDIENCE

This book will be beneficial for academicians, researchers, developers, engineers, and practitioners working in or interested in the research trends and applications of artificial and computational intelligence. This book is expected to serve as a reference book for developers and engineers working in the intelligent computing domain and for those pursuing a graduate/ postgraduate course in computer science and engineering/information technology.

Acknowledgments

We are extremely thankful to the authors of this 14-chapter book, who have worked very hard to bring this unique resource forward for helping students, researchers, and community practitioners. We feel that it is important to mention that as the individual chapters of this book are written by different authors, the responsibility of the contents of each of the chapters lies with the relevant authors for the chapter/s.

We would like to thank Randi Cohen, Publisher – Computer Science & IT, and Gabriella Williams, Editor, who worked with us on the project from the beginning for their professionalism. We also thank all the team members of the publisher who tirelessly worked with us and helped us in the publication process.

This book is a part of the research work funded by "Seed Grant to Faculty Members under IoE Scheme (under Dev. Scheme No. 6031)" awarded to Anshul Verma at Banaras Hindu University, Varanasi, India.

Chapter 1

A new method of range selection in global best–worst particle swarm optimization

*Lalit Kumar, Manish Pandey,
and Mitul Kumar Ahirwal*

1.1 INTRODUCTION

Metaheuristic algorithms (MAs) have been rapidly inspiring the nature-inspired swarm-based algorithms for high-dimensional optimization problems. The particle swarm optimization (PSO) algorithm is one of the main population-based algorithms inspired by the flight pattern of bird species [1, 2]. In the past few years, many improvements have been made in PSO [3–6] to get an optimal solution by using different initialization strategies, hybridization of equations, updated strategies, etc. [7]. Recently, Kumar et al. [8] proposed Global Best–Worst Particle Swarm Optimization (GBWPSO) which is a fully inherent parallel version of PSO by modifying the equations and strategy of PSO.

There are known shortcomings of most MAs [7, 9, 10]. When these algorithms are applied to a large amount of data in a high-dimensional search space, data should effectively be analyzed in a high dimension, slowing down the process to reach an optimal solution. In other words, higher exploration rate slows down the process or may not provide a real solution, and higher exploitation rate may make the process converge faster resulting in a premature resolution and lack of a global solution [11–13]. Binkley and Hagiwara [11] used velocity-based reinitialization approach to improve the optimum solution of PSO by providing a balance between exploitation and exploration of process. In 2013, Arani et al. [14] proposed a collision operator in PSO to control the movement of the algorithm throughout the search process. An adaptive exploration robotic PSO has been proposed by Garg et al. [15] to enhance the chances of exploring unexplored regions by adapting inertia weights. Rao and Yan [16] proposed a new version of PSO based on the information-sharing mechanism and competition strategy to enhance the global search ability. It is therefore important to find an approach that enhances the search space in terms of local and global search processes.

In this chapter, an innovative and simple Range Selection (RS) approach has been introduced in GBWPSO, Range Selection in Global Best–Worst Particle Swarm Optimization (RSGBWPSO), for exploration and refinement of search space to ensure its convergence to a global optimum. The RSGBWPSO

DOI: 10.1201/9781003433941-1

1

algorithm is tested by several benchmark functions. Compared to the GBWPSO algorithm, the RSGBWPSO has been found to achieve superior performance in terms of global solution value for the same number of iterations used in GBWPSO.

In Section 1.2, we will introduce the related work of the GBWPSO algorithm. Then we will discuss the basic idea of proposed RSGBWPSO with flow of implementation in Section 1.3. Section 1.4 provides the experimental results of proposed algorithm with their analysis. Finally, Section 1.5 concludes the chapter with a discussion on the scope of future work.

1.2 GLOBAL BEST–WORST PARTICLE SWARM OPTIMIZATION

GBWPSO algorithm is an extended version of PSO proposed by Kumar et al. [8]. It is based on the principle of Jaya algorithm, meaning tracking the path of the global best particle and avoiding the global worst particle. In other words, the velocity of the particle is improved using the updation equation of the Jaya algorithm.

Algorithm 1: Global Best–Worst Particle Swarm Optimization

Inputs: Population/Swarm size N, Number of dimensions M, Number of maximum iterations R, Acceleration constants $\psi_1 = \psi_2 = 1.5$
   Output: Solution with best fitness value (Optimal Solution)
   Perform Optimization:

   1: *For i = 1,…, N*
   2: Initialize Vel_i and Pos_i of particle randomly
   3: Calculate fitness of particle using objective function
   4: *End of For*
   5: *While* number of maximum iterations are not met
   6: Choose *best* (Pos_{best}) and *worst* (Pos_{worst}) solutions
   7: *For i = 1,…, N*
   8: Update the velocity and position of particle using Equations (1.1) and (1.2):

$$Vel_i^m(r+1) = w * Vel_i^m(r) + c_1 b_1 * \left(Pos_{best} - \left| Pos_i^m(r) \right| \right)$$

$$-c_2 b_2 * \left(Pos_{worst} - \left| Pos_i^m(r) \right| \right) \tag{1.1}$$

$$Pos_i^m(r+1) = Pos_i^m(r) + Vel_i^m(r+1) \tag{1.2}$$

   9: *If* fitness of updated particle ≤ fitness of previous particle **then**
   10: Replace the previous particle with the updated particle

11: *Else* Retain the original particle as it is
12: *End If*
13: *End of For*
14: *End of **while** loop*

In the above algorithm, *Vel* shows the velocity of particular particle, *Pos* refers to the position of particular particle, r is the latest iteration, m is the particular dimension of particle, inertia weight is taken as $w = 1$, h_1 and h_2 are the random numbers in (0, 1), and Ψ_1 and Ψ_2 are the positive acceleration constants. Figure 1.1 shows the flow diagram of GBWPSO.

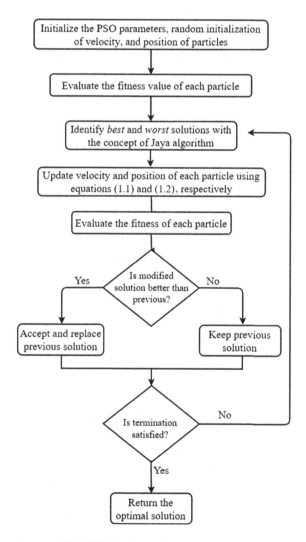

Figure 1.1 Flow diagram of GBWPSO.

1.3 PROPOSED RANGE SELECTION APPROACH IN GBWPSO

MAs with huge amount of data and domain should be effectively analyzed in terms of exploitation and exploration to achieve optimal solution for any particular problem. Here we have presented a range selection approach which provides best range to the particles within the search space (domain). Basically, this approach provides better global optimal solution and overcomes the limitations of MAs [3] such as premature convergence and slowdown of algorithm's process. In this approach, we first divide the total population and range in P and R partitions, respectively, where $P = R$. There are equal numbers of particles in each partition of the population. So, we have $P*R$ total combinations of population partitions with the respective range. Each combination uses the GBWPSO algorithm for one iteration and finds optimal value individually. At last, we have to find the average of all the optimal values with respect to each range and provide the best range based on the behavior of optimization problem. Now, the total population with selected best range and remaining iterations are provided to the GBWPSO algorithm for achieving improved optimal solution. Figure 1.2 shows the implementation process of proposed approach.

1.4 EXPERIMENTAL RESULTS

1.4.1 Benchmark functions

The performance of the proposed RSGBWPSO method is tested using several experiments performed on different benchmark functions from References [17, 18] with different properties. Table 1.1 shows the functions with their bounded ranges and global minimum value, where dimension, search space size, and optimum solution are represented as M, $Lb \leq x_i \leq Ub$, and $f(X^*)$ respectively.

1.4.2 Experiment results and discussions

In this work, the swarm size is assumed to be 40/80/100 and the dimension to be 10/50/500/1000/1500/4000 for all functions with a fixed number of maximum iterations of 30 (Tables 1.2–1.4) [19]. Both algorithms—GBWPSO and RSGBWPSO—are used to collect the experimental results from ten independent runs, each run including 30 iterations for each benchmark function. Table 1.2 shows the data obtained from ten independent runs of the two mentioned algorithms in terms of mean (average of optimal values), best (minimum of optimal values), worst (maximum of optimal values), and Std. (standard deviation between optimal values). Also, Figure 1.3 shows the graphical representation of mean function optimal value for both the functions on the

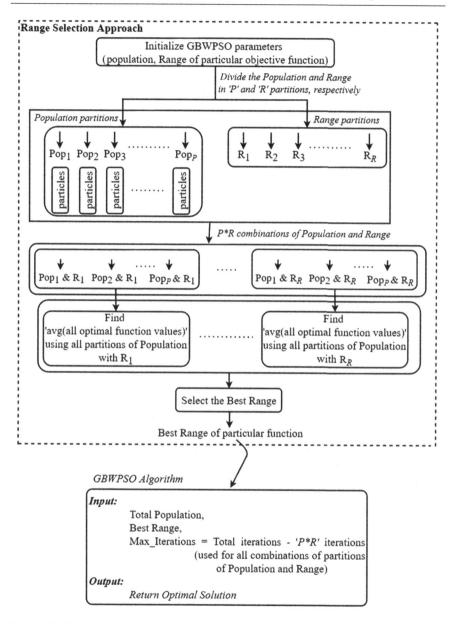

Figure 1.2 Flow diagram of proposed algorithm.

above-mentioned algorithms with various population size and dimension. From Figure 1.3, we can see that proposed RSGBWPSO has the high ability to reach the global optimum for all functions used in this study within the same number of maximum iterations as used in the original GBWPSO.

Table 1.1 Details of benchmark functions

Name of function	Nature	Function	Domain	Global minima (optimal solution)
Powell Sum	Unimodal	$f_1(X)=\sum_{i=1}^{M}|x_i|^{i+1}$	$-1\le x_i \le 1$	$f_1(X^*)=0$
Ackley	Multimodal	$f_2(X)=\exp(1)$	$-32\le x_i \le 32$	$f_2(X^*)=0$

$$-20\cdot\exp\left(-0.2\sqrt{\frac{1}{M}\sum_{i=1}^{M}x_i^2}\right)$$

$$\exp\left(\frac{1}{M}\sum_{i=1}^{M}\cos(2\pi x_i)\right)+20$$

Table 1.2 Comparison of optimal solutions on GBWPSO and RSGBWPSO for swarm size 40

Functions	Experiment details (Pop = 40, Max_itr = 30)	GBWPSO Mean value	Best value	Worst value	Std.	RSGBWPSO (for 'P = R = 4') Mean value	Best value	Worst value	Std.
f_1	Dim = 10	7.33 E^{-03}	3.52 E^{-03}	1.60 E^{-02}	3.50 E^{-03}	**1.64 E^{-04}**	3.67 E^{-09}	5.27 E^{-04}	2.22 E^{-04}
	Dim = 50	6.43 E^{-03}	3.71 E^{-03}	1.28 E^{-02}	2.73 E^{-03}	**9.53 E^{-05}**	2.30 E^{-06}	2.21 E^{-04}	8.41 E^{-05}
	Dim = 500	1.24 E^{-02}	4.41 E^{-03}	2.69 E^{-02}	7.31 E^{-03}	**9.33 E^{-05}**	7.59 E^{-06}	2.11 E^{-04}	6.57 E^{-05}
	Dim = 1000	1.96 E^{-02}	4.99 E^{-03}	9.21 E^{-02}	2.58 E^{-02}	**1.12 E^{-04}**	5.98 E^{-06}	3.49 E^{-04}	1.21 E^{-04}
	Dim = 1500	1.48 E^{-02}	4.63 E^{-03}	2.43 E^{-02}	5.62 E^{-03}	**4.31 E^{-04}**	4.87 E^{-05}	1.81 E^{-03}	5.19 E^{-04}
	Dim = 4000	5.68 E^{-02}	1.30 E^{-02}	1.04 E^{-01}	2.32 E^{-02}	**3.17 E^{-04}**	5.36 E^{-05}	9.68 E^{-04}	3.40 E^{-04}
f_2	Dim = 10	1.29 E^{+01}	1.12 E^{+01}	1.53 E^{+01}	1.32 E^{+00}	**2.43 E^{-01}**	1.55 E^{-02}	3.84 E^{-01}	1.25 E^{-01}
	Dim = 50	1.57 E^{+01}	1.48 E^{+01}	1.73 E^{+01}	6.47 E^{-01}	**8.15 E^{-01}**	6.27 E^{-01}	9.28 E^{-01}	9.70 E^{-02}
	Dim = 500	1.73 E^{+01}	1.66 E^{+01}	1.77 E^{+01}	4.10 E^{-01}	**1.15 E^{+00}**	1.13 E^{+00}	1.17 E^{+00}	1.14 E^{-02}
	Dim = 1000	1.74 E^{+01}	1.68 E^{+01}	1.79 E^{+01}	3.35 E^{-01}	**1.17 E^{+00}**	1.15 E^{+00}	1.18 E^{+00}	1.02 E^{-02}
	Dim = 1500	1.74 E^{+01}	1.68 E^{+01}	1.78 E^{+01}	2.55 E^{-01}	**1.17 E^{+00}**	1.16 E^{+00}	1.19 E^{+00}	1.14 E^{-02}
	Dim = 4000	1.77 E^{+01}	1.72 E^{+01}	1.82 E^{+01}	3.87 E^{-01}	**1.19 E^{+00}**	1.17 E^{+00}	1.20 E^{+00}	8.31 E^{-03}

1.5 CONCLUSIONS AND FUTURE DIRECTIONS

A range selection approach RSGBWPSO has been proposed. This approach achieved the best suitable range for total population within the same number of maximum iteration for all the steps as used in the original GBWPSO. Powell Sum and Ackley functions are used to examine the proposed approach for optimal solution. From the results, it can be very well concluded that RSGBWPSO approach outperformed GBWPSO in terms of fitness value (objective function value). The proposed RSGBWPSO algorithm is more

Table 1.3 Comparison of optimal solutions on GBWPSO and RSGBWPSO for swarm size 80

Functions	Experiment details (Pop = 80, Max_itr = 30)	GBWPSO				RSGBWPSO (for 'P = R = 4')			
		Mean value	Best value	Worst value	Std.	Mean value	Best value	Worst value	Std.
f_1	Dim = 10	5.65 E^{-03}	1.64 E^{-03}	1.27 E^{-02}	3.58 E^{-03}	**1.19 E^{-04}**	8.68 E^{-10}	4.70 E^{-04}	1.35 E^{-04}
	Dim = 50	7.10 E^{-03}	1.12 E^{-03}	1.37 E^{-02}	3.40 E^{-03}	**4.92 E^{-05}**	1.73 E^{-06}	1.33 E^{-04}	4.35 E^{-05}
	Dim = 500	7.36 E^{-03}	4.53 E^{-03}	1.23 E^{-02}	2.48 E^{-03}	**6.42 E^{-05}**	1.83 E^{-07}	1.84 E^{-04}	7.17 E^{-05}
	Dim = 1000	6.30 E^{-03}	3.40 E^{-03}	1.30 E^{-02}	2.81 E^{-03}	**1.38 E^{-05}**	2.30 E^{-06}	2.32 E^{-05}	6.68 E^{-06}
	Dim = 1500	1.05 E^{-02}	6.29 E^{-03}	1.76 E^{-02}	3.40 E^{-03}	**2.23 E^{-05}**	3.54 E^{-07}	9.98 E^{-05}	3.01E^{-05}
	Dim = 4000	4.61 E^{-02}	1.03 E^{-02}	1.88 E^{-01}	5.38 E^{-02}	**3.39 E^{-05}**	1.49 E^{-06}	8.05 E^{-05}	2.70 E^{-05}
f_2	Dim = 10	1.26 E^{+01}	8.78 E^{+00}	1.44 E^{+01}	1.49 E^{+00}	**5.79 E^{-02}**	−4.44 E^{-16}	1.42 E^{-01}	5.58 E^{-02}
	Dim = 50	1.55 E^{+01}	1.45 E^{+01}	1.64 E^{+01}	6.34 E^{-01}	**7.88 E^{-01}**	7.18 E^{-01}	8.68 E^{-01}	4.93 E^{-02}
	Dim = 500	1.68 E^{+01}	1.65 E^{+01}	1.73 E^{+01}	2.63 E^{-01}	**1.12 E^{+00}**	1.10 E^{+00}	1.14 E^{+00}	1.32 E^{-02}
	Dim = 1000	1.72 E^{+01}	1.68 E^{+01}	1.76 E^{+01}	2.16 E^{-01}	**1.15 E^{+00}**	1.13 E^{+00}	1.17 E^{+00}	1.01 E^{-02}
	Dim = 1500	1.74 E^{+01}	1.70 E^{+01}	1.77 E^{+01}	2.46 E^{-01}	**1.16 E^{+00}**	1.14 E^{+00}	1.18 E^{+00}	1.05 E^{-02}
	Dim = 4000	1.72 E^{+01}	1.67 E^{+01}	1.79 E^{+01}	4.24 E^{-01}	**1.17 E^{+00}**	1.16 E^{+00}	1.18 E^{+00}	6.69 E^{-03}

Table 1.4 Comparison of optimal solutions on GBWPSO and RSGBWPSO for swarm size 100

Functions	Experiment details (Pop = 100, Max_itr = 30)	GBWPSO				RSGBWPSO (for 'P = R = 4')			
		Mean value	Best value	Worst value	Std.	Mean value	Best value	Worst value	Std.
f_1	Dim = 10	3.42 E^{-03}	4.96 E^{-04}	6.47 E^{-03}	1.55 E^{-03}	**2.54 E^{-05}**	0.00 E^{+00}	9.49 E^{-05}	3.60 E^{-05}
	Dim = 50	7.98 E^{-03}	4.07 E^{-03}	1.55 E^{-02}	3.84 E^{-03}	**2.70 E^{-05}**	2.27 E^{-06}	1.93 E^{-04}	5.86 E^{-05}
	Dim = 500	5.07 E^{-03}	2.51 E^{-03}	9.08 E^{-03}	2.54 E^{-03}	**2.22 E^{-05}**	2.46 E^{-08}	4.30 E^{-05}	1.70 E^{-05}
	Dim = 1000	8.60 E^{-03}	2.72 E^{-03}	1.44 E^{-02}	3.82 E^{-03}	**1.96 E^{-05}**	1.89 E^{-06}	5.37 E^{-05}	1.91 E^{-05}
	Dim = 1500	9.29 E^{-03}	3.22 E^{-03}	2.47 E^{-02}	6.32 E^{-03}	**5.04 E^{-05}**	4.03 E^{-06}	1.28 E^{-04}	4.81 E^{-05}
	Dim = 4000	2.97 E^{-02}	8.48 E^{-03}	1.17 E^{-01}	3.28 E^{-02}	**2.30 E^{-05}**	9.48 E^{-07}	7.46 E^{-05}	2.34 E^{-05}
f_2	Dim = 10	1.19 E^{+01}	1.04 E^{+01}	1.42 E^{+01}	1.10 E^{+00}	**8.17 E^{-02}**	−4.44 E^{-16}	2.04 E^{-01}	6.58 E^{-02}
	Dim = 50	1.51 E^{+01}	1.47 E^{+01}	1.58 E^{+01}	3.33 E^{-01}	**8.23 E^{-01}**	7.71 E^{-01}	8.86 E^{-01}	3.71 E^{-02}
	Dim = 500	1.69 E^{+01}	1.63 E^{+01}	1.75 E^{+01}	4.16 E^{-01}	**1.10 E^{+00}**	1.09 E^{+00}	1.12 E^{+00}	1.14 E^{-02}
	Dim = 1000	1.72 E^{+01}	1.65 E^{+01}	1.78 E^{+01}	4.48 E^{-01}	**1.14 E^{+00}**	1.13 E^{+00}	1.16 E^{+00}	9.30 E^{-03}
	Dim = 1500	1.71 E^{+01}	1.64 E^{+01}	1.78 E^{+01}	3.93 E^{-01}	**1.15 E^{+00}**	1.14 E^{+00}	1.17 E^{+00}	1.05 E^{-02}
	Dim = 4000	1.73 E^{+01}	1.70 E^{+01}	1.77 E^{+01}	2.75 E^{-01}	**1.16 E^{+00}**	1.15 E^{+00}	1.17 E^{+00}	6.60 E^{-03}

effective compared with GBWPSO since it achieves the better optimal function value within the same number of maximum iterations as used in GBWPSO. Results show that optimal solution achieved by proposed method is approximately 99% and 94% better than GBWPSO for Powell Sum and Ackley functions, respectively. Experiments show that the ability to explore and refine the search space makes the proposed method applicable to both unimodal and multimodal functions. Some future research needs to be done

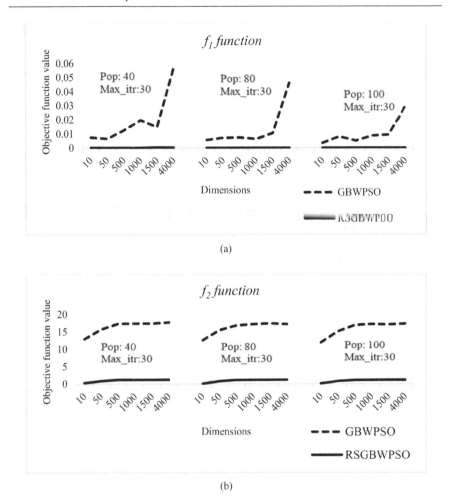

Figure 1.3 Optimal value on different population and the dimension on each function. (a) Powell Sum function. (b) Ackley function.

on the proposed method. First, we will test the RSGBWPSO for more complex benchmark functions. Second, we will use RSGBWPSO method to solve the complex real-world applications. Finally, we will provide some modification to make all the processes of proposed algorithm in both serial and parallel mode so that RSGBWPSO achieves better solution even in less computation.

REFERENCES

1. Kennedy, J.: Particle swarm optimization. In: Encyclopedia of Machine Learning, pp. 760–766, Springer, New York (2011)

2. Marini, F., & Walczak, B.: Particle swarm optimization (PSO): A tutorial. In: Chemometrics and Intelligent Laboratory Systems, 149, pp. 153–165 (2015)
3. Patel, V. P., Rawat, M. K., & Patel, A. S.: Analysis of search space in the domain of swarm intelligence. In: Proceedings of International Conference on Machine Intelligence and Data Science Applications, pp. 99–109, Springer, Singapore (2021)
4. Kumar, L., & Bharti, K. K.: A novel hybrid BPSO–SCA approach for feature selection. In: Natural Computing, 20, pp. 39–61 (2019)
5. Boudt, K., & Wan, C.: The effect of velocity sparsity on the performance of cardinality constrained particle swarm optimization. In: Optimization Letters, 14(3), pp. 747–758 (2020)
6. Orlando, C., & Ricciardello, A.: Analytic solution of the continuous particle swarm optimization problem. In: Optimization Letters, 15(6), pp. 2005–2015 (2021)
7. Chen, S., Bolufé-Röhler, A., Montgomery, J., & Hendtlass, T.: An analysis on the effect of selection on exploration in particle swarm optimization and differential evolution. In: *IEEE Congress on Evolutionary Computation (CEC)*, pp. 3037–3044, IEEE (2019)
8. Kumar, L., Ahirwal, M. A., & Pandey, M.: Parallel global best–worst particle swarm optimization algorithm for solving optimization problems. In: Applied Soft Computing, 142, p. 110329 (2022)
9. Choi, K. P., Kam, E. H. H., Lai, T. L., Tong, X. T., & Wong, W. K.: Exploration enhancement of nature-inspired swarm-based optimization algorithms. *arXiv: 2103.11113* (2021)
10. Huang, C., Li, Y., & Yao, X.: A survey of automatic parameter tuning methods for metaheuristics. In: IEEE Transactions on Evolutionary Computation, 24(2), pp. 201–216 (2019)
11. Binkley, K., & Hagiwara, M.: Balancing exploitation and exploration in particle swarm optimization: Velocity-based reinitialization. In: Information and Media Technologies, 3(1), pp. 103–111 (2008)
12. Islam, M., Li, X., & Mei, Y.: A time-varying transfer function for balancing the exploration and exploitation ability of a binary PSO. In: Applied Soft Computing, 59, pp. 182–196 (2017)
13. Çomak, E.: A particle swarm optimizer with modified velocity update and adaptive diversity regulation. In: Expert Systems, 36(1), p. e12330 (2019)
14. Arani, B. O., Mirzabeygi, P., & Panahi, M. S.: An improved PSO algorithm with a territorial diversity-preserving scheme and enhanced exploration–exploitation balance In: Swarm and Evolutionary Computation, 11, pp. 1–15 (2013)
15. Garg, V., Shukla, A., & Tiwari, R.: AERPSO: An adaptive exploration robotic PSO based cooperative algorithm for multiple target searching. In: Expert Systems with Applications, 209, p. 118245 (2022)
16. Rao, X., & Yan, X.: Particle swarm optimization algorithm based on information sharing in Industry 4.0. In: Wireless Communications and Mobile Computing, 2022, pp. 1–11 (2022)
17. Ardeh, M. A.: BenchmarkFcns toolbox: A collection of benchmark functions for optimization, 48, (2016)

18. Momin, J., & Yang, X. S.: A literature survey of benchmark functions for global optimization problems. In: Journal of Mathematical Modelling and Numerical Optimization, 4(2), pp. 150–194 (2013) doi: 10.1504/IJMMNO.2013.055204
19. Kumar, L., Pandey, M., & Ahirwal, M.K.: Parallel global best-worst particle swarm optimization algorithm for solving optimization problems. In: Applied Soft Computing, 2023, pp. 110329 (2023)

Chapter 2

Automatic speech recognition for cleft lip and cleft palate patients using deep learning techniques

Srinivasa Reddy K., Brahma Naidu K.,
Adi Narayana Reddy K., and A. Mallikarjuna Reddy

2.1 INTRODUCTION

Cleft lip and cleft palate (CLP) are birth defects that affect the upper lip and/or the roof of the mouth. Cleft lip occurs when there is a gap or split in the upper lip, while cleft palate occurs when there is a gap or split in the roof of the mouth. These defects occur due to incomplete development of the facial structures during fetal development, and can occur alone or in combination with each other. CLP are relatively common, affecting approximately 1 in 700 newborns worldwide. However, the incidence varies widely across different populations and regions. For example, the incidence is highest among Native American and Asian populations, while it is lowest among African populations. The exact causes of CLP are not fully understood, but they are believed to be a combination of genetic and environmental factors. Certain medications, alcohol, tobacco use, and nutrient deficiencies during pregnancy may increase the risk of these defects. CLP can have a significant impact on a child's health and quality of life. They can cause difficulties with feeding, breathing, and speaking, as well as hearing problems and increased risk of ear infections. Additionally, children with cleft lip and/or cleft palate may experience social and emotional challenges due to their appearance and communication difficulties. Treatment for CLP typically involves surgery, which is usually performed within the first year of life. Additional surgeries may be required as the child grows and develops. Speech therapy, dental care, and other supportive services may also be necessary to help the child achieve optimal health and development. CLP occur when a fetus' lips or mouth do not develop normally during pregnancy. Around the world, 1.41 infants have an orofacial cleft for every 1,000 live births, and almost 195,000 infants are born with clefts every year. When the velopharyngeal (VP) mechanism does not function properly, an overt or submucous cleft palate can cause hypernasality, which is when too much air escapes via the nose. Velopharyngeal insufficiency (VPI) is a significant factor in speech issues caused by cleft palate. Therefore, hypernasality and speech impairment in CLP may result from the presence of a cleft in the palate, velopharyngeal dysfunction (VPD), an oronasal fistula, or a combination of all three. Without

DOI: 10.1201/9781003433941-2

using any intrusive techniques, hypernasality may be automatically detected in connected speech on automatically segmented data. Cephalometric indicators of future orthognathic surgery requirement in children with repaired unilateral CLP can be found using machine learning (ML) in kids. The primary symptom observed for the cleft palate is hypernasality, which mainly causes excessive nasal resonance in pronunciation and speaking. This makes it difficult for patients who have hypernasality to spell and pronounce vowels and consonants clearly like other people. As a result, the extent to which a velopharyngeal tube connecting the mouth and nasal cavities opens and closes determines the severity of hypernasality. The important indicator in treating the patients to design the further treatment is to observe their speech patterns by speech therapy, estimating the hypernasality and the pharyngoplasty. The traditional way of observing these patterns is estimated with the scores given by the speech-language pathologists (SLPs). However, this is a laborious task, the expert has to be experienced to find the level of difficulty in the hypernasality-affected patients. This score also depends on the method of score given by the SLPs to various conditions. To solve this problem, a field of researchers and the scientific community attempted to analyse various possibilities of detecting hypernasality using machines and instruments. Nasometer is one of the results of these studies that measure the nasalance capabilities of the patients ranging from 0 to 100. However, the developed instruments are not capable of developing the correlation between the clinical examinations. Hence, it becomes inevitable again to study various techniques in understanding the speech patterns of the hypernasality patients. In the modern era, various complex problems are being solved with the advent of the latest ML techniques. A ML-based automatic speech recognition (ASR) system was developed and it gained a good amount of attention. The existing works only focused on cleft palate speech signal processing exhibiting a spectrum of different features. In order to accomplish categorisation using support vector machines (SVMs) and Gaussian noise mixture models, ML-based algorithms first extract acoustic features such as Mel-frequency cepstral coefficients (MFCC) or filter banks. The existing works focused on developing neural networks for hypernasality estimation. Nevertheless, many of these methods used best feature selection or extraction modules in the framework. Instead, they developed a stacked neural network over the acoustic features to show the classification. These approaches relied on learning hypernasality by ignoring the acoustic features which contain a lot of information compared to the hypernasality features. It is a notable advantage that the ASR models can extract a high-quality acoustic feature representation. The large-scale text-to-speech dataset enhances the model to completely understand the acoustic features. We believe that utilising the ASR model for initiation is advantageous for predicting hypernasality because transfer learning has been successful in previous tasks. Hence, in this work, a novel technique to escalate ASR model for hypernasality estimation is proposed with transfer learning.

2.1.1 Background study

Feng and Castelli [1] presented a comprehensive analysis of the 11 French vowels' nasalisation in the context of pole-zero evolutions which enables the recommendation of a universal method for analysing all vowels, allowing a true nasal vowel to be placed into this nasalisation frame. Accurate measurements of the nasal tract area function were achieved by Bjuggren and Fant. The latter's acoustic characteristics enable the establishment of a topological schema of pole-zero development patterns for the nasalisation of the 11 French vowels. An effective technique for examining the acoustic characteristics of nasal and nasalised vowels appears to be the introduction of a η-like configuration as a target for vowel nasalisation. Although the complexity of real nasal vowel spectra necessitates more complex simulations, in which the nasal tract would be better described and the effects of the source be taken into consideration, their research was a key step towards its interpretation and modelling. Zhang et al. [2] validated the diagnostic efficacy of 43 candidate SNPs previously observed using GWAS, by taking blood samples from control and NSCL/P infants in Han and Uyghur Chinese populations. Using several ML techniques, they developed predictive models using the verified SNPs and evaluated the accuracy of their predictions. Their findings demonstrated that logistic regression (LR), as measured by the area under the curve (AUC), performed the best for risk assessment. They developed the models using seven widely used ML models from the Python scikit-learn package, including SVM, LR, NB, RF, KNN, DT, and ANN. During the training phase, the tenfold cross-validation method to evaluate the AUC score value was performed to indicate the overall performance for each model. Vikram and Nagaraj Adiga [3] developed a two-stage speech enhancement technique based on signal processing to get the perceptual benchmark to compare the signal post-surgery or therapy. The nasal formant was suppressed in the first step to improve the CLP speech, and the spectral peak-valley augmentation was used in the second stage to lessen the hypernasality that is associated with the CLP speech. The improved speech signals were better than speech following prosthesis or surgery, according to the findings of the perceptual evaluation. The work may also be expanded to improve consonant sounds like stops and fricatives, which are negatively impacted by CLP.

Another study using the long short-term memory (LSTM) model was proposed by Gupta [4] to detect pathological voice disorders and test its effectiveness on a real-time 400 testing samples without any labels from FEMH voice disorder detection dataset. Before using an LSTM model for classification, several feature extraction techniques such as spectral contrast, chroma, spectral centroid and MFCC were used in data pre-processing to produce the optimal collection of features. The results achieved were 22% sensitivity, 97% specificity, and 56% unweighted average recall. In order to enhance the results, more tests with other hyperparameters should be conducted in the future, along with the usage of additional feature extraction methods. Mathad et al. [5] introduced a clinical-free, healthy speaker–based objective hypernasality measure (OHM) algorithm using a DNN nasality model. The hypernasal speech served as direct training for the algorithm. The findings revealed a substantial correlation between the OHM and the Americleft database's perceptual hypernasality scores ($r = 0.797$, $p < 0.001$) as well as the New Mexico Cleft Palate Center (NMCPC) database ($r = 0.713$, $p < 0.001$). In order to correct the acoustic discrepancy between the adult and kid speech, a pitch modification algorithm was applied. This modification work focuses on improving the model by fine-tuning hyperparameters using a corpus of cleft speech, or it may convert to a supervised model by using linear regression across several phrases to get speaker-level hypernasality ratings. Sudro et al. [6] studied a few methods of data augmentation to enhance CLP voice recognition. VTLP, reverberation, speaking rate, pitch modification, and speech feature modification using Cycle GAN were some of the approaches used for data augmentation. They investigated data gathered in the Kannada language using CLP and regular speech. Reverberation-based approaches produced somewhat better outcomes than the pitch- and speaking-rate-based approaches and Cycle GAN-based speech feature modification methods increase VTLP. A substantial difference is observed on comparing recognition performance to other data augmentation methods used in this study. Additionally, when compared to pitch and speaking rate adjustment techniques, VTLP and reverberation-based approaches provided comparatively superior outcomes. Cesari et al. [7] provided a clinical investigation that was done to compare the results with Praat, one of the most widely used voice analysis tools in clinical practice, in order to examine the clinical efficacy of the proposed m-health solution in classifying a voice as healthy or pathological. When a pathology is present, the results of using a rule-based algorithm to classify a voice as healthy or pathological demonstrate that Vox4Health is more adept than Praat at spotting the existence of a pathological voice, paying close attention to the performance of jitter and shimmer. The jitter or shimmer value produced the greatest accuracy of 72.6% in the diagnosis of vocal disorders when using a rule-based system. The best sensitivity, which is around 96%, was consistently attained by applying jitter. Finally, the Fundamental Frequency was used to reach the highest specificity, which is equivalent to 56.9%. A proper diagnosis of a voice issue requires further tests, such as a laryngoscopy, an invasive procedure that only a medical professional can do to see the vocal folds and any potential changes.

Shafi et al. [8] presented a ML-based approach to prevent clefts in the mother's pregnancy and identify embryos having CLP. In Reference [8], a dataset made up of 1,000 samples is used for performing feature selection, scaling, and cleaning. Identified crucial features accurately develop a cleft prediction model. The CLP–MLP was a superior model for cleft data categorisation, yielding 92.6% accuracy on unseen test data, according to their experimental tests. Maier et al. [9] showed that hypernasality can be automatically detected in connected speech on automatically segmented data, without any invasive means. On the basis of phoneme confusion data, they identified pronunciation characteristics. With a word level classification of up to 66.6% (CL) and 86.9% (RR), hypernasal speech was identified; 62.3% (CL) and 90.3% (RR) of the on-frame level rates were achieved. According to the results, the TEO's performance varied depending on the phoneme, and it performed less well in our situation than it had in other studies using adult speakers and manually segmented consonant–vowel and consonant–vowel–consonant clusters. Pham et al. [10], from the FEMH dataset, developed a useful model to distinguish between the many forms of voice disorders, such as normal, neoplas, phonotrauma, and vocal palsy. Various classification techniques were utilised, including SVM, random forest, k-nearest neighbour, and gradient boosting. The ensemble learning algorithm, which combines these learners and chooses the most well-liked prediction, was also applied. Although the models' accuracies are acceptable, they are substantially lower than those observed in earlier research, whose accuracies are all above 90%. It is perhaps a good idea to focus on phonotrauma in future study to enhance the accuracy of machine-driven voice disorder identification. Dhillon et al. [11] attempted to define the different applications and present state of artificial intelligence (AI) for helping people with cleft lip and/or palate. Using the search phrases artificial intelligence and cleft lip and/or palate, a search in the PubMed, Embase, and IEEE Xplore databases was carried out. A Google Scholar search was conducted for grey literature. The PRISMA-ScR standards were followed for conducting the study. They analysed that AI seems to be a hopeful solution that can benefit those who have cleft lip and/or palate. Currently, it has been used for diagnosis – prenatal, photographic, and identification of cephalometric features and mid-facial plane in participants – as well as for risk prediction of development of non-syndromic CLP. AI has also been applied to diagnose speech pathology, assist in pre-surgical orthopaedics, and anticipate surgical needs. The models created thus far exhibit encouraging outcomes in controlled situations. The severity and reliability issues related to the auditory perceptual evaluation of nasality in speech was examined by Brunnegård et al. [12] to see whether they may affect patients' daily lives or treatment decisions and whether nasometry could successfully lessen them. In perceptual assessment tasks, speech samples from 52 of these speakers and samples from a reference group of 21 speakers without cleft palate, velopharyngeal disability, or speech problems were used. Additionally, nasometric evaluations were performed on 14 speakers from the clinical population and 11 speakers from the reference population. To establish normative data for the nasometer, nasometry was used to analyse an additional reference sample of 220 children from three Swedish cities, whose ages were similar with those used for clinical assessments of infants born with cleft palate. The author came to the conclusion that even when sound technique was used, expert SLPs' judgements of speech nasality factors, notably hypernasality, might have low inter- and intra-rater reliability.

Chu et al. [13] examined the effectiveness of an ASR system that was trained on anechoic and reverberant speech in various types of rooms, and they trained a speech synthesiser to produce speech from the text that the ASR system predicted. The methods they followed were reverberation model, ASR model, speech synthesis model, listening test procedure, listening experiment and finally data analysis. The accuracy in the anechoic condition was 90%, the left and right channels in the office were 83.1% and 84.1%, respectively, and the left and right channels in Aula Carolina were 29.1% and 28.1% respectively,. The outcomes demonstrated that the approach enhanced speech understanding under previously unobserved conditions and that the ASR-synthesis approach may be advantageous to CI users in typical reverberant surroundings.

Modak et al. [14] used a learning system which is an open-source learning management system (LMS) for detecting two learner profiles, i.e. students with learning disability (LD) and without learning disability (non-LD). ML was used to determine if the user has LD (dyslexia in this case) or not. Binary classification is carried out using two ML techniques, LR and SVM, with the classes of the dataset being LD (1) and non-LD (0). They came to the conclusion that informal testing on the e-learning platform known as Moodle can help kids aged 11–13 who have learning disabilities. While performing detection based on the given dataset, the LR method for ML performs better than the SVM. Huqh et al. [15] analysed the current clinical uses of AI/ML techniques in diagnosis and treatment prediction in kids with CLP and created a qualitative summary of the studies retrieved, using databases like PubMed, Scopus, and the Web of Science Core Collection. They came to the conclusion that AI-enabled computer programming software offers a cutting-edge technology that can be used for precise landmark identification, quick digital cephalometric analysis, clinical decision-making, and treatment prediction. Kummer [16] indicated that all at-risk patients should undergo a test of their speech, resonance, and VP function shortly after age 3. The type of issue and its likely aetiology can be identified by a skilled and educated SLP. The speech features will reveal the extent of the VP gap if there is VPI. A VP opening's position may be determined via nasopharyngoscopy, which is helpful for surgical planning. Nasometry can offer unbiased information on changes following surgical treatment. In order to provide coordinated treatment and achieve the best possible results, children with clefts or other craniofacial defects should be handled by a craniofacial team. Vucovich et al. [17] developed a computer learning system to assess cleft speech. They discern between normal speech, VPD, and articulatory speech mistakes using their automated cleft speech evaluator, which analyses resonance and articulatory cleft speech faults. The evaluator was trained on 60 cases before being put to test on the next 13 patients. A 77% score was obtained by the cleft speech evaluator on its finest sentence, while a median of 65% was obtained for all sentences. The steps followed were developing the speech recognition engine, training the speech recognition system, and testing the speech recognition system.

HennaRaunak et al. [18] investigated the relationship between instrumental and perceptual examination of hypernasality in children with corrected $CP \pm L$. The kappa coefficient was computed to examine the inter- and intra-rater reliability for the two judges. Using multivariate analysis of variance (MANOVA), the mean nasalance scores of the two groups were compared. Using the Pearson product moment correlation, the association between the perceptual judgement of hypernasality and its instrumental measure, i.e. nasalance, was analysed. Therefore, when particular speech stimuli are used, there is a high connection between the perceptual and nasalance assessments of hypernasality (using the nasal view) in children with $CP \pm L$. However, the results were only applicable to the Marathi language, and more research must be done in other languages with bigger study populations in order to generalise the conclusions. Girish et al. [19] sought to compare the nasalance readings from the nasometer and the ASP software for children with and without repaired cleft palate (RCP) and typically developing children (TDC). Between the clinical group (RCP) and the control group (TDC), between the stimulus types (oral sentences, nasal sentences, and oronasal sentences), and between the instruments, the nasalance values were compared (ASP software and nasometer). The findings of the mixed ANOVA showed that there was a significant interaction between the stimulus type and participant group, the instrument type and participant group, as well as the stimulus type, instrument type, and participant group. They came to the conclusion that the ASP software was effective in detecting nasalance in TDC and in children with RCP. An autoregressive (AR) model for the vocal tract system of a patient with hypernasal speech is not correct because zeros emerge in the frequency response of the vocal tract system; therefore, a new quantitative technique is provided by Ehsan et al. [20] to estimate hypernasality. Vowels (/a/) taken from 392 utterances made up of disyllables (/pamap/) were uttered by 22 healthy persons and 13 people with cleft palate for this study. The subject's utterances were classified using a suggested index using K-means and the Bayes theorem. They concluded that comparing the 120 normalised cepstrum coefficients of the AR model with 10 poles to the ARMA model with two zeros and the same number of poles produced the best results. In this case, they were able to classify topics with an accuracy of up to 97.14% and utterances up to 81.12%. Suthar et al. [21] studied the use of landmark (LM) analysis, a method for automatically identifying speech disorders in children. It describes acoustic events occurring as a result of sufficiently accurate articulatory motions. To determine the efficacy of the novel features in separating speech disorder patients from healthy speakers, they tested several linear and non-linear ML classification approaches based on the raw characteristics and the suggested features. Monte-Carlo cross-validation and testing (MCVT) is a reliable method for contrasting various modelling approaches and evaluating their capabilities with a limited number of test samples. In particular, when there are more features than observations, as there were in this study, feature selection is a powerful method for preventing overfitting and lowering test variance. Last but not least, SMOTE can help solve the issue by producing synthetic samples. Xie et al. [22] emphasised the usefulness of ML-based methods for examining speech-evoked neurophysiological reactions. They proposed two types of ML-based methods: decoding models, which utilise characteristics from neurophysiological responses to provide an output for a speech stimulus, and encoding models, which employ speech stimulus features to forecast neurophysiological responses. They came to a conclusion that modern ML-based methods for analysing neurophysiological reactions to speech signals are helpful supplements to more conventional methods. In this chapter, we introduce a novel deep learning-based approach to enhance the ASR systems for the patients with the problem of hypernasality in an easy way.

2.2 PROPOSED METHODOLOGY

2.2.1 Architecture of the proposed model

The architecture of the decoder in the framework for autoregressive reenacting of the pseudocodes of the corresponding source speech is included in the model architecture of the proposed model for pretraining. The encoder network samples implicit speech manifestations from untreated acoustic data inputs and learns contextualised speech illustrations. Relative positional encoding boosts the encoder system and decoder system simultaneously. The outline of the proposed model architecture is given Figure 2.1.

As seen on the left section of Figure 2.1, the network that connects the encoders follows the XLNet-based design and consists of an encoder net, a

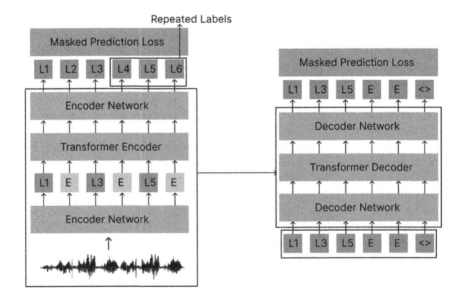

Figure 2.1 Outline of the proposed encoder–decoder network.

Transformer encoder. More precisely, the encoder network is a convolutional network with seven 1024-channel layers and strides [4, 10] and kernel widths [3, 6, 20] that is used for conditioning the waveforms. Twenty-four layers, a model diameter of 1,528, an inner dimension of 6,052, and 24 focus points make up the transformer encoder. The projection layer and the code embedding layer, which are included in the encoder-post network, are used to transform concealed states into pseudocodes.

Along with the transformer decoder, the decoder system also includes a decoder network. An embedding vector is created from a code index by the pre-net. The cross-attention and the so-called masked self-attention are absent from the transformer decoder's design but are present in the transformer encoder. Finally, using the post-net, the hidden state is converted into a probability distribution of sequences that has been normalised using the SoftMax function.

2.2.2 Pre-training of the proposed model

Speech-only data is available for the initial training method of learning for the proposed hybrid model. We present two pre-training tasks, which include masked projection loss on the encoder and reconstruction loss for the decoder, for pre-training the encoder–decoder model.

2.3 MODEL PREDICTION LOSS

The encoder network of the proposed model creates a characteristic sequence S from the speech frequency during pre-training by downsampling, and the transformer encoder uses the masked acoustic features to ingest hidden states hS. Additionally, the encoder network is optimised to forecast the discontinuous target pattern, in which each $S_t \in [CC]$ is a classification variable of the C-class. The generalised distribution of codewords is given in Equation (2.1).

$$P_f(CC \mid \underline{S}, tS) = \frac{\log\left(\mathrm{sim}(hS, W)/\varrho\right)}{\sum_{CC=1}^{C\hat{C}} \log\left(\mathrm{sim}(hS, W)/\varrho\right)} \tag{2.1}$$

2.4 ASR CONCEPTUALISATION

ASR is a technology that analyses human voice input to determine the text that corresponds to acoustics produced. Assume that the ASR corpus is (S, T), where S and T stand for the audio files and accompanying language representations, respectively. When synthesising audio data, a series of acoustic features (such as Mel filter bank features, the length and emphasis of the individual sounds) are first applied at the frame level before being sent into the model. In order to address ASR tasks, we often use an encoder–decoder framework [22, 23] at which decoder is structured in an autoregressive way and the hyperparameters are defined as $\alpha = \{\alpha_{enc}, \alpha_{dec}\}$. The goal of the ASR system is to estimate the most accurate text that corresponds to the provided speech, or arg max $P(T \,|\, S)$. Maximum likelihood estimation (MLE) is used to maximise the objective function, as given in Equation (2.2).

$$\tau_{ASR} = -\sum_{(s,t)}^{(S,T)} \sum_{k=1}^{|t|} \log P\big(t_k| \, t_{<i}, \, s{:}\alpha_{enc}, \alpha_{dec}\big) \qquad (2.2)$$

where (s, t) is a relationship of speech and text, P $(ti|ti|ti, s; \{\alpha_{enc}, \alpha_{dec}\})$ is a prediction of the ith token in the textual succession based on prior positioning as well as the specified speech, and (s, t) is a couple of speech and text. The encoder of this ASR model can generate deep representations using acoustic data, allowing the decoder to reliably determine the related text. As a result, by optimising Equation (2.1), we can create a really good ASR model in the broad framework.

2.5 HYPERNASALITY ESTIMATION FORMULATION

The purpose of hypernasality estimation is to assess the degree of hyper-nasality in CLP individuals' speech. Hypernasality estimates can be further divided into hypernasality recognition and hypernasality measurement by using various evaluation criteria. The first is a binary classification task that involves determining the degree to which cleft palate acoustic nature contains hypernasality. The latter is a more difficult multi-class categorisation task that involves predicting the hypernasality assessment of the associated cleft palate speech to evaluate the severity of hypernasality. In this study, the inten-sity of hypernasality is graded on a scale from 0 to 3 (normal, mild, moderate, severe), where each number corresponds to a different class in the multi-class categorisation test. A 2-tuple (X, Y) can be used to describe the CLP dataset, wherein X and Y stand for the samples of CLP acoustic set and the accom-panying hypernasality rating, respectively. To ensure consistency, we use the same pre-processing technique for CLP speech to produce features that are comparable to those used in ASR tasks (i.e. Mel filter bank features). We use an encoder framework with a classification layer to do hypernasality estimation, the parameters of the network are defined as $\hat{\alpha} = \left\{ \widehat{\alpha_{enc}}, \widehat{\alpha_{dec}} \right\}$. Hence, the objec-tive function for the ASR in hypernasality estimation is given as Equation (2.3). As a result, the formulation serves as the purpose of hypernasality estimation, which is given as Equation (2.3):

$$\tau_{CLS} = -\sum_{(i,j)}^{(I,J)} \log P\big(j \, | \, i; \, \widehat{\alpha_{enc}}, \, \widehat{\alpha_{dec}}\big) \qquad (2.3)$$

where $\left\{ \widehat{\alpha_{enc}}, \widehat{\alpha_{dec}} \right\}$ stand for the encoder's and classifier's respective parameters, respectively. The classifier is a linked SoftMax function with a column vector to scale the dimensionality of the encoder inputs as the number of categories |C|. For hypernasality assessment and detection, |C| is set to 2 and 4, respectively.

2.6 TRANSFER LEARNING

The ASR encoder–decoder network can be thought of as a potent acoustic feature representation with the aid of large-scale speech samples and the annotated text, as was discussed above. Therefore, we conclude that the encoder with ASR training, due to its capacity to learn high-quality audio representation, is preferable for hypernasality estimation. To fulfil this target, we require the architecture of encoder used in the ASR task and hypernasality estimation to be completely identical, and same as the input acoustic features (Mel filter bank). More specifically, we perform a hypernasality estimate job based on an ASR encoder after training an encoder–decoder architecture in an ASR goal. Hence, the objective function of the proposed model is as given in Equation (2.4).

$$\tau_{CLS} = -\sum_{(i,j)}^{(I,J)} \log P\left(j \mid i; \alpha_{enc}, \widehat{\alpha_{dec}} \right) \tag{2.4}$$

where α_{enc} is the ASR encoder–decoder network parameters in Equation. (2.1). Additionally, Figure 2.2 provides a brief explanation of our training pathway.

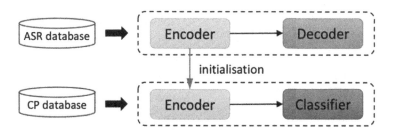

Figure 2.2 The training process for our strategy. The ASR dataset is used in the first row to build the model, and the ASR-trained encoder–decoder framework is then initialised to perform an evaluation of hypernasality on the cleft palate dataset.

2.7 EXPERIMENTS AND RESULTS

2.7.1 Dataset

The New Mexico Cleft Palate Research Center [8], which is primarily made up of English native speakers with cleft palate, compiled the NMPMC–CHN dataset as shown in Table 2.1. In this dataset, there are 41 patients affected with hypernasality, and 25 healthy speakers were chosen as the control group to create speech samples. Majority of the people who helped in curating the dataset are in the age group of 10.7 ± 1.7 years. A small subset curated randomly with the candidate sentences must be recorded by each patient. For every patient, a score between 0 and 3 will be defined based on the captured acoustic data (0 stands for regular and 3 means severe). Patients who score between 1 and 3 are considered to have hypernasality for the purpose of detection. A Chinese hospital constructed the CNH–CLP dataset, which comprises cleft palate patients of all ages, from infants to adults. In the CNH–CLP dataset, every patient speaks Chinese. Each patient's audio gathering process follows a similar process to that of the NMCPC–CLP dataset. A sizeable dataset for voice recognition in the English language is called Librispeech. For training the model, Librispeech offers 960 hours of speak data, sampled at 16,000 Hz, together with the relevant text. We choose dev-clean/dev-other as the validation set for the ASR training. Due to the fact that both the datasets are in the English language, we utilise Librispeech in training the ASR model before using it on the NMCPC–CLP dataset. In the field of Chinese ASR, Aishell-1 is a frequently used dataset. The training/validation set of the Aishell-1 dataset consists of 150/10 hours of audio. Each audio file includes the appropriate text and is compiled at 16,000 Hz. For all ASR datasets and CLP datasets, we first resample audios at 16,000 Hz before extracting 80-channel log Mel filter bank features (25 ms window size and 10 ms shift). Fairseq-S2T is a development toolkit used in this approach. The encoder and decoder framework proposed for the ASR task is made up of a stack of transformer layers with cross-attention modules and two convolutional layers for sub-sampling. For data augmentation during the ASR training phase, we employ SpecAugment. ADAM is the default optimiser used in this approach. Table 2.2 reports the detailed hyperparameters of the proposed model. We also assess our categorisation accuracy using fivefold cross-validation to diminish variation. All evaluations are tested at the speaker level.

Table 2.1 Statistics of NMPMC and CHN cleft palate datasets

Ratings of images	NMPMC	CHN
Regular	35	257
Mild	14	193
Slacken	17	514
Severe	19	119

Table 2.2 Hyperparameters of the proposed model

		ASR	CLS
	stride_value	3	3
CNN	width_of_kernel	8	8
	channel_value	1,024	
	layer_value	17	
Transformers	filter_dimension	1,024	
	Dropout	0.6	
	batch_size	512	64
Optimisation	learning_rate	2e-4	2e-7
	epoch	150	57

2.8 RESULTS

2.8.1 Estimation accuracy

We use accuracy as a criterion to examine how well our model performs in assessing hypernasality. The obtained results of the proposed model are presented in Table 2.3. Our starting point 2048*2 is the fundamental model without the ASR encoder–decoder. We also provide certain baselines [8] that employ statistical attributes as a point of comparison. We can draw the following conclusions from Table 2.3: (1) In both the NMPMC and CHN cleft palate datasets, our method significantly outperforms the baseline method when configured with an ASR encoder–decoder architecture, including hypernasality detection and assessment. (2) When compared to statistical methods, our method also shows significant improvement, particularly in hypernasality detection. These advancements also show how successful our approach is. Additionally, our approach is generalizable and may be employed with any neural network that has been used in earlier research [10, 12].

We also visualise the confusion matrix of our model by utilising ASR encoder–decoder framework in hypernasality speech estimation, and the

Table 2.3 Performance metrics of the proposed model

Method	NMPMC		CHN	
	HD	HA	HD	HA
Baseline	91.7 ± 0.8	79.2 ± 0.8	94.1 ± 0.3	73.1 ± 0.3
+ ASR	95.9 ± 0.2	87.8 ± 0.2	95.4 ± 0.2	80.8 ± 0.3
MFCC [8]	87.04	64.69	90.1 ± 0.4	70.5 ± 0.6
CQCC [8]	85.27	73.19	–	–
SFFB [8]	90.04	84.62	–	–

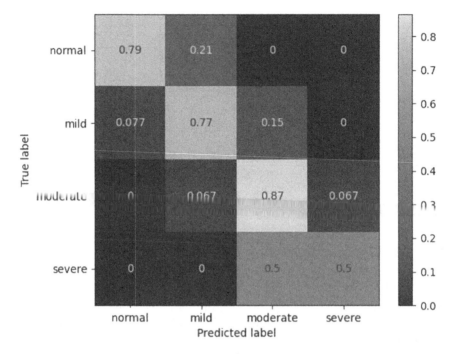

Figure 2.3 Confusion matrix of the proposed model for hypernasality estimation on both the datasets.

results are shown in Figure 2.3 to highlight how generalised our model is in predicting hypernasality. Figure 2.2 shows that, particularly in regular, mild, and moderate patients, our model is effective in explaining each label. Although CHN is an imbalance dataset (moderate and severe patients make up 50% and 10% of the total population, respectively), our model's performance in predicting severe cases is still respectable. Overall, these findings show that our model can successfully prevent overfitting and achieve higher generalisation performance.

We also show the hidden unit of encoder–decoder framework output to more clearly illustrate the benefits of our approaches in recognising auditory features. In more detail, we consider the encoder–decoder output to be $h \in R \ L \times D$, where L and D are the frame length and concealed size, respectively. As a result, we determine h's mean score first, and then we utilise its absolute value as the ith frame's active value. Figure 2.4 displays the outcome together with the Mel spectrum that goes with it. The results of our model show a higher activation value and are more sensitive to acoustic data than the network without ASR, because it is too smooth to discern the semantically of acoustic signals. This result supports our claim that high-quality auditory features can be extracted using an ASR model.

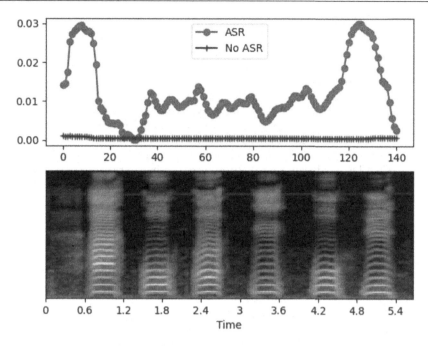

Figure 2.4 Comparative spectrum distributions between our solution and the industry standard without employing ASR in the encoder output's activated value.

2.9 CONCLUSION

Using the ASR model as our lens, we present a straightforward and practical method for enhancing hypernasality estimates in this study. More precisely, we point out that existing neural network–based approaches can only extract low-quality representation for acoustic characteristics, which is helpful for hypernasality estimate, and stack many neural network layers for classification. We suggest fine-tuning the encoder–decoder framework, which is pre-trained with the ASR objective, for hypernasality estimation of speeches to alleviate this shortcoming. Such a design enables our model to profit from the ASR model in two ways: (1) ASR corpus typically contains more audio data, allowing for improved generalisation; (2) ASR corpus labelling text directs model to extract acoustic aspects more accurately. The effectiveness of our methods in assessing hypernasality is also demonstrated by experimental results on two cleft palate datasets. We anticipate concentrating on two areas of research in the future: (1) Is it possible to perform hypernasality prediction in cleft palate utterance using more powerful and effective pre-trained speech frameworks, such as wav2vec [24]. (2) Traditional methods for hypernasality estimation typically designed some sophisticated analysis acoustic features, so we want to investigate the possibility of combining neural network–based features and statistical features to more accurately estimate hypernasality.

REFERENCES

1. Feng, G., Castelli, E. Some acoustic features of nasal and nasalized vowels: A target for vowel nasalization. Journal of the Acoustical Society of America. 1996, 99(6):3694–3706. doi: 10.1121/1.414967.
2. Zhang, Shi-Jian, Meng, Peiqi, Zhang, Jieni, Jia, Peizeng, Lin, Jiuxiang, Wang, Xiangfeng, Chen, Feng, Wei, Xiaoxing. Machine learning models for genetic risk assessment of infants with non-syndromic orofacial cleft. Genomics, Proteomics & Bioinformatics. 2018, 16(5):354–364. doi: 10.1016/j.gpb.2018.07.005.
3. Vikram, C. M., Nagaraj, A., Mahadeva Prasanna, S. R. Spectral Enhancement of Cleft Lip and Palate Speech, 2016, Interspeech, San Francisco, USA.
4. Gupta, Vibhuti. Voice disorder detection using long short-term memory (LSTM) model. 2019. doi: 10.13140/RG.2.2.17433.88165.
5. Mathad, V. C., Scherer, N., Chapman, K., Liss, J. M., Berisha, V. A deep learning algorithm for objective assessment of hypernasality in children with cleft palate. IEEE Transactions on Biomedical Engineering. 2021, 68(10):2986–2996. doi: 10.1109/TBME.2021.3058424.
6. Nomo Sudro, Protima, Das, Rohan, Sinha, Rohit, Prasanna, S. Significance of Data Augmentation for Improving Cleft Lip and Palate Speech Recognition, 2021, IEEE.
7. Cesari, Ugo, De Pietro, Giuseppe, Marciano, Elio, Niri, Ciro, Sannino, Giovanna, Verde, Laura. Voice disorder detection via an m-health system: Design and results of a clinical study to evaluate Vox4Health. BioMed Research International. 2018, 2018:8193694. doi: 10.1155/2018/8193694.
8. Shafi, Numan, Bukhari, Faisal, Iqbal, Waheed, Asif, Muhammad, Almustafa, Nawaz, Zubair. Cleft prediction before birth using deep neural network. Health Informatics Journal. 2020, 26:2568–2585. doi: 10.1177/1460458220911789.
9. Maier, Andreas, Reuß, Alexander, Hacker, Christian, Schuster, Maria, Noeth, Elmar. Analysis of hypernasal speech in children with cleft lip and palate. International Conference on Text, Speech and Dialogue, 2008, 389–396. doi: 10.1007/978-3-540-87391-4_50.
10. Pham, Minh, Lin, Jing, Zhang, Yanjia. Diagnosing voice disorder with machine learning. 2018 IEEE International Conference on Big Data, 2018, 5263–5266. doi: 10.1109/BigData.2018.8622250.
11. Dhillon, Harnoor, Chaudhari, Prabhat Kumar, Dhingra, Kunaal, Kuo, Rong-Fu, Sokhi, Ramandeep Kaur, Alam, Mohammad Khursheed, Ahmad, Shandar. Current applications of artificial intelligence in cleft care: A scoping review. Frontiers in Medicine, 2021, 8. doi: 10.3389/fmed.2021.676490.
12. Brunnegård, Karin. Evaluation of nasal speech: A study of assessments by speech-language pathologists, untrained listeners and nasometry. 2008.
13. Chu, K., Collins, L., Mainsah, B. Using automatic speech recognition and speech synthesis to improve the intelligibility of cochlear implant users in reverberant listening environments. 2020 IEEE International Conference on Acoustics, Speech and Signal Processing (ICASSP 2020), 2020, pp. 6929–6933. doi: 10.1109/ICASSP40776.2020.9054450
14. Modak, M., Warade, O., Saiprasad, G., Shekhar, S. Machine learning based learning disability detection using LMS. 2020 IEEE 5th International Conference on Computing Communication and Automation (ICCCA), 2020, pp. 414–419. doi: 10.1109/ICCCA49541.2020.9250761

15. Huqh, Mohamed Zahoor Ul et al. Clinical applications of artificial intelligence and machine learning in children with cleft lip and palate: A systematic review. International Journal of Environmental Research and Public Health. 2022, 19(17):10860. doi: 10.3390/ijerph191710860
16. Kummer, Ann W. Evaluation of speech and resonance for children with craniofacial anomalies. Facial Plastic Surgery Clinics of North America. 2016, 24(4): 445–451. doi: 10.1016/j.fsc.2016.06.003
17. Vucovich, Megan et al. Automated cleft speech evaluation using speech recognition. Journal of Cranio-Maxillo-Facial Surgery: Official Publication of the European Association for Cranio-Maxillo-Facial Surgery. 2017, 45(8):1268–1271. doi: 10.1016/j.jcms.2017.05.002
18. Tak, HennaRaunak, Waknis, Aarti, Kulkarni, SnehaPrakash. Perceptual and instrumental analysis of hypernasality in children with repaired cleft palate. Journal of Cleft Lip Palate and Craniofacial Anomalies. 2016, 3:67. doi: 10.4103/2348-2125.187508
19. Girish, K. S., Mariswamy, Pushpavathi, Abraham, Ajish, Vikram, C. M. Automatic speech processing software: New sensitive tool for the assessment of nasality – A preliminary study. Journal of Cleft Lip Palate and Craniofacial Anomalies. 2022, 9:14–23. doi: 10.4103/jclpca.jclpca_22_21
20. Akafi, Ehsan, Vali, Mansour, Moradi, Negin, Baghban, Kowsar. Assessment of hypernasality for children with cleft palate based on cepstrum analysis. Journal of Medical Signals and Sensors. 2013, 3:209–215. doi: 10.4103/2228-7477.128302
21. Suthar, K., YousefiZowj, F., Speights Atkins, M., He, Q. P. Feature engineering and machine learning for computer-assisted screening of children with speech disorders. PLoS Digit Health. 2022, 1(5): e0000041.
22. Reddy, Srinivasa, Rao, P. Venkateswara, Reddy, A. Mallikarjuna, Reddy, K Sudheer, Narayana, J. Lakshmi Narayana, Silpapadmanabhuni, Sri. Neural network aided optimized auto encoder and decoder for detection of COVID-19 and pneumonia using CT-SCAN. Journal of Theoretical and Applied Information Technology. 2022, 100(21):6346–6360.
23. Xie, Zilong, Reetzke, Rachel, Chandrasekaran, Bharath. Machine learning approaches to analyze speech-evoked neurophysiological responses. Journal of Speech Language and Hearing Research. 2019, 62:587–601. doi: 10.1044/2018_JSLHR-S-ASTM-18-0244
24. Schneider, Steffen, Baevski, Alexei, Collobert, Ronan, Auli, Michael. WAV2VEC: Unsupervised pre-training for speech recognition, Facebook AI Research, 2019.

Chapter 3

Dynamics of underwater acoustic signal processing

An underwater acoustic marine habitat monitoring application perspective

Mishachandar B. and Vairamuthu S.

3.1 INTRODUCTION

The marine life has always fascinated humans, in particular, the cetaceans have attracted humans towards the ocean for centuries. However, the increasing human indulgence in ocean-based activities has made the lives of these underwater species challenging [1]. In many parts of the world, cetaceans like whales, dolphins, and porpoises are on their verge of extinction owing to their difficulty in sustaining in a frequently changing soundscape like oceans due to increasing anthropogenic activities [2, 3]. This scenario has disturbed the ocean habitat, especially the cetaceans that use sound to navigate, communicate, avoid predators, and find prey in its ecosystem. Adverse effects like physical injury, physiological and behavioural modifications, and masking make animal life in oceans undesirable [4]. Recent scientific data have proved that high-level impacts like a hindered animal-to-animal communication, altered locomotive and communication behavior, and stress in the ocean habitat are due to the increased anthropogenic activities. Increasing consequences of these anthropogenic activities on marine life have drawn the attention of ecosystem managers to conserve the ocean life that deserves our respect and protection. However, the lack of data owing to data collection in a harsh environment like underwater challenges its development [5]. Growing research efforts and contributions in this regard can help revive this condition at its earliest. Unlike terrestrial animals, observing the activities of marine animals visually using IF and RADAR data collection methods are costly and demand equipment requiring a large-scale laboratory setup [6]. Moreover, most marine species reside in deep oceans causing visual monitoring and inspection infeasible. Besides, factors like distant topology, cetacean's high mobility, and less surface appearance hinder visual observation largely [7]. Earlier research efforts attempted underwater communication using electromagnetic waves, radio frequency waves, and optical waves but properties like high-frequency range and severe attenuation in water made EM waves inappropriate for underwater communication. Optical waves suffered limited transmission range and high scattering. RF waves used in terrestrial communication experienced a swift decrease in its transmission range

DOI: 10.1201/9781003433941-3

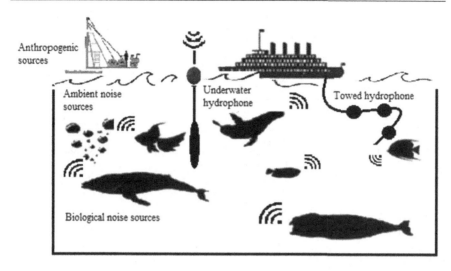

Figure 3.1 Ocean noise sources.

making it highly incompatible for signal transmission in oceans [8]. In this case "acoustics" was found to be a promising alternative that uses the sound-producing ability of marine species. The property of sound to travel faster in water than light aids in utilizing sound propagation to send and receive messages in the underwater environment [9]. Figure 3.1 refers to the typical real-time scenario in underwater with multiple acoustic systems producing sound that is recorded using static and mobile passive acoustic monitoring (PAM).

Marine mammals produce different sounds depending on their emotional behaviour to sense, detect, navigate, communicate, and perform echolocation [10]. The use of sound for communication has drawn attention of the researchers to record and study cetacean behavior with ease. Acoustic monitoring can be either active or passive [11]. PAM is extensively used among the scientific and research community to record and study the marine habitat's temporal and spatial behaviour through the use of underwater microphones known as hydrophones for its non-intrusive characteristic. PAM also aids in mitigating the adverse effects caused due to the proliferation of human activities such as increased ship traffic, ocean exploratory activities, and military and civilian activities. Amidst PAM, where cetaceans are detected acoustically by listening and recording their sounds, active acoustic monitoring (AAM) uses devices like whale finding sonar to listen to the reflected echoes from the animal without the need for marine species to produce any sound [12]. AAM risks the lives of these animals due to the increased sound produced for better reflection and to capture echoes in the sonar [13]. This chapter primarily aims to articulate a marine habitat monitoring approach to monitor and preserve the depleting ocean life due to the varying soundscape of the oceans. A complete solution to marine habitat monitoring from

Figure 3.2 Stages of the acoustic marine habitat monitoring approach.

data collection to application deployment is approached with acoustic audio recording as the source of data. Figure 3.2 shows the stages of the acoustic habitat monitoring approach.

The marine habitat monitoring approach observes marine life and makes repeated observations of its condition to measure the changes from its previous status over time [14]. Research efforts in this field are mostly aimed at designing monitoring applications only for cetaceans and little or no regard is given to fishes and invertebrates [15]. In oceans, the main victim of varying soundscape of the oceans due to the increasing anthropogenic activities is cetaceans, if viewed from the aspect of impact. But the intensity of harm caused to the fishes and the invertebrates is equally intensive. The degraded acoustic quality of diverse habitats has broadened the impact on marine mammals, leading to more probable repercussions for fishes and invertebrates. This chapter aims to design a marine habitat monitoring approach covering all the marine species build on this fact. The contributions of this chapter are threefold: (1) An acoustic marine habitat monitoring application is reviewed upon. (2) An in-depth review of the possible options is given for each step of the proposed approach and the ideal choice for the approach is briefed upon at the end of each section. (3) The scope for future applications is discussed to give an idea of the conceptualization of the proposed reviewed approach as real-time monitoring applications.

This chapter is structured as follows. Section 3.1 discusses the need for a marine habitat safe monitoring technique. Data collection and pre-processing are touched upon in Section 3.2. An in-depth insight into feature extraction is given in Section 3.3. In Sections 3.4–3.6, each step of the approach is discussed in detail with its related works. The scope for future applications is dealt with in Section 3.7. Finally, Section 3.8 concludes the chapter with a focus on the future work.

3.2 DATA COLLECTION AND PRE-PROCESSING

Data collection and pre-processing is the first step in an automated application development. Marine species vocalization as acoustic audio recording is the data for any audio-based automated work like classification, detection, and localization. Data as either text or images of the marine species were found to be ineffective in the past works [16]. The audio form of data used in this work are underwater sounds recorded using underwater microphones known as hydrophones. Emphasizing the marine habitat–friendly nature of the proposed work, the sounds are recorded using PAM. The recording in PAM is done in two ways: mobile and stationary [17]. In mobile PAM, the hydrophones are attached to a ship or to an ocean glider to cover larger ocean area in a limited time duration. Stationary PAM, on the contrary, is deployed at a fixed location for a longer duration of time [18]. The next important factor post the choice of method for data collection is the deployment pattern of the hydrophones. The conventional ways are the array set-up with multiple hydrophones: a minimum of at least four and single hydrophone deployment [19]. The most preferred choice is the multi-array hydrophone set-up that facilitates capturing the animal call in all three dimensions. But owing to its drawbacks of ambiguity and the expense incurred, it is overruled by the single hydrophone set-up that is both cost-effective and performance-efficient in strident conditions. In reality, the sounds recorded underwater are extremely raw and complex with overlapping vocalizations from multiple cetaceans that mostly move in clusters added to the presence of anthropogenic noise. The raw acoustic audio data collected from the ocean environment usually comprises (a) sounds produced by marine species, including marine mammals, fishes, and invertebrates; (b) natural sources of noise from the physical oceanographic processes like gushing waves sounds, rain, and seismic activities such as underwater earthquakes and volcanoes; (c) anthropogenic noise sources, including shipping activities, sonars, UANs that contribute largely to the overall noise of the ocean environment [20]. Various other factors that make data collection underwater highly challenging are the non-stationary nature of the marine species; harsh ocean environmental conditions that lead to displacement and biological fouling of hydrophones; difficulty in deployment and covering vast ocean fronts, and above all the difficulty in recharging the batteries through renewable energy source is highly non-feasible in an environment like underwater [21]. Amidst the environment favouring nature of PAM, its performance is largely dependent on the techniques employed to separate the signal of interest from the other interfering signals in the data [22]. This condition is highly applicable for remote sources and sounds with a low signal-to-noise ratio (SNR). Numerous audio sources separation techniques like principal component analysis (PCA), vector quantification, singular value decomposition, independent component analysis (ICA), non-negative matrix factorization (NMF), and deep neural networks (DNN) [23, 24] are employed to separate the correlated signals of interest from the mixture of interfering signals. It can also serve as a prerequisite for performing tasks like detection and classification for better results.

The data pre-processing stage consists of recovering the raw audio data in waveform with the information pertaining only to the time and converting it to a time–frequency representation known as power spectrum with both the time and frequency information and further converting it to spectrogram which is an image representation of the audio data with the time–frequency–amplitude

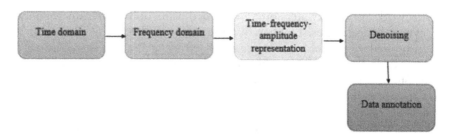

Figure 3.3 Data pre-processing pipeline.

information of the acoustic audio recordings. The spectrograms are even further converted to log spectrogram and Mel-frequency spectral coefficient (MFCCs) and other feature extraction techniques to extract more profound features from the audio. The choice of feature extraction depends on the type of audio signals to be processed. A spectrogram suffices for the preliminary data pre-processing. The quality of the audio is enhanced in the denoising phase where the acoustic recordings are cleaned to remove the artefacts interfering the background noises. The denoised audio is annotated to locate the occurrence of vocalization in time, and this is done mostly manually by human experts through visual inspection. Lately, it is annotated seamlessly by many open-source and paid software [25]. The start and end of an animal call is identified and marked to form an annotation and a frame with a single identification is called a label. The final annotated samples form as training and testing data to perform detection and classification tasks. The nature and the property of the captured signals changes drastically with the deployed environment such as shallow water, freshwater and deep water. Figure 3.3 shows the data pre-processing pipeline.

3.3 FEATURE EXTRACTION

Feature extraction is the process of extracting useful information from the data to enhance the performance of the automated tasks [26]. The use of feature extraction is needed when the detector or the classifier is a machine learning model dealing with handcrafted features [27], whereas in the case of a deep learning model the need for feature extraction is not required as the model involves learning benchmark features and the classifier is capable of self-learning the features [28]. The non-stationary nature of the underwater signals due to the presence of interfering noise from biological, non-biological, and ambient noise sources degrades the performance of the system. Hence, the need for a feature extractor to extract useful information from the raw acoustic recordings has become a prerequisite. Audio data recorded using underwater hydrophones are usually correlated as mixed signals in their raw form as a channelized recording is usually infeasible. The redundant information in the raw data is removed via feature extraction or feature selection. Feature selection is the selection of relevant feature variables and feature extraction is the elimination of irrelevant feature variables in the dataset [29]. In the feature extraction phase, the data in the audio format is converted into a series of two-dimensional frames of images known as spectrograms. Spectrograms are energy-band representations of the noises recorded in the acoustic audio recording. The diverse noises recorded are depicted as peaks with varying intensity and timbre. Unlike processing a 2D image, the processing of a spectrogram representation takes up an altogether different approach as spectrograms are represented as an image but do not possess features like that of an ordinary image [30]. Table 3.1 shows the feature extraction methods for marine species sounds. In this section, we will address feature extraction wholly from the aspect of marine species signal analysis and not just limit it to cetaceans. The signals in the audio data are interpreted and converted into a set of feature vectors that depict highlighted signals in the acoustic recordings. Further, the classifier or the detector is selected based on the methodology and the application developed. Refer to Figure 3.4 for the feature extraction pipeline.

The feature extraction of an acoustic audio recording takes up a series of steps to extract useful midlevel features like pitch- and beat-related descriptors such as note onsets, fluctuation patterns, and MFCCs from the raw audio data. At the initial stage, time-domain information is captured from the waveform with time and amplitude information in the x- and y-axes. Analysing marine mammal vocalization or any audio data requires frequency information as the nature of audio data is non-static and it varies with time. Time–frequency representations express how the spectral components in a signal evolve. The time-domain signal is converted to a frequency-domain signal, also known as the power spectrum, by applying the Fourier transform (FT) on it. The frequency-domain representation provides an idea of all the frequencies that make up the sound with magnitude and frequency information in the x- and y-axes. A spectrogram representation of the audio data is obtained by combining both time- and frequency-domain signals. In spectrograms, the time and frequency information is represented in x- and y-axes. Different frequency components at varied time and the frequency band distribution at a particular time instance are denoted using colours. The intensity of the colour denotes the contribution of the sound. Spectrograms have information about frequency, temporal, intensity, and energy of the sound that help in extracting the mid-level perceptual features. Log spectrograms and MFCCs are more profound representation of the spectrogram. MFCC gives a consistent human-interpretable image over time of the entire signal and is the recommended choice for feature extraction for the proposed approach as it suits best for detecting and classifying all marine species sounds. The various other options for feature extraction methods with their advantages and disadvantages are provided in Table 3.1 and their choice is mostly done based on the type and the nature of the sounds to be detected. Similar to MFCCs,

Table 3.1 Feature extraction methods for marine species sounds

Method	Signal type	Advantages	Disadvantages
STFT	Non-stationary signals of all marine species	Time and frequency information of the signal is available	The fixed size of the sliding window results in limited spectrogram resolution
WT	Short-lived non-stationary signals like sperm whale only	• The size of the window is adjusted according to the frequency for better spectrogram resolution • Performs feature extraction covering the whole spectrum without a dominant frequency band	• Poor signal discrimination • Uniform resolution distribution
HHT	Bioacoustics signals of odontocete whales	• Detects underwater acoustic signals efficiently compared to STFT and wavelet transform. • Better data utilization • Facilitates easier interpretation of results and Data Thirsty	Fails in case of signals with low-energy component
EMD	Cetacean signals of whales	• For human interpretation, labelling is not required • Data-driven model • Avoids the needs for pre-processing and large training dataset	• Highly sensitive to interfering background noises • Difficulty in distinguishing feeble noise of fishes and invertebrates. • Lacks quick detection without prior knowledge • Affected by extreme values in the signal
LPC	Pulsed calls of whales	• Facilitates easier calculation and interpretation • Suits best for low- and medium-frequency sounds	• Sensitive to ambient noises • Requires knowledge about past samples
MFCC	Loud distinctive calls of whales, seals, and pinnipeds	• Easy human interpretation • Unique distinguishing spectrogram representation • Highly preferred feature extraction method due to low computational complexity	• Focuses only high-frequency sounds • Unsuitable for fishes and marine invertebrates sounds classification

Gammatone frequency cepstral coefficient (GFCCs) is another popularly used feature extraction method inspired by the design of cochlea of a human ear [31]. It is the best method for handling data from the noisy acoustical environment. Figure 3.5 shows the steps involved in the MFCC feature extraction process.

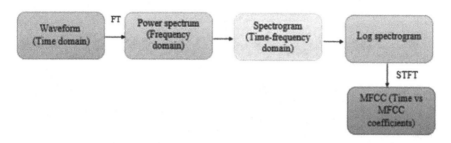

Figure 3.4 Feature extraction pipeline.

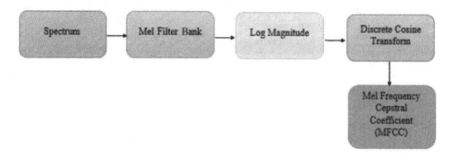

Figure 3.5 MFCC feature extraction process.

Amidst these methods, there are various other feature extraction methods developed by researchers compatible with their work in classifying marine mammal sounds. Few popular ones include Teager energy operator (TEO) [32] and Weyl transform [33]. Amidst modelling unique features, the idea of aggregating different features has gained significance recently. Feature fusion technique has proven to improve the accuracy of the model compared to the performance of a single feature [34, 35]. Exploring feature extraction methods imposes scope for future research in designing a single-feature extraction method capable of extracting features of all sounds. Figure 3.3 represents three types of audio data representation, namely waveform, spectrogram representation, and peak frequency spectrogram representations. The waveform, spectrogram, and peak frequency spectrogram representation of a marine mammal call is shown in Figure 3.6.

3.4 DETECTION

An underwater acoustic scene consists of several noise sources that contribute to the soundscape of the oceans. The idea is of perceiving relevant information from these audio sources to perform sound source detection. Sound source detection techniques – in particular, audio-based detection techniques – are commonly employed to detect the presence of animal activity amidst

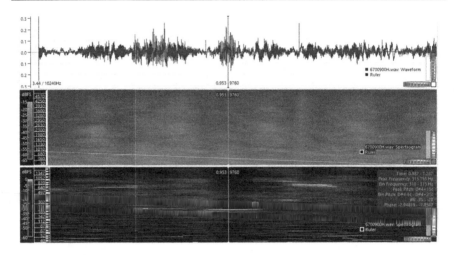

Figure 3.6 Waveform, spectrogram, and peak frequency spectrogram representation of a marine mammal call.

the highly interfering ocean noises in the acoustic audio recording using the audio fingerprinting technique [36]. In this technique, the audio form of data is converted into a two-dimensional spectrogram and peak finding or fingerprint hashing algorithms are used to define the peaks or fingerprints in the acoustic recording. In our case, the peaks in the acoustic recordings denote the presence of animal activity through vocalizations produced by marine species. Cetacean vocalization ranges from low to high frequencies occupying a wide frequency band with different characteristics. The influencing characteristics include varying vocals among and between species and the temporal and geographical variations. Cetaceans vocalization is mainly of four types: clicks, whistles, songs, and pulsed class. Similarly, fish sounds are commonly classified as drums, grunt, and impulse. Figure 3.7 shows a

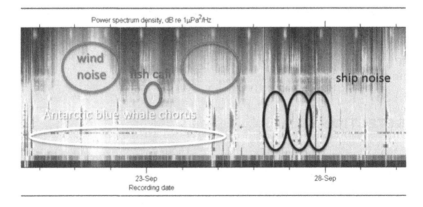

Figure 3.7 Marine soundscape of Perth Canyon, Australia [22].

manually annotated marine soundscape of Perth Canyon in Australia with diverse acoustic sources contributing to the ocean soundscape data. Framewise activity detection in sound source detection is approached using various supervised classification task methods [37]. Some of the most popularly used classifiers include the Gaussian mixture model, hidden Markov model (HMM), fully connected neural network, recurrent neural network, convolutional neural network [38], and convolutional recurrent neural network. The choice of classifier depends on the nature of the signal and the application to be developed.

Noise from diverse ocean noise sources like biological sources that consist of marine mammals, fishes, and invertebrates; non-biological sources like sonars and UANs; natural sources like rain, underwater earthquake, ocean waves, and few other unidentified sources are the predominant sources for detection. Of all the marine species, cetaceans are the species of interest for researchers for decades for their significance to the marine ecosystem and their lucrative values. Their sound-producing ability is used for communication, echolocation, and forging. The sounds produced as upcalls, clicks, songs, or grunts range from very short- to long-range sounds. PAM recording devices are deployed underwater for a substantially longer duration of time as months due to their high-cost incurring nature. Hence, the data recorded in these devices are of huge volumes that make manual inspection and interpretation completely infeasible. Therefore, a detection algorithm is needed to perform automatic detection of signals produced by diverse ocean-dwelling marine species. Factors like time–frequency difference in the vocal collection, the technique adopted, nature of the signal, and the real physical environment strongly influence the detection [39]. No single detection algorithm is ideal for detecting and classifying all the 82 varieties of marine species due to variability in time and frequency, amplitude among species vocal repertoire, and their physical environment as a monitoring approach needs a suite of such algorithms to achieve reduced misdetection.

Factors that influence the detection accuracy of a model in general are as follows: (i) *Data* – The nature of the type of data used has a strong influence on the performance of the detector. Marine species vocalizations being continuous, data is fed sequentially for precise detection. Added to the nature of the data, combined datasets are found to perform better compared to models trained and tested using a dataset from a single source. (ii) *Data collection method and its location* – The method of data collection plays an important role in the detection as the method determines the timbre of the acoustic recording. Location in oceans denotes the depth as deep water or shallow water. The characteristic and propagation pattern of sound in both these regions vary drastically leading to inappropriate results when compared. (iii) *SNR* – It is a measure of signal strength over background noise. It plays a significant role in determining the accuracy of the detector. Acoustic recording with interfering white noise hinder precise detection and lead to misleading results. (iv) *Size and variance of the dataset* – The size of the vocalization data is generally large owing to the data collection method and duration. Increasing the variance of the dataset increases the performance of the model [24]. Automatic sound detection is performed using many tools. HMM is one such popular tool largely used in detecting cetaceans sounds. Ogundile et al. [40] tested the efficiency of HMM over a novel feature extraction method known as the selective time-domain feature extraction method that adapted easily to the tool. They claim that the challenges faced in employing regular feature extraction methods like Mel-scale frequency cepstral coefficients (MFCC) and linear predictive coding (LPC) are overcome using the proposed feature extraction method. The efficiency of the model was tested on a continuous acoustic recording of Bryde's whale vocalizations collected from a single location. The results proved that the technique offered high sensitivity and false discovery rates compared to other traditional feature extraction methods. Recently, the increasing ocean noises have drawn attention of the researchers to propose an experiment called the Quiet Ocean Experiment where the scientists quest for quitter seas [41]. This massive project aimed at studying the response of all marine organisms to the noise. Of all the effects, the authors claim the incident at the coasts of North America to be the most distressing where hundreds of whales were washed ashore dead due to anthropogenic activities like vessel collisions and fishing activities. Inspired by the efforts of this experiment in Reference [42], a complete end-to-end detection using a region-based convolutional neural network (R-CNN) is developed. Three varieties of the endangered whale were detected in both time and frequency domains amidst a background of highly interfering ambient and non-biological noise sources. The challenges of sound event detection is shown in Figure 3.8.

In a recent study, the communication characteristic of cetaceans was found to differ from their habitat. Marine mammals in the ocean exhibit different cognitive abilities compared to a river-dwelling mammal [43] – similarly to the one in captivity to the one in its environment. Likewise, its communication pattern is strongly linked to its nature of adaptability [44]. In proposing an automated detection system, all such aspects need to be taken into account for a precise oceanic organisms detection. The most popular detectors detect the presence of a particular species vocalization in an acoustic recording as click or no click. Luo et al. [45] proposed a CNN-based method to detect odontocetes clicks as click and non-click by analysing the spectrograms. The detector is generalized to detect echolocation clicks of other different species. Figure 3.7 is a long-duration false colour spectrogram of Perth Canyon scoundscape in Australia with various noise sources detected manually by an expert. A comparison of automated detection results with those of manual detection shows that automated detection achieves quite a comparable accuracy at a faster rate.

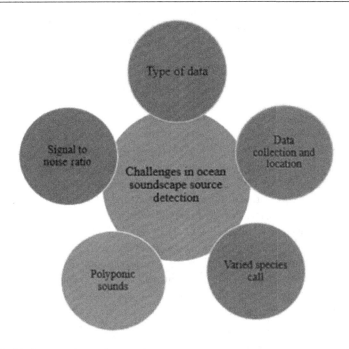

Figure 3.8 Challenges of sound event detection.

3.5 CLASSIFICATION

Understanding underwater data is a less investigated topic owing to the difficulty in assessing a diverse range of ambient noise from a noisy environment like ocean. Its automation finds use in many applications such as marine life monitoring. Accessing the impact of anthropogenic noise sources on the marine ecosystem is gaining huge importance among the research community using scoundscape analysis. Audio classification refers to the process of listening and analysing audio recordings. The three main distinguishing factors that help in audio classification are amplitude, frequency, and timbre. Amplitude denotes the loudness, frequency refers to the pitch, and timbre indicates the intensity or quality of the sound. Marine species classification from recorded acoustic recordings is quite tedious due to the following challenges: (i) *Varying noise sources:* The noises in an environment like the ocean are highly transitory and non-stationary, covering the entire frequency spectrum ranging from low-frequency grunts of invertebrates to high-frequency calls from cetaceans. Amidst classifying marine species sounds, artificial acoustic systems being a mimicked version of the natural acoustic systems produce similar frequency sounds hindering precise classification [46]. In this case, the efficiency of the model is dependent on the robustness of the classifier and the training dataset. (ii) *Sensor deployment:* The physical deployment environment of a sensor plays a key role in determining its performance. Environmental properties like long propagation delay, environmental noise, path loss, Doppler spread, and multipath effect affect underwater acoustic communication [47]. Other than environmental properties, the depth of the ocean as deep and shallow ocean contributes to the sensor's performance. Shallow water properties like high-temperature gradient, multipath effect, surface noise, and large propagation delay vary largely from deep ocean characteristics demanding suitable sensor configuration and properties [48]. Deployment as either static deployment or dynamic deployment also plays a major role in classification. The choice of region of deployment or the deployment scheme depends on the application developed [49]. (iii) *Overlapping vocalization pattern:* For most marine mammals, the nature of sounds produced is mostly continuous, broad-spectrum with frequencies close enough to the background noise causing difficulty in signal detection amidst reverberating ocean noises. Both acoustic sound detection and classification face the challenge of background noises overshadowing the foreground sound events [50]. Figure 3.9 pictorially represents the challenges in sound source classification.

Audio-based classification aims at automating the classification of sound sources in an acoustic recording, but most automated algorithms require large volumes of the training dataset. Kerri et al. [51] have presented a signal decomposition technique known as empirical mode decomposition (EMD). The need for a large training dataset and pre-processing is evaded facilitating hasty detection of all sound events in the recordings without any prior

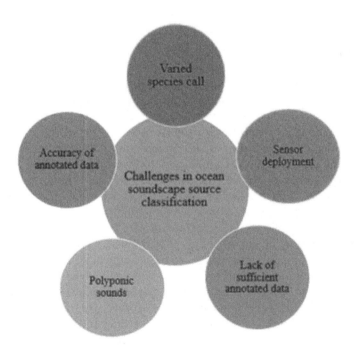

Figure 3.9 Challenges of sound source classification.

knowledge. The detection and classification are carried out in two phases: EMD detection and EMD classification. In the detection phase, all possible sound events in the dataset are extracted with minimum pre-processing; and in the classification process, the detected signals are uniquely identified and labelled. Amidst its benefits, the model was found to poorly perform in the presence of extreme values in the captured signal.

In a similar effort to reduce data pre-processing followed by a time-consuming manual validation, Zhong et al. [52] have proposed an ensembled deep learning CNN model to classify vocalizations of an endangered variety of whale known as beluga as true or false to study the cause of its declining population. As a drawback, the accuracy of the model depends on a large training dataset. About the past works, no single classifier is capable of classifying all the possible varieties of marine species. Moreover, classifying multiple sounds produced by a single source was also a tedious task as the model needs extensive training to classify variants of a single source like whistles, calls, and speaks that vary significantly. In Reference [53], such an effort is taken to classify marine mammal vocalization based on an independent ensemble methodology with 1/6 octave analysis–based feature extraction. According to the computational model, outputs of four parallel feed-forward neural networks are combined to effectively classify 11 classes of marine mammals. In acoustic scene classification [54], classifying diverse ocean noises is grabbing the interests of bio acousticians and ecologists to study the varying soundscape of oceans and its effects on marine life. To aid such efforts, Thomas et al. [55] have attempted to classify ocean noises of biological, non-biological, and ambient noise sources. An acoustic representation of stacking multiple spectrograms fetched from different STFT parameters is proposed. The performance of the classifier deteriorated with species mix in the passive acoustic moorings.

3.6 LOCALIZATION

Marine species are known for their locomotive skills, of which cetaceans, in particular, are renowned travellers. A typical migration pattern of marine mammals spans over hundreds of miles across ocean basins. Fishes and invertebrates owing to their size take up shorter distances limited to few kilometres as the energetic cost of travel proportionally decreases with the animal's size [41]. The movement pattern of a cetacean has a strong influence on factors like their birth and mating habits, distribution of food in space, and time [42]. The breeding and raising of their young ones have a strong interdependence with their locomotion. An aquatic animal's movement can be viewed from different temporal and spatial scales. The annual persistently long distant movement between two destinations as migrations and short animal home range movement throughout the year are the two common localization patterns of a marine animal. Owing to the strong connection of an animal's movement with its survival, it is of foremost importance to localize and track them to effectively monitor and record their characteristics. Logging the data as coordinates or frequently followed patterns of movement or trajectories can help avoid anthropogenic activities like shipping near the movement zone of the animal that cause harm through noise that obstructs their communication and through physical injury caused due to oil spills and vessel collision with marine mammals [43]. However, localizing a marine mammal faces some challenges: (i) *Non-Gaussian and non-stationary sounds:* Marine species are highly mobile as they are constantly moving in search of prey. Localizing a moving body is quite tedious as the position of the animal is constantly changing with respect to time. (ii) *Dynamically changing ocean environment:* The ocean environment tends to change drastically compared to that of a terrestrial environment. Environmental factors such as interfering background noises, moving sound sources, and reverberations change dynamically in the real world. Climate plays a huge role in determining ocean phenomena. Strident ocean environment affects data collection by disturbing the deployment of the hydrophone. (iii) *Polyphonic sounds:* Overlapping vocalizations from multiple sounds recorded in PAM is a natural characteristic of marine species as their movement is mostly in groups and their vocalizations are random. Identifying a single animal call from the polyphonic sounds is a recent research topic in audio AI. (iv) *Physical layout of the ocean:* Localizing a sound-producing source fetches best results mostly for an indoor deployment as the area for position prediction is defined as a closed surface. In the case of a vast and lively environment like the ocean, the positions are always approximated by assuming the physical layout of the ocean to be of any equally dividable geometrical shape [24]. Refer to Figure 3.10 for challenges in sound source localization.

Localization using acoustic audio recordings locates the vocalizing animal using sound source localization (SSL). The idea of SSL is to locate the sound-producing acoustic source directly in its environment using the signals captured by the microphone arrays. Sounds produced by marine species are highly non-stationary. In this case, continuous tracking at each varying position finds purpose than estimating a single position of the animal [44]. The methods adopted for SSL falls into three important categories: time delay–based method [45], beamforming-based method [46], and self-localizing sensor nodes [43]. The time delay–based method, also known as indirect method, uses time as the parameter for localizing the source. The time difference of arrival (TDOA) between pairs of spatially distributed microphones is estimated using the generalized correlation function (GCF). The TDOAs are combined with the stationary deployment position of the microphone to estimate the location of the sound-producing source. It suits best for static sources as its rate of movement is relatively low with respect to the analysis frame [47]. The beamforming-based method of SSL estimation is computed based on the intensity of signal power received by the microphone when steered towards the direction of the source. SRP-PHAT is one of the popularly

Figure 3.10 Challenges in sound source localization.

used beamforming-based SSL estimation algorithms. This method of SSL is a preferred choice by researchers for its robustness in any noisy and reverberant environment. The conventional idea of node deployment in UWSN is to be static, but, practically, the nodes deployed in an environment like underwater change their location over time. Due to this reason, the frequently displacing position of the underwater hydrophone needs to be self-calibrated or self-localized as in the case of self-localizing sensor nodes. Similar to the sensor node deployment, the ocean depth as deep water or shallow water influences the localization result drastically. Like deep oceans, the acoustic properties of shallow waters hugely depend on the main influencing factors of ocean depth, temperature, and salinity. Differed acoustic properties and sound propagation pattern in shallow water makes deep ocean localization algorithms incompatible for shallow water [48]. Figure 3.11 shows the broad classification of sound source localization algorithms.

Unlike cetaceans, localizing fishes using SSL takes up a different approach as their nature of receiving sounds differs from the directional hearing characteristic of most terrestrial vertebrates. So, the question of whether fishes move in the direction of sound or leave sound samples while swimming towards the source and how to locate a sound-producing fish in three dimension are still open questions to locate underwater vertebrates. But the fact is designing a single-activity model for the whole of marine species is not feasible and also localizing different marine species needs a deeper

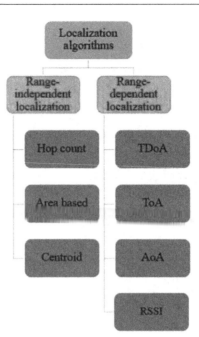

Figure 3.11 Classification of sound source localization algorithms.

understanding of their distinct hearing mechanism. As one such effort in Reference [49], the authors have studied the hearing behavior of fishes in detail to aid researchers in proposing an SSL chiefly for fishes. About multiple hydrophone deployment of PAM in Reference [50], a stationary source is localized using passive 3D SSL method. The geometric configuration is adopted for the multiple array of PAM deployment using three sound field microphones to cover sounds from three dimensions. A closed-form solution based on two TDOAs and three AOAs is derived. As their findings, the authors have observed that longer observations of the stationary source fetch higher accuracy. In previous works, sound event detection and sound source localization when performed separately experienced data association problems. To overcome this limitation in Reference [51], the authors have attempted polyphonic sounds localization and detection together as SELD in a three-dimensional space using deep neural network architecture. The temporal activities on each time frame are detected and from there localization is performed to estimate the 3D Cartesian points using a single DOA for every sound event. In addition to localization, the mobile sound source is also tracked with respect to time. Phase and magnitude components of the spectrogram are taken to be the features for the model, thereby evading the need for feature extraction. A drawback of the SELD method is that multiple instances of the same overlapping class cannot be obtained using a single DOA.

Sound source localization is performed in two variants: time delay–based localization and live localization. In time delay–based localization, the position of a sound event is delayed to the actual occurrence of the event, which is estimated as possible trajectories. Underwater microphones deployed underwater are retrieved and the recorded acoustic audio recordings serve as the data to perform time-delayed SSL. Results of this kind help in studying the animal's characteristic in its environment over a while and in finding the region of dwelling or frequent movement pattern of the animal. Most outdoor localizations are time delay–based as the feasibility of data collection and transmission is less. Live localization, on the other hand, facilitates live position estimation. In this case, the developed model is completely automated like robots and suits best for an indoor environment. An example of live source tracking in Reference [52] is the sound source localization and tracking system using both DOA estimation and SRP-PHAT algorithm. The power maps from SRP-PHAT are used as input features of the model with a 3D convolutional neural network to perform tracking. The challenge was to perform it in a highly noisy and reverberant environment. The efficiency of the model is improved by using random trajectories and an infinite size of the dataset to train the model. The logged detected and classified data can help in identifying the trajectories of the localizing animal. With the commonly followed pattern of movement or trajectory to be known, estimating the future location of the non-stationary becomes obvious. Following this idea of SSL evades huge disturbances caused due to the deployment of a real-time localizing model.

3.7 SCOPE FOR FUTURE APPLICATION DEVELOPMENT

Monitoring is the core activity in conservatory biology and biodiversity conservation. It serves as the base for conserving nature across the globe. Unfortunately, many monitoring applications follow a baseless approach leading to more harm than benefit. Monitoring is an art of making observations, measuring the level of impact, assessing its consequences, and drawing a conclusion as to how the interdependence between species and its ecosystem is changing over time and space. Its changes are prone to either naturally or deliberate human intervention. This section on the scope for future applications is an open perspective of how "sound" as a medium of communication can favour real-time applications at a large scale, especially in oceanic organism research. Sound localization under water can aid a whale in finding its prey and can help humans to observe the characteristics of a marine species. Likewise, acoustic multilateration as a method is gaining huge popularity in studying the life of aquatic animals that are challenging to observe visually. Exploring biological ocean sounds opens the scope for numerous applications in this regard. The very idea of discussing it from the application point of view is for the better conceptualization of the proposed approach. The categorization for sound source–based marine species monitoring applications is generally done for five main purposes:

1. *Animal Behaviour Analysis:* Variation in behavioural patterns among the population has a strong influence on the management efforts either to intensify or to subside conservation. Hence, before the decision on conservatory measures for a species, analysing the scale and spread of its behavioural style with its impact is of foremost importance. Behavioural analysis of an animal provides a deeper understanding of its character- istics for better monitoring and conservatory measures. The response of an animal to varied situations in its environment provides an insight into its breeding pattern, population distribution, habitat requirements, and dwelling region. Animal behaviour analysis helps in exploring plenty of rare and elusive species in the ocean. Matching similar characteristics like vocalization patterns, the region of dwelling, feeding habitats, and physical and behavioural characteristics can help in identifying this rare species.

2. *Marine Bioacoustics:* Bioacoustics is the study of an animal's interde- pendence with its habitat and surrounding with the use of acoustical perception of sound [53]. Amidst observing the oceanic life, its sur- rounding habitat and environment need to be studied for its interre- lation with the marine species. A better ocean environment leads to healthy ocean life. In this regard, acoustic scene classification of ocean noises to study the soundscape of oceans is an open research idea. A sub-link in the list of monitoring applications is water quality monitor- ing. The quality of water plays a major role in determining the health of its dependent species. Disaster-related applications like monitoring oil spills, pipelines, and cables are all crucial concerning issues in recent times [54]. Likewise, the very idea of marine habitat monitoring leads to many applications that need novel approaches and a better understand- ing of ocean life.

3. *Population Monitoring:* Population monitoring is estimating the popu- lation density of a species to get useful information on the status of marine life. It ensures the normal functioning of life in its environment with a count of its reproducing ability. Ill effects of anthropogenic activ- ities in the ocean first affect the reproductive behaviour of an animal. It causes a decline in poor larvae formation and premature rupturing of fish eggs and unhealthy offspring in mammals. Observing the popula- tion of a marine species provides information about mortality, migra- tion, and population structure like age, sex ratio, fragmentation, and genetic diversity. The location or the region of dwelling to be known, the operation of artificial acoustic systems like UAN and sonars can be distant to avoid its ill effects on marine life. Other than monitor- ing, logging this population-related data can help numerous research

efforts in a long run. In Reference [55], the authors have proposed a novel marine habitat–friendly marine habitat monitoring framework that emphasizes on performing monitoring without affecting the marine life. Applications like (i) abundance estimation, (ii) habitat and behavioural analyses, (iii) monitoring rare and elusive species, (iv) logging acoustic information, and (v) absence estimation or mitigation are few others applications. In abundance estimation, the density of the animal population at a given area is calculated to obtain an estimate of the abundance of the species of interest. The prevalence of a species is estimated in a single number or clusters. Habitat and behaviour analyses have attracted attention of the ecologists to observe and study the distribution pattern of different species in the ocean. In a recent research finding, the dwelling pattern or distribution of cetaceans was found to be non-uniform, showing spatial and temporal heterogeneity [56]. One key solution to reduce the impact of anthropogenic activities on the cetaceans is mitigation or absence estimation. In observing the animal's movement, the intensity of anthropogenic activities can be adjusted and altered to reduce its impact. In the case where the habitat area of the species is too vast to be surveyed and the species that cannot be detected by listening, PAM in its monitoring rare and elusive species application finds purpose. Commonly, data collection through PAM results in a large repository of data due to the long acoustic surveys. Logging this data provides detailed detection history and data processing post-survey that aids the application.

4. *Physiology:* Stress monitoring applications is a new perspective in monitoring applications as to measure the level of stress an animal is subject to due to anthropogenic activities. Stress affects marine life causing diseases, reduced reproduction, and chances of survival. The factors that cause stress are identified to be diseases, lack of food, and predominately the human-caused factors like noise, pollutions, and physical injury [57]. Recorded acoustic vocalizations of marine species serve as a great source for identifying the level of "stress impact". Stress monitoring application for marine species is an open new idea for application development in this chapter. Applications of this nature can save the marine life in distress.

5. *Methods Development:* Designing non-invasive artificial acoustic systems by adjusting the operating power of acoustic data transmission is a much dealt research topic in recent times but the results achieved are mostly unsatisfactory. In this case, maintaining the performance of artificial acoustic systems with no intrusion to marine life can be addressed using an approach as proposed. The baseline for the development of any conservatory method relies on the nature of the approach. Hence the scope for these applications is as vast as the ocean. A plenty of other problems in the ocean that hinder ocean life need to be identified and addressed for a healthy ocean ecosystem.

3.8 CONCLUSION AND FUTURE WORK

In this chapter, PAM is viewed from a different direction in the cetacean research opening scope for research in this field. In underwater acoustic sensor networks, it is necessary to design a marine habitat monitoring application to evade the impact caused due to anthropogenic activities. The idea of proposing such an approach is to support diverse monitoring applications that do more harm than benefit to marine life. In proposing such an approach, utmost care is ensured to the marine habitat and their communication. In this way, the perspective of audio signal processing in an underwater acoustic sensor network application is explored and the challenges are presented as future research direction in this field. The future indented work in this area is to design a real time end to-end underwater cognitive acoustic monitoring application effectively addressing a real-time problem. This chapter is an effort to change the idea of monitoring applications that the ocean and its habitat can benefit best.

3.9 CONFLICT OF INTEREST

The authors declare that they have no known competing financial interests or personal relationships that could have appeared to influence the work reported in this chapter.

REFERENCES

1. K. M. Awan, P. A. Shah, K. Iqbal, S. Gillani, W. Ahmad, and Y. Nam, "Underwater wireless sensor networks: A review of recent issues and challenges," Wirel. Commun. Mob. Comput., vol. 2019, 2019, pp. 1–20.
2. W. Yonggang, S. M. Ieee, T. Jiansheng, P. Yue, and H. Li, "Underwater communication goes cognitive," *OCEANS 2008*, IEEE, 2008.
3. R. Williams et al., "Impacts of anthropogenic noise on marine life: Publication patterns, new discoveries, and future directions in research and management," Ocean Coast. Manag., vol. 115, pp. 17–24, 2015.
4. J. Hildebrand, "Impacts of anthropogenic sound," in J. E. Reynolds III et al. (eds.), Marine Mammal Research: Conservation beyond Crisis, Johns Hopkins University Press, pp. 101–124, 2005.
5. R. P. Morrissey, J. Ward, N. Dimarzio, S. Jarvis, and D. J. Moretti, "Passive acoustic detection and localization of sperm whales (*Physeter macrocephalus*) in the tongue of the ocean," Appl. Acoust., vol. 67, pp. 1091–1105, 2006.
6. G. Qiao, M. Bilal, S. Liu, Z. Babar, and T. Ma, "Biologically inspired covert underwater acoustic communication: A review," Phys. Commun., vol. 30, pp. 107–114, 2018.
7. M. Stojanovic and P. Beaujean, "Acoustic communication," Springer Handbook of Ocean Engineering, Springer, 2003.

8. J. Pires, M. Colombo, J. Gallardo, C. De Maziani, and R. Alcoleas, "Vertical underwater acoustic channel model in sensor networks for coastal monitoring," IEEE Lat. Am. Trans., vol. 11, no. 1, pp. 382–388, 2013.

9. M. Bittle and A. Duncan, "A review of current marine mammal detection and classification algorithms for use in automated passive acoustic monitoring," in T. McMinn (ed.), Proceedings of Acoustics: Science, Technology and Amenity, Victor Harbour, South Australia: Australian Acoustical Society, pp. 1–8, November 17–20, 2013.

10. C. D. Pyc, M. Geoffroy, and F. R. Knudsen, "An evaluation of active acoustic methods for detection of marine mammals in the Canadian Beaufort Sea," Mar. Mamm. Sci., vol. 32, no. 1, pp. 202–219, 2016.

11. P. Subramanian, T. Nantha Kumar, and J. Jayashankar, "Underwater wireless sensor networks," Int. J. Chem. Sci., vol. 14, no. June, pp. 809–811, 2016.

12. M. Murad, A. A. Sheikh, M. A. Manzoor, E. Felemban, and S. Qaisar, "A survey on current underwater acoustic sensor network applications," Int. J. Comput. Theory Eng., vol. 7, no. 1, 2015.

13. K. De Jong et al., "Predicting the effects of anthropogenic noise on fish reproduction," Rev. Fish Biol. Fish., vol. 30, no. 2, pp. 245–268, 2020.

14. E. Guirado, S. Tabik, M. L. Rivas, D. Alcaraz-segura, F. Herrera, and S. Clara, "Whale counting in satellite and aerial images with deep learning," Sci. Rep., vol. 9, pp. 14259, 2019.

15. T. Guilment, D. Pastor, F. Socheleau, and S. Vallez, "Classification of marine mammal vocalizations in seismic environment." https://www.whoi.edu/wp-content/uploads/2020/01/2020_01_22_abstract.pdf

16. X. Li, Y. Sun, Y. Guo, X. Fu, and M. Pan, "Dolphins first: Dolphin-aware communications in multi-hop underwater cognitive acoustic networks," IEEE Trans. Wirel. Commun., vol. 16, no. 4, pp. 2043–2056, 2017.

17. E. M. Grais, G. Roma, A. J. R. Simpson, and M. D. Plumbley, "Two stage single channel audio source separation using deep neural networks," IEEE/ACM Trans. Audio Speech Lang. Process., vol. 25, no. 9, pp. 1469–1479, 2017.

18. W. Heo, H. Kim, and O. Kwon, "Source separation using dilated time-frequency DenseNet for music identification in broadcast contents," Appl. Sci., vol. 10, no. 5, pp. 1727, 2020.

19. A. Pandey, S. Member, and D. Wang, "A new framework for CNN-based speech enhancement in the time domain," IEEE/ACM Trans. Audio Speech Lang. Process., vol. 27, no. 7, pp. 1179–1188, 2019.

20. A. K. Ibrahim et al., "Automatic classification of grouper species by their sounds using deep neural networks," vol. 144, pp. EL196–EL202, 2018.

21. U. K. Verfuss et al., "Comparing methods suitable for monitoring marine mammals in low visibility conditions during seismic surveys," Mar. Pollut. Bull., vol. 126, pp. 1–18, 2018.

22. P. Zhuang, L. Xing, Y. Liu, S. Guo, and Y. Qiao, "Marine animal detection and recognition with advanced deep learning models species recognition on coral reef videos," Conference and Labs of the Evaluation Form, 2017.

23. A. M. Usman and O. O. Ogundile, "Review of automatic detection and classification techniques for cetacean vocalization," IEEE Access, vol. 8, pp. 105181–105206, 2020.

24. D. K. Mellinger and C. W. Clark, "Recognizing transient low-frequency whale sounds by spectrogram correlation," J. Acoust. Soc. Am., vol. 107, no. 6, pp. 3518–3529, 2014.

25. H. Park, C. D. Yoo, and S. Member, "CNN-based learnable gammatone filterbank for environmental sound classification," IEEE Signal Process. Lett., vol. 27, pp. 411–415.

26. V. Kandia and Y. Stylianou, "Detection of sperm whale clicks based on the Teager–Kaiser energy operator," Appl. Acoust., vol. 67, pp. 1144–1163, 2006.

27. Y. Xian, A. Thompson, Q. Qiu, and L. Nolte, "Classification of whale vocalizations using the Weyl transform, International Conference on Acoustics, Speech and Signal Processing (ICASSP), Brisbane, Australia, 2015.

28. X. Dong, "Environment sound event classification with a two-stream convolutional neural network," IEEE Access, vol. 8, pp. 125714–125721, 2020.

29. V. Bountourakis, L. Vrysis, and K. Konstantoudakis, "An enhanced temporal feature integration method for environmental sound recognition," Acoustics, vol. 1, pp. 410–422, 2019.

30. O. S. Kirsebom et al., "Performance of a deep neural network at detecting North Atlantic right whale upcalls," J. Acoust. Soc. Am., vol. 147, pp. 2636–2646, 2020.

31. F. Han, J. Yao, H. Zhu, and C. Wang, "Marine organism detection and classification from underwater vision based on the deep CNN method," Math. Probl. Eng., vol. 2020, p. 3937580, 2020.

32. C. Erbe, A. Verma, R. Mccauley, A. Gavrilov, and I. Parnum, "The marine soundscape of the Perth Canyon," Prog. Oceanogr., vol. 137, pp. 38–51, 2015.

33. S. Nanaware, R. Shastri, Y. Joshi, and A. Das, "Passive acoustic detection and classification of marine mammal vocalizations," 2014 International Conference on Communication and Signal Processing, IEEE, pp. 493–497, 2014.

34. S. Adavanne, A. Politis, and J. Nikunen, "Sound event localization and detection of overlapping sources using convolutional recurrent neural networks," IEEE J. Sel. Top. Signal Process., vol. 99, pp. 1–15, 2018.

35. O. O. Ogundile, A. M. Usman, O. P. Babalola, and D. J. J. Versfeld, "Ecological informatics a hidden Markov model with selective time domain feature extraction to detect inshore Bryde's whale short pulse calls," Ecol. Inform., vol. 57, p. 101087, 2020.

36. I. L. Boyd et al., "An international quiet ocean experiment," Oceanography, vol. 24, no. 2, pp. 174–181, 2011.

37. M. Thomas, B. Martin, K. Kowarski, B. Gaudet, and S. Matwin, "Detecting endangered baleen whales within acoustic recordings using R-CNNs," *AI for Social Good workshop at NeurIPS (2019)*, Vancouver, Canada, pp. 1–5, 2019.

38. P. A. Van Walree, "Propagation and scattering effects in underwater acoustic communication channels," IEEE J. Ocean. Eng., vol. 38, no. 4, pp. 614–631, 2013.

39. P. C. Bermant, M. M. Bronstein, R. J. Wood, S. Gero, and D. F. Gruber, "Deep machine learning techniques for the detection and classification of sperm whale bioacoustics," Sci. Rep., vol. 9, pp. 1–10, 2019.

40. W. Luo, W. Yang, and Y. Zhang, "Convolutional neural network for detecting odontocete echolocation clicks," J. Acoust. Soc. Am., vol. 145, pp. EL7–EL12, 2019.

41. G. Yao, Z. Jin, and Y. Su, "An environment-friendly spectrum decision strategy for underwater acoustic networks," J. Netw. Comput. Appl., vol. 73, pp. 82–93, 2016.

42. S. Climent, A. Sanchez, J. V. Capella, N. Meratnia, and J. J. Serrano, "Underwater acoustic wireless sensor networks: Advances and future trends in physical, MAC and routing layers," Sensors (Switzerland), vol. 14, no. 1, pp. 795–833, 2014.

43. Z. Zou and M. Badiey, "Effects of wind speed on shallow-water broadband acoustic transmission," IEEE J. Ocean. Eng., vol. 43, pp. 1–13, 2017.
44. D. Pompili, T. Melodia, and I. F. Akyildiz, "Deployment analysis in underwater acoustic wireless sensor networks," Proceedings of the 1st International Workshop on Underwater Networks, Association for Computing Machinery, pp. 48–55, 2006.
45. M. A. Aslam, M. U. Sarwar, M. K. Hanif, R. Talib, and U. Khalid, "Acoustic classification using deep learning," Int. J. Adv. Comput. Sci. Appl., vol. 9, no. 8, pp. 153–159, 2018.
46. Kerri D. Seger et al., "An empirical mode decomposition-based detection and classification approach for marine mammal vocal signals," J. Acoust. Soc. Am., vol. 144, 3181–3190, 2018.
47. M. Zhong et al., "Beluga whale acoustic signal classification using deep learning neural network," J. Acoust. Soc. Am., vol. 147, 1834–1841, 2020.
48. F. R. González-Hernández, L. P. Sánchez-Fernández, S. Suárez-Guerra, and L. A. Sánchez-Pérez, "Marine mammal sound classification based on a parallel recognition model and octave analysis," Appl. Acoust., vol. 119, pp. 17–28, 2017.
49. T. Virtanen et al., Proceedings of the Detection and Classification of Acoustic Scenes and Events 2016 Workshop (DCASE2016), Tampere University of Technology, 2019.
50. B. Martin, K. Kowarski, and B. Gaudet, "Marine mammal species classification using convolutional neural networks and a novel acoustic representation," U. Brefeld et al., (eds.) Machine Learning and Knowledge Discovery in Databases, vol. 11908, Springer, Cham, pp. 1–16, 2020.
51. C. Gervaise et al., Optimal passive acoustic systems for real-time detection and localization of North Atlantic right whales in their feeding ground off Gaspé in the Gulf of St. Lawrence, Can. Tech. Rep. Fish. Aquat. Sci., vol. 3345, pp. 1–58, 2019.
52. R. Darlene, "Marine mammal auditory systems: A summary of audiometric and anatomical data and its implications for underwater acoustic impacts," Polarforschung., vol. 72, no. 2, pp. 79–92, 2004.
53. M. Cobos, F. Antonacci, A. Alexandridis, A. Mouchtaris, and B. Lee, "A survey of sound source localization methods in wireless acoustic sensor networks," Wirel. Commun. Mob. Comput., vol. 2017, 2017, p. 3956282.
54. E. Nosal, "Methods for tracking multiple marine mammals with wide-baseline passive acoustic arrays," J. Acoust. Soc. Am., vol. 134, pp. 2383–2392, 2013.
55. R. Diamant, H. P. Tan, and L. Lampe, "LOS and NLOS classification for underwater acoustic localization," IEEE Trans. Mob. Comput., vol. 13, no. 2, pp. 311–323, 2014.
56. G. Han, C. Zhang, L. Shu, and J. J. P. C. Rodrigues, "Impacts of deployment strategies on localization performance in underwater acoustic sensor networks," IEEE Trans. Ind. Electron., vol. 62, no. 3, pp. 1725–1733, 2015.
57. B. Mishachandar and S. Vairamuthu, "An underwater cognitive acoustic network strategy for efficient spectrum utilization," Appl. Acoust., vol. 175, p. 107861, 2021.

Chapter 4

Visual question answering (VQA) on radiology images

A survey of methods and techniques

Jinesh Melvin Y.I. and Sushopti D. Gawade

4.1 INTRODUCTION

Visual question answering (VQA) in the medical field is a very challenging domain. This system aims to give the correct answer to the input questions which are taken from the clinical image. It also helps to obtain feedback to patients' queries and make them more informative. The normal VQA focuses on visual perceptual tasks which require some common perceptual abilities shared by humans. For example, doctors and even children can easily answer the question on an image with several mobile phones in a box: "How many mobile phones in the box?" But if the question is what size the phone is? Then it is a difficult task to give correct answers to such kind of questions. The system requires more skills. Most existing systems design simple tasks.

VQA is a task where the question is asked on the images which are given as input by the user with the help of feature extraction method. The image gets trained and tested, which is supposed to frame an answer for the question which is typically a word or a phrase. One of the major directions for visual question answers in research is deep learning using various image recognition such as CNN and RNN for NLP. The system will answer the question similar to humans. It will learn the images and textual knowledge from the input images and question, this we name as training phase, after that it combines two data streams and finally use advanced knowledge to generate the accurate answers for suitable questions from the input medical image. The literature survey of VQA is depicted in Figure 4.1.

The remaining part of the chapter is as follows: Section 4.1.1 gives an overview of neural network with single neuron example. Section 4.1.2 deals with the basics of supervised learning with different classification. In Section 4.2, different techniques used in image feature extraction and textual feature extraction are studied. Section 4.3 mentions the problem statements and explores the proposed system of medical visual question answering system with latest algorithms. Methodology, system architecture, and evaluation matrix are presented in Sections 4.4 and 4.5. Section 4.6 concludes the survey of methods and techniques.

 DOI: 10.1201/9781003433941-4

Figure 4.1 Literature survey.

4.1.1 Neural network

Neural network is a deep learning technique which performs more efficiently and fast. It helps to cluster and classify the data by extracting the features that are fed to other algorithms. By combining the multiple artificial neurons, we can make a neural network. This network takes data, learns from the data, and when given new related data, it can predict the result of the data. It contains three sets of layers: input layer, hidden layer, and output layer. We use image pixels in the input layer, which turn into one or more connected hidden layers; here the actual processing is done using activation function and dependencies. The output of a neural network is calculated using the trained data and the propagation method and it is used for further analyzing and testing purposes [1].

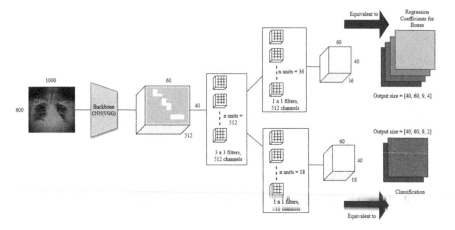

Figure 4.2 Neural Network architecture.

Suppose we want to classify the male and female images using a neural network. So we first train the images by giving a huge amount of male and female images. It classifies the images using parameters. The lines which connect one node to another are called weights. The weight will change if it predicts wrongly. Single neuron is called a perceptron.

The products of all the inputs and weights are taken and a bias is added to it. Bias is a real number which is used to train during learning the process. Then the results are taken as sigmoid (Z) (see Figure 4.2).

Sigmoid is the function which takes any number as an input. If the number is a positive number, then it returns the value between 0.5 and 1; if the number is negative, then it returns the value between 0 and 0.5. Just get the output and the probability between 0 and 1. The same process will happen for multiple neural networks.

The following are the three steps to obtain probability:

Step 1: Inputs = [X1, X2, X3] and Weights = [W1, W2, W3]

Step 2: $Z = [(X1 * W1) + (X2 * W2) + (X3 * W3)] + B$

Step 3: $Y = \dfrac{1}{1 + e - 2}$

4.1.2 Supervised learning

Supervised learning is also a machine learning task which underlies the relationship between data and labels, and develops the capability to predict the input data. In Reference [1], different types of images are used as an unbalanced dataset for image classification and feature extraction. Some of the image binary classification algorithms used in Reference [2] are logistic regression with perceptron (LRP), multi-layer perceptron (MLP), and deep multi-layer perceptron (DLP). The performance matrix is used for each algorithm. Here it distinguishes two different classes, namely, food and non-food for food dataset, which train and test how accurately it recognizes the class objects by using auto-recognizing tools.

4.2 LITERATURE SURVEY

Some recent papers have been referred to study common VQA systems [3–7]. Free form and open-ended questions are used for an image. It provides natural language answers. Some of the capability answers to the open-ended questions are mentioned in this chapter: fine-grained recognition, activity recognition, object detection, knowledge based reasoning, and common sense reasoning [3]. Also, Reference [5] considers the question generated from the templates of objects, attributes, relationship between objects, etc. [4]. Answer the questions by using workers crowdsourced about visual content asked by visually impaired users, train, validate, and test the images by using Microsoft Common Objects in the context (MS COCO) [8] datasets. Two methods for answering the questions are open answer and multi-choice answer [3].

The Document Visual Question Answering paper mentions the challenges in VQA for document images [9]. CVPR 2020 dataset is used for document VQA. The challenge comprised two different tasks: VQA on single-document image and VQA on collection of document images. In Reference [10], Co-Attention Network with Question Type (CAQT) is proposed for VQA task. It is integrated with the co-attention mechanism and question type into one unified model for VQA. Three key values [10] are self-attention to assign greater weights, knowing the question type before answering could compact the candidate answer space, and datasets should be feasible and effective for CAQT. The contribution of Reference [10] is attending to the image regions which are most relevant to the question and when calculating textual attention, it does not use image features which decrease the computational burden.

4.2.1 Convolutional neural network (ConvNet/CNN)

CNN is one of the categories of neural networks which has proven to be very effective in image recognition and classification. It is also used as smart grid application. CNN architecture has three different layers: convolution layer (with ReLU activation), pooling layer, and fully connected or dense layers. Convolutional layer extracts the information from the input images. It preserves the spatial relationships between the inputs by learning its input features. It converts input image into filter (f), the input image (x) is $(n \times n)$ matrix, that is, 5×5, which is converted into filter as 3×3 image and it produces the convolutional output $(n - f + 1) \times (n - f + 1)$, which is also 3×3 images. Convolutional layer output $Y = \sum_{i}^{m} x * f$. The ReLU layer is an activation function $f(x) = \max(0, x)$. Pooling layer will reduce the extracted data which is also called downsampling layer. There are three types of pooling: max pooling, average pooling, and sum pooling, among which max pooling is predominantly used in CNN. The flatten layer converts matrix into vector and the dense layer is used to classify the input image into class to which it belongs. Finally, the output layer predicts the proper output using softmax techniques.

Md. Ahsen Habib Raj, Md. A.I. Mamum, and Md. Farukuzzaman Feruk used CNN to predict diabetic retinopathy status using Fundus images [11]. Feature extraction and classification are the two phases mentioned in this paper. Using feature extraction and image recognition with CNN [12], it performed image feature extraction with different functional layers of CNN structure. It describes each layer of a separate functional block. The recognition process and results were stored into the MNIST database. CNN is applied in many practical fields such as vocal recognition, pattern recognition, NLP, and video analysis [13]. CNN is an integral transformation operation, which functions through a specific operator. Also, CNN manages to scan images and extract objects with much lower compute cost. In Reference [14], neural image question answers an end-to-end formulation. CNN features are fed into images to answer a question and CNN has also raised the bar on image classification [15].

4.2.2 Long short-term memory (LSTM)

LSTM is an artificial recurrent neural network (RNN) architecture used in the field of deep learning. It has feedback connection. Also, it does not process only single-data points but the entire sequence of data. Traditionally, RNNs are not good at capturing long-range dependencies; for example, when we work with huge datasets and multiple RNN layer, we are at the risk of vanishing gradient problem, which means when we train a very deep neural network, the gradient decreases exponentially as it propagates down the layer. There will not be any weight update because the gradients vanish. So to overcome this vanishing gradient problem in RNN, LSTM was introduced. It is used to modify the RNN's hidden layer; it is also capable of remembering the weights and their inputs over a very long period of time. In the hidden layer, the cell state is passed down to the next block.

LSTM captures the long-range dependencies that can always have memory of previous inputs for a very extended time duration. There are three gates in the LSTM: forget gate, input gate, and output gate. Forget gate removes the information that is no longer useful in the cell state: $f^{(t)} = \sigma\left(W^f\left[h^{(t-1)}, x^{(t)}\right] + b^f\right)$; second, by the input gate, additional information to the cell state is added: $i^{(t)} = \sigma\left(W^i\left[h^{(t-1)}, x^{(t)}\right] + b^i\right)$; finally, at the output gate, additional useful information to the cell state is added by an output $O^{(t)} = \sigma\left(W^o\left[h^{(t-1)}, x^{(t)}\right] + b^o\right)$. This gating mechanism of LSTM has allowed the network to learn the conditions for when to forget, ignore, or keep information in the memory cell. $\underline{C}$ denotes the modified cell state; so the equation is $\underline{C}^{(t)} = \tan h\left(W^c\left[h^{(t-1)}, x^{(t)}\right] + b^c\right)$, here $\tan h$ distributes gradients, hence it prevents vanishing. $c^{(t)}$ and $h^{(t)}$ denote two vectors for the input and hidden gate, respectively: the equation form of input and hidden vectors are, respectively, as follows:

$$c^{(t)} = f^{(t)}C^{(t-1)} + i^{(t)} \underline{C}^{(t)} \tag{4.1}$$

$$h^{(t)} = tanh\left(c^{(t)}\right) \times o^{(t)} \tag{4.2}$$

The leap-LSTM [16] has different text categorization tasks, such as sentiment analysis, news categorization ontology, and topic classification. Syntactic matching between question and answer is a traditional approach [17]; dependency tree model is recently used for matching general question and answer [18, 19]. Linear chain conditional random field extracts the answers, as the answer sequence labeling problem of the tree editing sentence [20], as lexical model used in [21].

4.3 MEDICAL VISUAL QUESTION ANSWERING SYSTEM

Compared with the existing domain, this is a very challenging problem, because medical-related questions are very difficult but the user will expect accurate answers. Systems have a high responsibility to give accurate answers to users' questions about the input images, its human health- and safety-related aspects. VQA problem combines two modalities such as text and image. There are some base perceptual tasks which recognize the image modality named CT and MRI.

Textual question answering is a task which automatically identifies the correct answer to a question. The traditional definition of extraction method can easily cause error propagation while defining features. Its purpose is to create textual answers for a specific question, any type of question from input images. The goal of this task is to resemble actions performed by users in the community such as ranting answers as applicable, selecting the best answer for a specific question, or identifying duplicate questions.

The problem statement of VQA and methodology with different algorithms like faster RCNN, BiLSTM, and MLP technology are discussed next. The evaluation matrix from a different existing system is also discussed.

4.3.1 Problem statement

To find answers to the given questions about the medical image is a very tremendous task, as the medical terms are very difficult to understand. Despite the developed technology, the patients do not have enough skills to check their reports to make them healthy. This system supports clinical decision-making and improves patient engagement. With the help of different algorithms, it generates an automated system which makes it faster. Also, the patients can access both structured and unstructured data of their health via medical portal to help them better understand their health conditions, including medical images.

4.3.2 Methodology

4.3.2.1 Faster R-CNN

Yiran Feng, Xueheng Tao, and Eung-Joo Lee proposed the classification of shellfish recognition based on improved faster R-CNN framework of deep learning. Faster R-CNN is the combination of region proposal network (RPN) and faster R-CNN. In Reference [22], dense block constitutes the feature extraction network, which allows extracting the deeper semantic information; it also accomplishes object identification and localization. Extracting the candidate regions by using RPN is provided in References [23, 24]. Faster R-CNN is composed [25–27] of three neural networks: feature network, region proposal network, and detection network.

Faster R-CNN with region sampling is dealt with in Reference [28]. Real-time object detection using RPN is described in Reference [29]. A region proposal algorithm is to generate bounding boxes or locations of possible objects in the images. Classification layer is to predict which class this object belongs to and the regression layer is to make the coordinates of the object bounding box more precise. Example faster RCNN structure is provided in Figure 4.3.

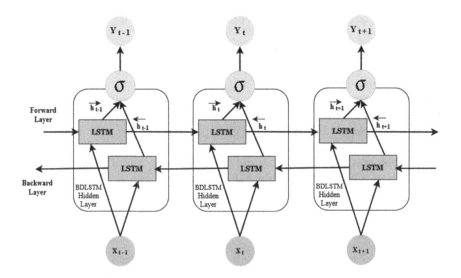

Figure 4.3 Fast RCNN structure.

4.3.2.2 Bidirectional LSTM

Bidirectional LSTM is an extension of traditional LSTM that can improve the models' performance on sequential classification problems, utilizing all the timestamps of input sequence and it trains two LSTM instead of one LSTM on an input sequence.

It connects two hidden layers of the opposite direction to the same output. The output layer can get the information from the past and future state simultaneously. It performs excellent sequential modeling problems for text classification. BiLSTM structure is shown in Figure 4.4. Melamud et al. [30] proposed BiLSTM based on word2vec's CBOW architecture. Hybrid model is used with attention mechanism to improve the text classification [31]. Liu [32] proposed an automatically extract and analyze semantic features for answer extraction. Attention weights are according to semantic similarity of question–answer pairs, which enables the network to focus on significant information and raises the probability of selecting correct answers. Cai [33] initiated a co-attention mechanism to extract the interaction between questions and answers with the combination of text similarity method using cosine and Euclidean to score the question and answer sentence. The contribution of this paper is to train the questions and answers dataset of ImageClef 2020, which is related to skeletal, using BiLSTM attention model. Map the questions and answers to the corresponding distribution vector to find the similarity. By using this method, different types of answers such as open-ended, close-ended, binary, and descriptions were displayed as an output.

4.3.2.3 Feedforward neural network

The encoding obtained is used for images and questions as input to the network from Visual Question Answer by Pankti [34]. In simple multilayer

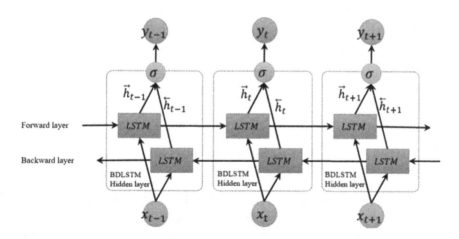

Figure 4.4 BiLSTM structure.

perceptron (MLP), there are more than 8,000 dimensions of dataset with images and questions for training, which has 3 fully connected dense layers and more than 1,000 nodes in each layer. Softmax is used for categorization in the final output layer. Riddhi et al. contribute MLP to combine the final results from the image and the questions [1]. Mourad proposed an autoencoders model which takes a medical question–image pair as input and it responds to the outputs in natural language [35]. Here the input features are images and questions. The CNN is used to obtain the visual feature and the LSTM is used to generate the textual feature. Finally, the model reconstructs both the input features using a simple MLP model which is a neural network with fully connected layers. MLP falls under the category of feedforward algorithm, because the image and question pairs were integrated with the initial weights in a weighted sum and subjected to the activation function, like the perceptron. There are many hidden layers present in MLP, each layer feeding the next one with the result of their computation, with their internal representation of the data. It moves through the hidden layer to the output layer. Also, it contains an information layer which manages to transfer the needed information highlights and a yield layer.

4.4 VQA SYSTEM ARCHITECTURE ON RADIOLOGY IMAGE

A system is needed to solve subproblems of other artificial intelligence models, which is a challenging aspect in the medical domain. The user uploads any kind of medical image where the system should answer for a given input image. The answer should be genuine and comprehensible to other users, besides being descriptive. Suppose the skull image is present as an input image, and the question is as follows "What organ system is primarily present in this image?" So the system generates the models and analyzes both the inputs for getting the accurate output as "skull and contents". Initiating the answers for the given question from the image is an important problem-solving aspect. Most of the answers come in minimum two to three words, but the idea is to try to generate long answers. Select more than 70% of most frequent answers in the VQA training datasets, so that the user can expect reasonable answers (see Figure 4.5).

4.5 COMPARISON OF EVALUATION METRICS FROM THE EXISTING SYSTEM

An essential component of the challenge is determining the quality of the question–answering system. The Med-VQA evaluates the time efficiency of reasoning models for question conditioned reasoning (QCR) and type conditioned reasoning (TCR), which compare with its base model [36]. The result

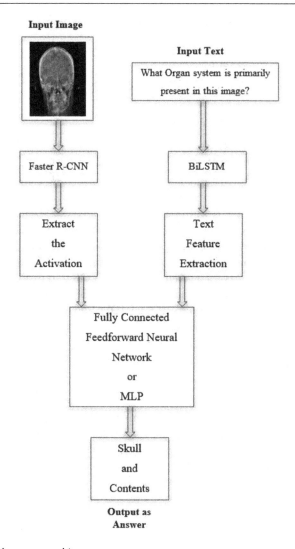

Figure 4.5 VQA system architecture.

is obtained from the averaging of training and testing time. Computational time slightly increases for training. The study of effectiveness of the QCR and TCR components are summarized in Table 4.1.

From Fuji and Zhou [37], the evaluation metrics is used to find the accuracy to compare the output result and the ground truth; here different methods are used to analyze the result: precision, recall, confusion matrix, and so on. Three other models were used to find the accuracy in comparison of textual data: BLEU score, accuracy score, and WBSS score. The final score of classification and generative model for VQA is provided in Table 4.2.

Table 4.1 Effectiveness of the QCR and TCR

BASE + QCR + TCR	
Time efficiency	0.57
Accuracy for opened and closed end	0.71

Table 4.2 Final score for VQA

Accuracy score	0.64
BLEU score	0.65
WBSS score	0.67

The evaluation metrics is found between two classifications short answer which is composed of only one word, and the long answer, which has multiple words or may be the answer is descriptive. The EM describes both the groups as metrics is based on information retrieval and natural language generation. It automatically generates the text for a given input. METEOR and BLEU were designed for automatic evaluation of machine translation [38, 39]; ROUGE-L [40] is developed for evaluation of text summarization; CIDEr and SPICE [41, 42] are developed for evaluation of image description and image captions.

4.6 CONCLUSION

The VQA system generates the answers for given questions from input images. The different types of information are trained by the system where the question refers to the task and classified the answer for a particular image. Textual question answering is the task of extracting an accurate answer in an open, closed, and descriptive way. This is to satisfy the users to get knowledge about the radiology images; visual and textual feature extraction will make sense for the input data to generate an automatic answer.

In the field of question answering, deep learning approaches have received a lot of attention. There are different deep learning models proposed in this domain. The models such as CNN, RNN, supervised learning, LSTM, faster R-CNN, and BiLSTM are used for the survey.

Several datasets are required for generating automatic question answering systems for both visual and textual analyses. In terms of comparison, the set of questions have at least one answer; VQA, CLEVR, ImageClef, and others provide datasets. Also, there is a possibility of collecting real-world datasets from the clinic.

REFERENCES

1. Riddhi N. Nisar, Devangi P. Bhuva, and Pramila M. Chawan, "Visual question answering using combination of LSTM and CNN: A survey," Int. Res. J. Eng. Technol., vol. 6, no. 10, pp. 780–783, 2019.

2. Reza Dea Yogaswara and Adhi Dharma Wibawa, "Comparison of supervised learning image classification algorithms for food and non-food objects," CENIM, IEEE, May 2019.

3. Stanislaw Antol, Aishwarya Agrawal, Jiasen Lu, and Margaret Mitchell, "VQA: Visual question answering," Computer Vision Foundation, IEEE, 2015.

4. J. P. Bigham, C. Jayant, H. Ji, G. Little, A. Miller, R. C. Miller, R. Miller, A. Tatarowicz, B. White, S. White, and T Yeh, "VizWiz: Nearly real-time answers to visual questions," User Interface Software and Technology, 2010.

5. D. Geman, S. Geman, N. Hallonquist, and L. Younes, "Visual Turing test for computer vision systems," Proc. Natl. Acad. Sci., vol. 112, no. 12, pp. 3618–3623, 2014.

6. M. Malinowski, and M. Fritz. A multi-world approach to question answering about real-world scenes based on uncertain input," NIPS, 2014.

7. K. Tu, M. Meng, M. W. Lee, T. E. Choe, and S. C. Zhu, "Joint video and text parsing for understanding events and answering queries," IEEE MultiMedia, 2014.

8. T.-Y. Lin, M. Maire, S. Belongie, J. Hays, P. Perona, D. Ramanan, P. Dollar, and C. L Zitnick, "Microsoft COCO: Common objects in context," ECCV, 2014.

9. Minesh Mathew, Rubèn Tito, Dimosthenis Karatzas, R. Manmatha, and C. V Jawahar, "Document visual question answering challenge 2020," arXiv: 2008.08899v2 [cs.CV], 18 July 2021.

10. Chao Yang, Mengqi Jiang, Bin Jiang, Weixin Zhou, and Keqin Li, "Co-attention network with question type for visual question answering," IEEE Access, vol. 4., pp. 40771–40781, 2019.

11. Md. Ahsan Habib Raj, Md. Al Mamun, and Md. Farukuzzaman Faruk, "CNN based diabetic retinopathy status prediction using fundus images," 2020 IEEE Region 10 Symposium (TENSYMP), 5–7 June 2020, Dhaka, Bangladesh.

12. Yu Han Liu, "Feature extraction and image recognition with convolutional neural networks," J. Phys. Conf. Series, vol. 1087, p. 062032, 2018.

13. J Koushik, "Understanding convolutional neural network," arXiv: 1605.09081, 2016.

14. Mateusz Malinowski, Marcus Rohrbach, and Mario Fritz, "Ask your neurons: A neural-based approach to answering questions about images," IEEE International Conference on Computer Vision, 2015.

15. A. Karpathy and L. Fei-Fei, "Deep visual-semantic alignments for generating image descriptions," CVPR, 2015.

16. Ting Huang, Gehui Shen, and Zhi-Hong Deng, "Leap-LSTM: Enhancing long short-term memory for text categorization," Proceedings of the Twenty-Eighth International Joint Conference on Artificial Intelligence (IJCAI-19), pp. 5017–5023, 2019.

17. V. Punyakanok, D. Roth, and W. Yih, "Natural language inference via dependency tree mapping: An application to question answering," Comput. Linguist., vol. 6, no. 9, pp. 1–10, 2004.

18. M. Heilman, and N. A. Smith, "Tree edit models for recognizing textual entailments, paraphrases and answer to questions," Human Language Technologies: The 2010 Annual Conference of the ACL, Association for Computational Linguistics, Los Angeles, CA, pp. 1011–1019, 2010.

19. M. Khan, F. Kuhn, D. Malkhi, G. Pandurangan, and K. Talwar, "Efficient distributed approximation algorithms via probabilistic tree embeddings," Distrib. Comput., vol. 25, no. 3, pp. 189–205, 2012.

20. X. Yao, B. V. Durme, C. Callison-Burch et al., "Answer extraction as sequence tagging with tree edit distance," Proceedings of the 2013 Conference of the North American Chapter of the Association for Computational Linguistics: Human Language Technologies, NAACL HLT, pp. 858–867, Atlanta, GA, June 2013.
21. G. Zhou, Y. Zhou, T. He, and W. Wu, "Learning semantic representation with neural networks for community question answering retrieval," Knowledge-Based Systems, vol. 93, pp. 75–83, 2016.
22. Yiran Feng, Xueheng Tao, and Eung-Joo Lee, "Classification of shellfish recognition based on improved faster R-CNN framework of deep learning," Math. Probl. Eng., vol. 2021, p. 1966848, 2021.
23. C. Peng, K. Zhao, B. C. Lovell et al., "Faster ILOD: Incremental learning for object detectors based on faster RCNN," Pattern Recognit. Lett., vol. 140, pp. 109–115, 2020.
24. Z. Liu, Y. Liu, T. Wang et al., "Detection approach based on an improved faster RCNN for brace sleeve screws in high-speed railways," IEEE Trans. Instrum. Meas., vol. 69, no. 7, pp. 4395–4403, 2019.
25. Github website: https://github.com/rbgirshick/py-faseter-rcnn.
26. Github website: https://github.com/facebookresearch/Detectron.
27. Tf-faster-rcnn, Github website: https://github.com/endernewton/tf-faster-rcnn.
28. Xinlei Chen, and Abhinav Gupta, "An implementation of faster RCNN with study for region sampling," arXiv:1702.02138 [cs.CV], February 2017.
29. Shaoqing Ren, Kaiming He, Ross Girshick, and Jian Sun, "Faster R-CNN: Towards real-time object detection with region proposal networks," arXiv: 1506.01497v3 [cs.CV], January 2016.
30. O. Melamud, J. Goldberger, I. Dagan, S. Riezler, and Y Goldberg, "context2vec: learning generic context embedding with bidirectional LSTM," Proceedings of the 20th SIGNLL Conference on Computational Natural Language Learning, Association for Computational Linguistics (ACL), Berlin, Germany, pp. 51–61, 2016.
31. Beakcheol Jang, Myeonghwi Kim, Gaspard Harerimana, Sang-ug Kang, and Jong Wook Kim, "Bi-LSTM model to increase accuracy in text classification: Combining Word2vecCNN and attention mechanism," Appl. Sci., vol. 10, no. 17, p. 5841, 2020.
32. Lan Liu, Yingxiang Li, Jiarui Zhang, Zehuan Yu, and Yongqiang Chen, "Attention-based BiLSTM model for answer extraction in question answering system, IEEE, 2019.
33. Linqin Cai, Sitong Zhou, and Xun Yan, and Rongdi Yuan, "A Stacked BiLSTM neural network based on coattention mechanism for question answering," Comput. Intell. Neurosci., vol. 2019, p. 9543490, 2019.
34. Pankti Kansara, "Visual question answering," SJSU ScholarWorks, Computer Sciences Commons, 2018.
35. Mourad Sarrouti, "NLM at VQA-Med 2020: Visual question answering and generation in the medical domain, CEUR-WS.org/Vol-2696, 2020.
36. Li-Ming Zhan, Bo Liu, Lu Fan, Jiaxin Chen, and Xiao-Ming Wu, "Medical visual question answering via conditional reasoning," MM'20: Proceedings of the 28th ACM International Conference on Multimedia, Association for Computing Machinery, ISBN 978-1-4503-7988-5/20/10.
37. Fuji Ren, Yangyang Zhou, "CGMVQA: A new classification and generative model for medical visual question answering," IEEE Access, vol. 8, pp. 50626–50636, 2020.

38. M. Denkowski and A. Lavie, Meteor universal: Language specific translation evaluation of machine translation," Proceedings of the Ninth Workshop on Statistical Machine Translation, pp. 376–380, 2014.
39. K. Papineni, S. Roukos, T. Ward, and W. J. Zhu, "BLEU: A method for automatic evaluation for any target language," Proceedings of the 40th Annual Meeting on Association for Computational Linguistics, 2002.
40. Rabia Bounaam, and Mohammed El Amine Abderrahim, Tlemcen University at ImageCLEF 2019 Visual Question Answering Task, September 2019.
41. R. Vedantam, C. Lawrence Zitnick, and D. Parikh, "Cider: Consensus-based image description evaluation," Proceedings of the IEEE Conference on Computer Vision and Pattern Recognition, pp. 4566–4575, 2015.
42. P. Anderson, B. Fernando, M. Johnson, and S. Gould, "Spice: Semantic propositional image caption evaluation," European Conference on Computer Vision, pp. 382–398, Springer, 2016.

Chapter 5

A comparative approach for speech emotion recognition using CNN and branch CNN

Pratik Kanani, Deepkumar Patel, Sanika Ardekar, Yash Joshi, Nancy Nadar, and Vishakha Shelke

5.1 INTRODUCTION

Decision-making and human behavior are significantly influenced by emotions. They enlighten us about our surroundings and direct our relations with others. Emotions also have an impact on cognitive functions like recollection and attention and help control physiological processes. It is essential for many disciplines, including psychology, sociology, and artificial intelligence, to recognize and understand feelings. Computer science and engineering study on emotion recognition is expanding quickly. There are many potential uses for the ability to automatically recognize and comprehend emotions from various kinds of data, such as text, speech, and audio, in a number of sectors, including health care, virtual assistants, and human–computer interface. As more data in various formats is generated, there is an increasing demand for automated emotion recognition.

Neural network models for machine learning are modeled after the function and organization of the brain of humans. They are composed of neurons or linked nodes arranged in layers that process incoming data and generate hypotheses or classifications. Typically, a sizable dataset of emotional expressions is used to teach a network of neural nets for speech emotion recognition (SER). The neural network can learn to identify patterns and relationships between various features of emotional expressions, such as facial expressions, vocal tones, and word choice, thanks to this dataset's labeling of specific emotions like joy, sadness, anger, and surprise.

The intended research will assess the performance of our proposed audio SER using RAVDESS [1] and TESS datasets [2]. The Ryerson Audio-Visual Database of Emotional Speech and Song (RAVDESS) [1] features 12 men and 12 women (24 professional performers), singing and speaking in two languages while expressing eight distinct emotions, including calm, joyful, surprised, sad, neutral, angry, disgusted, and fearful (English, Mandarin). There are 1,440 total files supplied, including audio-only and audiovisual recordings. The TESS (Toronto emotional speech set) dataset, on the other hand, includes more than 1,000 samples of actors (all female) speaking in eight distinct emotions (happy, sad, angry, fearful, neutral, calm, disgust, and surprised) and two languages (English and Spanish). Both datasets serve

DOI: 10.1201/9781003433941-5

Figure 5.1 Wave plot graph.

as a benchmark for our suggested approach and have been extensively utilized in the literature for testing audio-based emotion detection systems. The evaluation of the system uses these datasets and hence compares the findings through state-of-the-art methods.

Five emotions are taken into consideration: happy, sad, fear, disgust, and anger. Analysis of emotions from the audio wave plot can be difficult and complicated, hence convolutional neural networks (CNNs) are employed to ease the task of SER. Waveforms are one-dimensional representations of audio signals that lack the spectral content necessary to detect emotional signs in speaking. Although waveforms in Figure 5.1 can shed some light on the speech's acoustic characteristics, they are insufficient for using the RAVDESS dataset to forecast emotions. Therefore, models of deep learning like CNN and branch CNN (B-CNN) are used to predict emotions.

This chapter

1. Emphasizes the importance of B-CNN
2. Experiments with the dataset against B-CNN to improve accuracy and assess the loss
3. For improved results, compare CNN and B-CNN models on audio data

The remaining sections of the chapter are structured as follows: Section 5.2 lists the pertinent titles. Section 5.3 provides a summary of our recommended strategy, which also covers pre-processing and design. Section 5.4 offers comparative analyses of both approaches. Section 5.5 presents the result and Section 5.6 concludes the chapter.

5.2 RELATED WORK

Two layers of long short-term memory (LSTM) and 1D and 2D deep CNNs have been used to identify the emotions in spontaneous speech [3]. Both models learned local and global features using raw voice data and augmented (mid, right, side, and left) segment-level Mel spectrograms five local feature learning blocks, two LSTM layers, and a completely connected layer that make up the architecture of both models [4]. The importance of neural networks has been further emphasized by recurrent neural networks that predict categorical emotions in real time while taking into consideration the conversation context and the moods of each party [4]. The effectiveness of the proposed technique and model is evaluated using two benchmark datasets and an empirical evaluation of real-time prediction capability. The proposed method demonstrated an accuracy of 60.87% when weighted and 60.97% when unweighted for six basic emotions in the IEMOCAP dataset. Language differences have no bearing on the connection between prosody and emotion, according to the analysis of Marathi speech samples [5], which focuses on regional language SER using deep neural networks. Padman et al. [5] performed an acoustic analysis of voice and propose to introduce a classifier to reduce the confusion rate. Detailed efficient approach Mel cepstral frequency coefficients have been suggested as a solution to this issue. According to Patel et al. [6], applying autoencoders boosts the performance of the model. The paper provides a new path and insights into the impact of emotion detection from audio based on autoencoder representation [6]. It has been noted that using autoencoders improves the categorization precision of the feelings in the input audio files. To evaluate the robustness of the method, three classifiers—convolutional neural networks (CNN), support vector machines, and decision tree classifier—have been put into use. Additionally, the findings of a classification effort using Resnet50 and Alexnet are reported. Fractal-based SER using CNN was also used [7], which suggested a new feature vector. The study showed how effective the fractal features are at identifying feelings in speech data. Each dataset was classified individually for feature selection, then two datasets at a time, and, finally, all the datasets were combined and sent to the Resnet for classification in order to create a trustworthy SER system.

According to research on multimodal SER and ambiguity resolution [8], less complicated machine learning models that have been trained over a small number of manually created features are capable of performing on par with the most sophisticated emotion recognition method currently based on deep learning. This forms a basis for our research since B-CNN has been employed which proves to be less complicated. Wave2vec 2.0 outperforms pretrained audio neural networks, according to research on multilingual, multitask speech emotion detection [9]. The capacity to recognize emotions in speech across multiple languages can be improved by using model selection in automatic language recognition, according to research on how to better multilingual recognition of emotion in speech [10]. Four methods for selecting the best training group for the present language are compared: among speakers of the same family of languages, using every corpus that is accessible, choosing based on the automated LID, and language family.

Fahad et al. [11] demonstrate that MFCC vector features have been instrumental in extracting features and giving a boost to the model's metrics. The development of speaker adaptive models has made use of MFCC, epoch, and mixed characteristics [12, 13]. The models' performance has been assessed using the IEMOCAP database. When MFCC and epoch characteristics are used independently, the average accuracy for emotion detection systems is 59.25% and 54.52%, respectively. Combining MFCC and epoch characteristics boosts the identification rate to 64.2%. Zhou et al. [14] introduce a method without the need for parallel data, suggesting a one-to-many VAW-GAN-based framework for emotional style transmission. To define emotional prosody in a continuous space, deep emotional qualities from SER are used and the network can adapt an expressive style from an existing expression to one that has not yet been heard. Availing of a classification of PAN and MS in a two-branch CNN design [15] was carried out. Two sections make up the design: one for the MS source and one for the PAN. The final land cover category is created by combining the characteristics obtained by each branch, which yields superior quantitative and qualitative results than more recent classification methods for optical VHSR images. Another study [16] used concurrent convolutional neural networks to categorize peptides that engage with ion channels, along with multi-branch CNN. The results showed a 6–15% increase in accuracy for forecasting all three channel peptides, demonstrating that multi-branch CNN can not only sustain a high prediction performance on general test sets but can also achieve an acceptable performance when compared to traditional ML methods. Hence, B-CNN has shown to be effective for multimedia input and has only been employed for images and peptide file formats. We investigate the B-CNN approach for audio and aim at finding a robust model for SER streamlining the CNN approach. We compare our CNN model and the B-CNN model results to highlight the improved metrics and results.

5.2.1 Research gaps

Using unprocessed speech samples and enhanced segment-level Mel spectrograms, 1D and 2D deep convolutional neural networks with two layers of LSTM learned local and global features. Compared to speaker-dependent and independent speaker experiments, Amjad et al.'s mid-level spectrograms had poorer accuracy [3]. For six fundamental emotions, Chamishka et al.'s method gave 60.87% weighted accuracy and 60.97% unweighted accuracy which used recurrent neural networks that predict categorical emotions in real time while taking into consideration the conversation context and the moods of each part [4]. Borwankar et al. showed how effective the fractal features are at identifying feelings in speech data and removed the emotion of "disgust" to make the dataset balanced and accordingly only included neutral, sad, happy, fear, and angry [7].

5.3 DATA PRE-PROCESSING TECHNIQUE

Data preparation is crucial because it raises the data's standard and increases the models' precision. It entails a number of stages to clean, transform, and organize raw data into a format that can quickly assess. The data can be made more meaningful and helpful for training the models by removing unnecessary or redundant information, handling missing values, and scaling the features. In addition to preventing overfitting, proper data preparation can enhance the models' ability to generalize to new, untested data.

5.3.1 Voice augmentation

RAVDESS dataset has been augmented with various techniques like the injection of noise to increase its robustness. This increases the diversity and complexity of the data, making it more difficult for the model to overfit and better prepare it for real-world scenarios with more varied and unexpected input. By purposely distorting the data, the model's ability is improved to generalize previously unseen data, enhancing its overall accuracy and efficacy. Further, this voice has been stretched and pitch variation has been done to reduce the overfitting of the data.

5.3.2 Feature extraction

A crucial step in analyzing and discovering relationships between various objects is feature extraction. The audio data is converted and provided into a format that the models can comprehend To do this, feature extraction is used. The three vectors of the audio signal—time, amplitude, and frequency—represent its three dimensions.

5.3.2.1 Chroma STFT

To compute Chroma features, a short-term Fourier transformation is used. STFT encodes information about pitch classification and signal structure [15].

Chroma STFT is a technique that has been used to extract harmonic information from audio signals. Calculating the STFT of the signal, it is founded on the notion of representing the audio data in the frequency domain and then mapping the STFT magnitude values to a Chroma representation. The Chroma representation is a feature vector composed of 12 dimensions, with each dimension corresponding to a unique pitch class (C, C#, D, D#, etc.) [17]. Since its harmonic structure successfully retains the emotional content of an audio stream, Chroma representation is well-suited for emotion identification. Chroma can give key insights into the emotional content of the audio by evaluating the distribution of pitch classes, making it a strong tool for emotion recognition. Additionally, Chroma STFT is robust to variations in the timbre of the audio, making it a suitable feature for emotion recognition from different types of audio sources and recording conditions. Chroma STFT features are given as input to our proposed emotion recognition system, which is trained to predict the emotions present in the audio signals.

5.3.2.2 MFCC

MFCCs provide a compressed representation of the spectrum that is commonly used for speech identification and are a key feature in a variety of audio signal–related research fields. The Mel-frequency spectrum (MFC) in sound processing depicts the short-term power spectrum of a sound by using a linear cosine transform of a log power spectrum on a nonlinear Mel-scale of frequency [16]. Coefficients that make up an MFC are referred to as MFCCs.

The Mel Spectrogram is a useful feature for recognizing audio emotions. It represents the audio signal in the frequency domain by converting it to a spectrogram and then capturing the signal's spectral content with a Mel-scale filter bank. The Mel-scale belongs to how different frequencies are perceived by the ear of human beings, allowing the Mel Spectrogram to represent the audio signal in a more human-like manner. The Mel Spectrogram is a two-dimensional signal representation that captures the energy of specific frequency bands at specific time intervals. The frequencies in a Mel spectrogram have been transformed to the Mel scale.

After processing each extraction step, all the results are stored in the stack horizontally and the final result stack. Different functions were introduced for adding noise, shift, pitch, and stretch to the data to perform data augmentation in various ways. The function of noise is adding random amplitude to the data. The function of stretch is stretching the time or words in the audio. The function shift is shifting amplitude in various ranges, from –5 to +5, and the last function is a pitch where the audio of the data is more amplified and emotion is given more emphasis in this method.

Get features function that is used in the extraction algorithm. The function takes an argument of the file path from where the data augmentation process starts. Data is augmented in three ways, one with no augmentation, adding only noise to data, and adding stretch and pitch to the data. The augmentation part of the data is performed using extract feature functions where we create various columns for various features and a horizontal stack is created for ZCR, chromo STFT, mfc, rms, and Mel spectrogram. This procedure is repeated three times in three various augmentation features. Data is stored in a vertical stack for three different columns. Librosa library of Python is used to perform various features of mfcc, zcr, etc.

Algorithm for adding various features to data:

Step 1 – initialize 2 empty list
Step 2 – iterating each column of a single row in the index, path, emotion

Step 3 – get_features(path) - adding features to the audio file present at that path

Step 4 – storing feature in a 2d array in a variable called feature

Step 5 – Iterating a feature to and storing emotion in 1 list and ele in one 1 list

Step 6 – Make a data frame of 2 list

Step 7 – one hot Encoding of the elements of the Y list

5.4 ARCHITECTURE OF SINGLE CNN AND B-CNN

5.4.1 Architecture of single CNN

The audio file contains various emotions of men and women that are extracted using data pre-processing and the get_features algorithm. The audio of a human and the emotion are stored in two separate variables. The model aims to find the emotion of the audio from the given input audio file. In CNN, the initial layer, the input layer, is a tensor representing the audio data that is considered as input. Since the input data is audio file and input layer shape is tensor, it can be represented as (None, num_samples, num_channels), where num_channels is the number of audio channels.

The model or CNN architecture, as observed in Figure 5.2, consists of seven convolutional layers: Conv1, Conv2, Conv3, Conv4, Conv5, Con6, and Conv7. First, the input is taken in the form a Spectrogram and then Voice is passed to the First Convolutional layer.

The network is started by applying two 1D convolutional layers (conv_1 and conv_2) to the input tensor(input_x). In the input tensor, the number of audio samples is 162 and output form of the convolutional layer which is Conv1 is (None, 162, 256), with a single channel being used [18]. The layer has 256 filters which is applied on input data and a kernel size of (8,1) which is used to scan the input data and learn features as Zero padding is applied to the input to ensure the output shape has the same size as of input data. ReLU (rectified linear unit) is a activation function. This layer contains a total of 2,304 parameters [19].

The result of Conv_1 is further passed to another layer conv_2 and then the output of conv_2 is normalized with a batch normalization layer and passed through a dropout layer (drop_1) with a rate of 0.25 to prevent overfitting. The output of drop_1 is then passed through a max pooling layer(pool_2) with a pool size of 8 which gives output as (None, 20, 256)

The above output is passed as an input with a total of three sets of two 1D convolutional layers(conv_3 to conv_5,conv_6 to conv_7) and then the result is passed to batch normalization layer, a dropout layer, and a max pooling layer and a final result is obtained.

Finally, the output of conv_7 (None, 2, 64) is flattened with flatten layer and passed through a final dense layer (output) with an activation function of

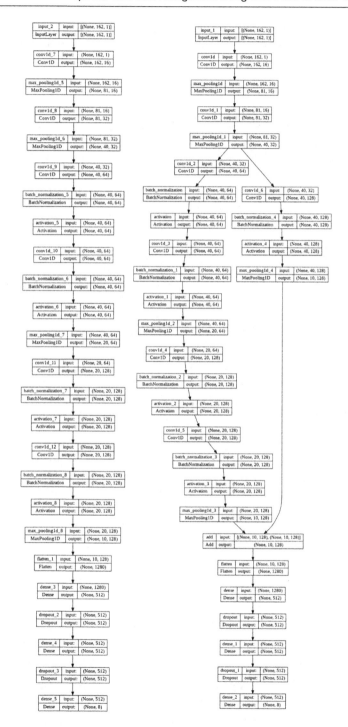

Figure 5.2 Single CNN and branch CNN architecture.

"softmax". As evidenced by the shape of the "y train" variable, the final dense layer has the same number of units as the number of classes in the training data.

5.4.2 Need of B-CNN

The audio data used as input became more complex after the addition of various features. The input shape is around 162 columns and 12,744 rows, as the model needs to be more complex. As observed in single-layer CNN, there is more variation in loss, which shows the complexity of the data. The need for B-CNN arises here to build a more complex model to handle multiple tasks simultaneously and also to provide different processing paths for different types of tasks and different types of inputs. B-CNN also provides improved accuracy and faster optimization and processing because it can handle multiple inputs and outputs, compared to a single CNN. B-CNN is known for the role it plays in the loss function of the model. Loss is also used to consider the performance of the B-CNN model during training and to optimize model parameters. There are several loss functions available, such as mean-square error, cross-entropy, and mean absolute error. The loss is an important step in the training process because it directs the optimization of the model parameters and allows the model to improve in accuracy over time.

In B-CNN, multiple paths or branches of computation are available, with each branch having its respective loss function. In single-layer CNN, only one loss function was available, which is considered the final loss of the model. While in B-CNN, the loss function of each branch is combined or added to form a final loss, which guides model parameters on how to optimize to give a faster and more accurate answer. B-CNN is designed in such a way that it can be used for multitask learning where each branch performs different tasks with different loss functions. Finally, all the branch losses are combined, and it works on the improvement or optimization of model parameters, which leads to an improvement in accuracy as compared to the single-stream models that can handle one task at a time. B-CNN is better at handling data for feature extraction and classification as compared to single-stream models which have single loss functions for all stages of processing.

5.4.3 Architecture of B-CNN

B-CNN is typically used in situations where it is essential to separate out various informational types or features from the input data. It is used as a multitask learning in computer vision where the same input image is for both object detection and classification tasks. Performing tasks like sentiment analysis or named object recognition requires various types of information to be extracted and analyzed separately from the input text. Here it is used to detect the SER in the following manner.

Considering the architecture of single-layer CNN, there were seven convolution layers used with max pooling, ReLU, and flattening. The B-CNN architecture also consists of seven convolutional layers, but the branching is applied after a certain layer. The audio file contains various emotions of men and women that are extracted using data pre-processing and the get_features algorithm. The audio of a human and the emotion are stored in two separate variables. In CNN, the input layer is a tensor representing the input data which is audio file. Since the input audio file and the layer shape is tensor, it can be represented as (None, num_samples, num_channels), where num_channels is the total number of audio channels.

In the layer which goes as an input to the B-CNN, the shape of the input is [None, 162, 1]. Here, the number of audio samples is 162, and the number of channels obtained from the audio data is 1. After the input layer is added, the network applies two 1D convolutional layers (conv_1 and conv_2) to the input tensor (input_x). The first layer Conv1 has 16 filters and a kernel size of (3,1), which are used to scan the input data and learn features. as same padding is applied to the input to ensure the result shape is of the same size as the input. The activation function ReLU is used in B-CNN. The total parameter used in this layer is 64. Where the output shape obtained is (None, 162, 16) before applying the next layer, max pooling is applied to the 1 layer output, and the audio shape is reduced to 81 from 162. Further, this is passed to the next layer (second layer), which has 32 filters and a kernel size of (3,1), and the activation ReLU total parameter obtained is 1,568. This layer output is passed through max pooling. From here, the concept of branching starts, and the model is divided into two branches. The first branch has four convolutional layers, which is termed as "big branch", while the second branch, dubbed a "small branch", has one convolutional layer.

The big branch has four convolutional layers, the first two of which have an identical structure with 64 filters and kernel size (3,1) with the same padding. The output obtained has a shape of the first layer that is normalized before applying the activation function, and the ReLU activation layer is applied to the normalized output shape. After two convolution layers with two times normalization and activation, the total parameter is 24,704. Another two layers follow a similar structure, with 128 filters and a kernel size (3,1) applied with the same padding; the layers are first normalized and then the ReLU function is applied to the normalized output. Here comes the end of a big branch. The other small branch contains one convolutional layer that has 128 filters and a kernel size (3,1) with the same padding. Before applying activation, the output is normalized and then the activation of ReLU is applied and max pooling of the output shape layer is done.

The two branches are then connected and their output shape is flattened and passed through a dense layer. There were two dense layers applied with the units of 512 and the activation function of ReLU. After each dense layer, a 0.4 dropout is applied to the layer. Following the second dropout, the final dense layer of total labels or emotions that are used in the dataset was applied. In total, eight emotions were used, which are applied as units in the final dense layer that is applied on the output obtained, and the activation of softmax is then applied. The model's architecture is now complete.

5.4.4 Compiling and fitting the model

The model is then compiled after it has been created. The model's learning process is configured using Keras' compile function. The arguments used to compile the B-CNN and single CNN models are the optimizer, also known as an optimization algorithm, which is used to change the model weights. Stochastic gradient descent (SGD), which has a learning rate of 0.01, a decay rate of 1e-6, and a momentum of 0.8, is the optimizer employed in both models. The performance of the model is assessed using the loss function; in this case, multi-class classification issues are frequently solved using categorical cross entropy. The model's performance is evaluated using the final measures. Here the accuracy is stated, which is the proportion of correctly identified samples. After calculating the summary of the model obtained by B-CNN, the total parameter used was 1,031,272, of which the trainable parameters were 1,030,248 and non-trainable parameters were 1,024. After calculating the metrics, we start with fitting the training data with the fit function of the Keras library with a batch size of 128 and with 100 epochs. To keep a check on the model, ReduceLROnPlateau is being used when the measure no longer shows evidence of progress and the learning rate is reduced. This callback monitors a quantity and pauses learning if there has not been any progress in a defined number of epochs.

5.5 IMPLEMENTATION AND RESULTS

Precision, recall, F1 score, ROC, AUC, and confusion matrix are just a few of the measures that may be used to gauge how well SER performs. Here, the model is evaluated using the Loss function and Confusion Matrix. A 3/4 division ratio was used to divide the data, with 25% used for testing and 75% for training.

5.5.1 Evaluation of loss

One of the most essential elements of neural networks is the loss function, which, along with the optimization functions, is directly responsible for adapting the model to the given training data. A loss function is used to compare the objective and predicted output values, revealing how well the neural network models the training data. The model works to narrow the output gap between the predicted and the goal during training. The loss over the training data is represented by the value of "Loss" at the conclusion of each epoch. The lower the number, the better because the optimization procedure with training aims to minimize this.

Classification cross-entropy loss is a metric for how closely a model's predictions fit a dataset's actual class labels. In order to forecast one of several potential classes for each input example, multi-class classification models are frequently used in deep learning. To improve the model's forecast accuracy, the loss must be minimized because it is computed as the negative log-likelihood of the true class. The Softmax activation function, where K is used to represent the number of classes or emotion in the classification task, returns a probability distribution over K classes after accepting a vector of real values as input. The function maps the input values to a probability space, such that the sum of the probabilities is 1. The loss calculated using the CNN model was 1.3011.

For the B-CNN, the loss came out to be 0.4934. Results show that the B-CNN achieved a 62.07% reduction in loss compared to the baseline model, demonstrating significant improvement in its ability to accurately identify emotions. When compared to CNN, the B-CNN model is able to more accurately capture the information because it uses numerous branches that concentrate on learning different features from the input data. Since the B-CNN uses various regularization techniques, like Dropout and Batch Normalization in each branch, to minimize the overfitting of the data, it has a lower loss function than the CNN model. Figure 5.4 shows a smoother and more gradual change than Figure 5.3 which indicates that splitting the emotions into branches and concentrating on their specific features has improved the SER task.

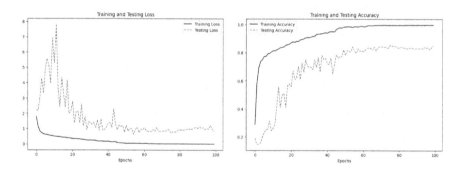

Figure 5.3 Single CNN loss graph.

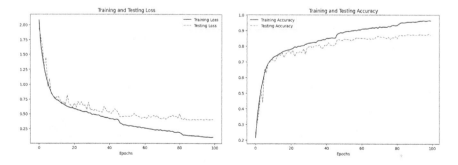

Figure 5.4 B-CNN loss graph.

5.5.2 Confusion matrix analysis for single CNN and B-CNN

Following the completion of the B-CNN model architecture, the results were visualized using a confusion matrix and classification report. The branch model performed well, as the loss obtained from B-CNN was much lower than that obtained from a single CNN in terms of emotion classification. In the confusion matrix produced by B-CNN, emotions are classified into eight different classes. The eight emotions used in the chapter are considered classes by the model. The first emotion shown in Figure 5.5 is anger, which is considered 92% accurate by the model, one of the most accurately predicted emotions.

The main emotion that proved B-CNN as one of the most effective models is calm; it worked 78% accurately while single CNN worked only 39% accurately. In single CNN, most of the calm emotions were predicted as disgust which in B-CNN is reduced drastically from 57% to 3%, which shows the best use of the model. Some calm emotions are also predicted as neutral and sad. The emotion disgust is predicted very well by single CNN as compared to B-CNN; the percentage accuracy for single CNN is 97%, whereas for branch CNN it is 87%. B-CNN did not perform accurately only for disgust emotions; for the rest of the emotions, it performed very well as compared to single CNN. The emotions fear, happy, neutral, sad, and surprise have an accuracy of 91%, 89%, 88%, 86%, and 89%, which is higher as compared to a single CNN.

The CNN model is able to predict emotions in speech with an accuracy of 82%. Of these predicted emotions, the proposed model is able to classify disgust and angry with the highest accuracy of 97% and 89%, respectively, and fear, happy, neutral, sad, and surprised with the highest accuracy of 83%, 82%, 84%, 72%, and 85%, respectively. The calm emotion has the lowest

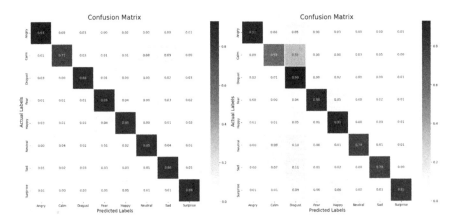

Figure 5.5 Confusion matrix for B-CNN and CNN.

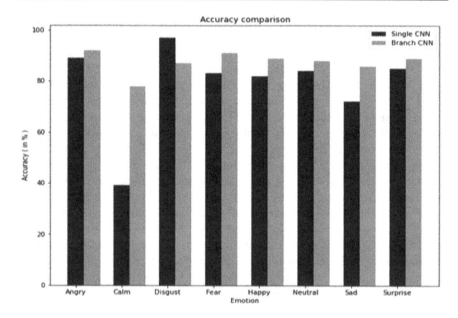

Figure 5.6 Comparison of accuracy.

accuracy of 39%. The proposed model shows the misclassification of the calm emotion and sad emotion as disgust emotion many times.

5.5.3 Accuracy graph

The bar graph in Figure 5.6 represents the distribution of emotional states in the dataset. The X-axis shows the different emotions, while the Y-axis represents the accuracy percentage achieved by the single CNN and B-CNN models in classifying each emotion. As can be seen in the graph, two models achieve high accuracy in angry, fear, happy, surprise, neutral, and sad. B-CNN outperformed CNN in all emotions except disgust emotion. Overall, the result suggests that B-CNN is best for predicting the SER for all emotions except disgust.

5.6 CONCLUSION AND FUTURE SCOPE

This chapter compares CNN and B-CNN methods for employing SER which was tested on RAVDESS and TESS datasets. While CNN's total accuracy is 82.36%, B-CNN's overall accuracy is 88.51%. The complexity of the data is illustrated by the greater variance in loss, as seen in single-layer CNN. Here, B-CNN is created for a more complex model that can handle numerous tasks at once and provide various processing pathways for each emotion and its specific features. Moreover, the training parameters for both models have been kept the same, highlighting the versatility of B-CNN over CNN. When giving better and finer predicting accuracies for each of the experimenting emotion class labels, the B-CNN model outperformed the CNN model impressively. In the RAVDESS and TESS dataset, disgust is found to be more difficult to forecast using B-CNN than the other seven emotions because B-CNN considers a variety of parameters when learning and predicting as opposed to CNN, which requires less complexity. It could efficiently support operations in a contact center, allowing for real-time monitoring of the feelings generated by phone calls. Despite the unique benefits of this research, there are still some difficulties and restrictions. First, we were unable to construct and test our models on bigger and more varied dataset due to the lack of speech datasets with emotions identified. Using a larger voice training dataset built from populations representing different populations in terms of language or culture when such a dataset becomes available could further improve the generalizability of our prediction models. Second, we discovered that predicting disgust from the speech was difficult. Future reference can therefore concentrate on discovering new descriptors that accurately capture this mental condition. For example, disgust emotion could be more accurately predicted by other forms such as the image of a person with a voice.

REFERENCES

1. Livingstone, S. R., & Russo, F. A. (2018). The Ryerson Audio-Visual Database of Emotional Speech and Song (RAVDESS): A dynamic, multimodal set of facial and vocal expressions in North American English. *PLoS One*, 13(5), e0196391. doi: 10.1371/journal.pone.0196391
2. Pichora-Fuller, M. K., & Dupuis, K. (2020). *Toronto emotional speech set (TESS)*. doi: 10.5683/SP2/E8H2MF
3. Amjad, A., Khan, L., Ashraf, N., Mahmood, M. B., & Chang, H.-T. (2022). Recognizing semi-natural and spontaneous speech emotions using deep neural networks. *IEEE Access*, 10, 37149–37163. doi: 10.1109/ACCESS.2022.3163712
4. Chamishka, S., Madhavi, I., Nawaratne, R., Alahakoon, D., De Silva, D., Chilamkurti, N., & Nanayakkara, V. (2022). A voice-based real-time emotion detection technique using recurrent neural network empowered feature modelling. *Multimedia Tools and Applications*, 81(24), 35173–35194.
5. Padman, S., & Magare, D. (2022). Regional language speech emotion detection using deep neural network. In *ITM Web of Conferences* (Vol. 44, p. 03071). EDP Sciences.
6. Patel, N., Patel, S., & Mankad, S. H. (2022). Impact of autoencoder based compact representation on emotion detection from audio. *Journal of Ambient Intelligence and Humanized Computing*, 13(2), 867–885.
7. Borwankar, S., Dogra, M., & Verma, J. P. (2021). Fractal-based speech emotion detection using CNN. In *Soft Computing for Problem Solving: Proceedings of SocProS 2020* (Vol. 1, pp. 741–755). Springer, Singapore.
8. Sahu, G. (2019). Multimodal speech emotion recognition and ambiguity resolution. arXiv:1904.06022.

9. Sharma, M. (2022, May). Multi-lingual multi-task speech emotion recognition using wav2vec 2.0. In *ICASSP 2022–2022 IEEE International Conference on Acoustics, Speech and Signal Processing (ICASSP)* (pp. 6907–6911). IEEE.
10. Sagha, H., Matejka, P., Gavryukova, M., Povolný, F., Marchi, E., & Schuller, B. (2016). Enhancing multilingual recognition of emotion in speech by language identification. In *Proceedings of Interspeech 2016* (pp. 2949–2953). doi: 10.21437/Interspeech.2016-333
11. Fahad, M. S., Deepak, A., Pradhan, G., & Yadav, J. (2021). DNN-HMM-based speaker-adaptive emotion recognition using MFCC and epoch-based features. *Circuits, Systems, and Signal Processing, 40,* 466–489.
12. Palaiahnakote, S., di Baja, G. S., Wang, L., & Yan, W. Q. (Eds.). (2020). Pattern Recognition: 5th Asian Conference, ACPR 2019, Auckland, New Zealand, November 26–29, 2019, Revised Selected Papers, Part I (Vol. 12046). Springer Nature.
13. Sultana, S., Iqbal, M. Z., Selim, M. R., Rashid, M. M., & Rahman, M. S. (2022). Bangla speech emotion recognition and cross-lingual study using deep CNN and BLSTM networks. *IEEE Access, 10,* 564–578. doi: 10.1109/ACCESS.2021.3136251
14. Zhou, K., Sisman, B., Liu, R., & Li, H. (2021, June). Seen and unseen emotional style transfer for voice conversion with a new emotional speech dataset. In *2021 IEEE International Conference on Acoustics, Speech and Signal Processing (ICASSP)* (pp. 920–924). IEEE.
15. Gaetano, R., Ienco, D., Ose, K., & Cresson, R. (2018). A two-branch CNN architecture for land cover classification of PAN and MS imagery. *Remote Sensing, 10*(11), 1746.
16. Yan, J., Zhang, B., Zhou, M., Kwok, H. F., & Siu, S. W. (2022). Multi-branch-CNN: Classification of ion channel interacting peptides using multi-branch convolutional neural network. *Computers in Biology and Medicine, 147,* 105717.
17. Jan, Č. (2021). *Multimodální rozpoznávání emocí z řeči* (Bachelor's thesis, České vysoké učení technické v Praze. Vypočetní a informační centrum).
18. Das, J. K., Ghosh, A., Pal, A. K., Dutta, S., & Chakrabarty, A. (2020, October). Urban sound classification using convolutional neural network and long short term memory based on multiple features. In *2020 Fourth International Conference on Intelligent Computing in Data Sciences (ICDS)* (pp. 1–9). IEEE.
19. Verma, G. K., Tiwary, U. S., & Agrawal, S. (2011). Multi-algorithm fusion for speech emotion recognition. In *Advances in Computing and Communications: First International Conference, ACC 2011, Kochi, India, July 22–24, 2011, Proceedings, Part III* (pp. 452–459). Springer, Berlin.

Chapter 6

Revolutionizing agriculture
A comprehensive review of artificial intelligence techniques in farming

Gautam Siddharth Kashyap, Prerna Kamani,
Malvika Kanojia, Samar Wazir, Karan Malik,
Vinay Kumar Sehgal, and Rajkumar Dhakar

6.1 INTRODUCTION

Currently, half of the world's population is still engaged in agricultural activities rather than being industrialized or urbanized. In India, for example, agricultural activities still employ two-thirds of the population. Some people believe that agriculture is an art form that not only raises a seed from the soil to a plant but also serves for human consumption. Agriculture is the country's backbone, playing a significant role in the alleviation of poverty of rural people and thereby improving the economy of the country. However, agriculture is currently facing the following two types of problems:

1. *Demand:* Meeting the food consumption demand of the population
2. *Supply:* Supplying agricultural products to the population

Demand and supply are directly proportional to each other, meaning as demand for food rises, so will the supply. According to the Food and Agriculture Organization of the United Nations (FAO), by the end of 2050, the world's population will have increased by 34%. At this point, problems will begin to arise when things do not work together. We need to take a more strategic approach to farming in order to be more productive, increase yield, reduce human labor, and accelerate the economic process. These goals can be met with the help of artificial intelligence (AI) techniques. Self-driving cars that use vision recognition systems, recommendation engines that offer items you might like based on previous purchases, and virtual assistants that use speech and language recognition all are examples of AI. AI is having a significant impact everywhere. Every industry is attempting to deploy intelligent machinery in order to automate specific operations, including the agriculture industry. Agriculture and farming are two of the oldest and most important occupations on the planet. It has a $5 trillion industry and is very important to the economy. In this chapter, we attempted to cover the following seven stages of agricultural challenges:

1. *Preparation of soil:* During this stage of farming, farmers prepare the soil for seeding. Large clumps of dirt are broken up, and debris like sticks, rocks, and roots are removed. Fertilizers and organic matter are

DOI: 10.1201/9781003433941-6

also added depending on the type of crop to create an ideal environment for crops.

2. *Sowing of seeds:* At this stage, the spacing between two seeds, as well as the depth at which the seeds should be planted, must be considered. During this stage, climate conditions such as temperature, humidity, and rainfall are critical.

3. *Adding fertilizers:* For the farmer to continue producing nutritious and healthy crops, soil fertility must be maintained. Farmers use fertilizers because they contain plant nutrients such as nitrogen, phosphorus, and potassium. Fertilizers are simply nutrients added to agricultural fields to supplement the elements already present in the soil. This stage also determines the quality of the crop.

4. *Irrigation:* This stage contributes to the preservation of soil moisture and humidity. Underwatering or overwatering can stymie crop growth and, if not done correctly, can result in crop damage.

5. *Weed protection:* Weeds are unwanted plants that grow in close proximity to crops or along agricultural boundaries. Weed control is critical because weeds reduce yields, increase production costs, obstruct harvesting, and degrade crop quality.

6. *Harvesting:* It is the collection of ripe crops from fields. This task necessitates the participation of a large number of laborers, making it a labor-intensive activity. The post-harvest process includes cleaning, sorting, packing, and refrigeration.

7. *Storage:* The products are stored in this stage of the post-harvest system to ensure food security outside of agricultural seasons. Packing and transportation of crops are also included.

However, in addition to the aforementioned challenges, several other challenges exist in the agricultural domain:

- Climate factors like rainfall, temperature, and humidity have a big impact on agriculture. Climate change is caused by increased deforestation and pollution, which makes it difficult for farmers to make decisions about how to prepare the soil, sow seeds, and harvest.
- Each crop requires a different type of soil nourishment. The soil requires three primary nutrients: nitrogen (N), phosphorus (P), and potassium (K). Crops of poor quality can result from a lack of nutrients.
- Weed control is critical, as evidenced by the preceding points. If not controlled, it can increase production costs as well as nutrient absorption from the soil, resulting in a nutrient deficit.

The agriculture industry is using AI to help produce healthier crops, control pests, monitor soil and growing conditions, organize data for farmers, reduce effort, and improve a wide range of agriculture-related operations throughout the food supply chain. AI in agriculture not only helps farmers automate their agricultural operations but also changes precise cultivation for increased crop yield and quality while using fewer resources. Companies involved in AI-based products or services, such as agricultural training data, drones, and automated machine manufacturing, will benefit from future technological advancements that will assist the world in dealing with food production issues for a growing population.

Because of the importance of this topic, several review articles have been published in recent years to investigate it. We chose some of the reviews from 2013 to 2020 based on their citation count, which is listed in ascending order: Barbedo [1] published a review on detecting and classifying plant diseases using digital image processing techniques. They only chose plants with visible symptoms on the leaves and stems. The authors organized their review into three sections: (1) detection, (2) classification, and (3) quantification. The survey's main goal is to assist vegetable pathologists and computer vision researchers who work in this field. Zareiforoush et al. [2] published a systematic review on the use of computer vision techniques for rice quality inspection. The authors concentrated their review on practical applications of rice harvesting and handling processing such as rice yield measurement, milling degree, fissure identification, shape and size analysis, color analysis, root estimation, internal damage assessment, and spikelet analysis. Their review combines technical and theoretical computer vision principles to provide a nondestructive quality assessment of rice. Vithu and Moses [3] published a review that employs machine vision techniques to assess grain quality. Their review delves into the recognition of foreign matter, insect infestation, microbial infections, and discolored grains. The scope of AI techniques for the grain quality evaluation monitoring system is explained in their review. They also talked about the scope and limitations of the proposed system. Shah et al. [4] published a survey that relies on rice plant infected images to detect rice plant disease using a variety of image processing and machine learning techniques. The authors also covered image processing and machine learning tasks. They have chosen 19 papers to conduct their survey. In their survey, they used various types of criteria such as image dataset size, the number of classes, pre-processing and segmentation techniques, and so on. Barbedo [5] investigated the difficulties in automatic disease detection. He has discussed the limitations and issues with previous studies. The author divides the challenges into two categories that can have an impact on the automatic disease detection process: (1) intrinsic factors and (2) extrinsic factors. He has also proposed some solutions to these problems. Kamilaris and Prenafeta-Boldú [6] published a review of deep learning techniques used in agriculture. Their survey paints a clear picture of the models that outperform commonly used image processing techniques in terms of accuracy. They have chosen 40 papers to conduct their survey. They also discussed the benefits, drawbacks, and future potential of deep learning in agriculture. Patrício and Rieder [7] published a review that employs machine vision techniques in the production of five popular grains. They have concentrated on the challenges and opportunities associated with the use of machine vision in disease detection, insect infestation, grain quality, and phenotyping and phenology. The authors attempted to identify gaps in previous studies and to provide future research aspects. They have chosen 25 papers to conduct their survey. Chlingaryan et al. [8] published a review on machine learning-based crop yield prediction and nitrogen estimation. The authors conducted the review using studies from the previous 15 years. They compared various machine learning techniques that perform the same tasks in precision agriculture. The authors also discussed cost-effective and comprehensive crop yield prediction and nitrogen estimation solutions. Zamora-Sequeira et al. [9] published a review of recent nano-electric sensor-based methods for quantifying pesticides in agricultural activities. The authors divided their review into six categories of sensors for agricultural pesticide detection: (1) electrochemical, (2) optical, (3) nano-colorimetric, (4) piezoelectric, (5) chemo-luminescent, and (6) fluorescent. They focused on bananas, but other vegetables and fruits are mentioned as well. In their review, they also mentioned the applications, limitations, and purpose of these sensors. Fue et al. [10] published a review of robotic cotton harvesting technologies. They divided their review into four categories: (1) recent agricultural robotic technologies, (2) exploring robotic harvesting technologies, (3) recent cotton harvesting robotic technologies, and (4) challenges in the development of robotic technologies They also discussed the benefits, drawbacks, and future potential of robotic technologies in cotton harvesting and agriculture. The studies mentioned above have provided an in-depth analysis of the techniques used in agriculture. However, we believe there is still a need for our review to assist researchers in exploring both AI techniques and the agriculture area in one place, as we have cited 77 papers from the last 21 years in this chapter. We have divided agricultural techniques into six categories: (1) intelligent systems, (2) fuzzy logic, (3) image processing, (4) machine learning, (5) deep learning, and (6) machine vision. We have divided the selected papers based on the techniques used.

The chapter is structured as follows. In Section 6.3, the methodology for selecting papers will be discussed. Section 6.3 provides a gentle overview of AI, fuzzy logic, machine learning, deep learning, and machine vision techniques. Section 6.4 discusses studies that use AI techniques in agriculture in six groups: intelligent systems, fuzzy logic, image processing, machine learning, deep learning, and machine vision. Section 6.5 concludes this chapter.

6.2 METHODOLOGY

This chapter reviews published works that have used AI techniques in agriculture. For identifying, evaluating, and interpreting the results relevant to the scope of this chapter, a simple protocol is used. For the literature searches, the Google Scholar search engine and the Scopus database were used. AI is such a hot topic that several papers have been published in this area. As a result, the search expression is defined: (1) (*"artificial intelligence"* OR *"machine learning"* OR *"deep learning"* OR *"machine vision"* OR *"intelligent systems"* OR *"fuzzy logic"*) AND (*"agriculture"*), (2) (*"artificial intelligence"*) AND (*"agriculture"*), (3) (*"intelligent systems"*) AND (*"agriculture"*), (4) (*"fuzzy logic"*) AND (*"agriculture"*), (5) (*"machine learning"*) AND (*"agriculture"*), (6) (*"deep learning"*) AND (*"agriculture"*), and (7) (*"machine vision"*) AND (*"agriculture"*). The time interval is set for the last 21 years, as shown in Figure 6.1. The work is evaluated in three categories: (1) identification, (2) screening, and (3) eligibility. The search expression is entered into the database during the

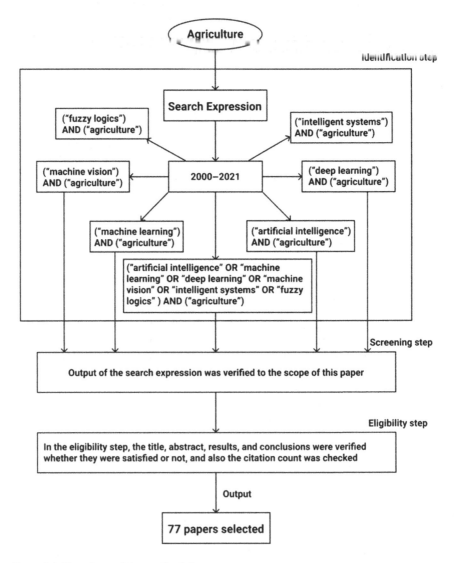

Figure 6.1 Flowchart of the methodology.

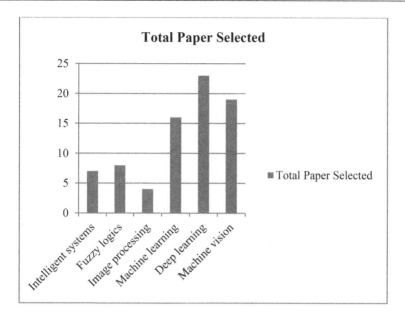

Figure 6.2 Bar graph distribution of selected techniques.

identification step. The output of the search expression was verified to the scope of this chapter during the screening step. In the eligibility step, the title, abstract, results, and conclusions were checked to see if they were satisfied, as well as the citation count. After all of these steps were completed, a total of 77 papers were chosen for this chapter, as shown in Figure 6.2. The chosen papers are intelligent systems (7 papers), fuzzy logic (8 papers), image processing (4 papers), machine learning (16 papers), deep learning (23 papers), and machine vision (19 papers). As shown in Figure 6.3, 58 papers are published in journals, 18 papers are published in international conferences, and 1 paper is published in the *IEEE magazine*.

6.3 A GENTLE INTRODUCTION TO AI, FUZZY LOGICS, MACHINE LEARNING, DEEP LEARNING, AND MACHINE VISION

AI is a science, and machine learning is the most common form of AI implementation. Deep learning is a subset of machine learning, and machine vision is a subset of AI techniques.

6.3.1 Background of AI

AI can be defined as any theory, method, or technique that assists computers in analyzing, simulating, exploiting, and investigating human behavior and

Paper Distribution

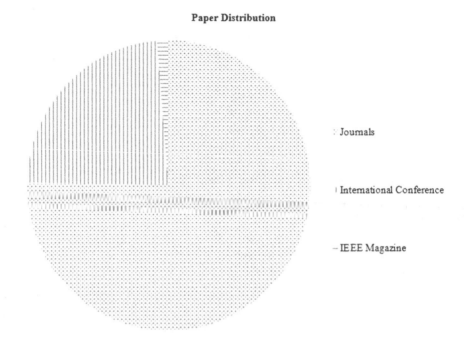

: Journals

ı International Conference

– IEEE Magazine

Figure 6.3 Pie chart distribution of selected papers.

thought processes. The primary goal of AI is to build an intelligent system capable of performing tasks that humans were previously incapable of performing intelligently. There are several instances where AI has demonstrated its capability. For example, in 1997, Russian chess grandmaster Kasparov was defeated by IBM *"Deep Blue"*. AI technology has evolved in three stages: (1) the initial stage (1956–1980), (2) the industrialization stage (1980–2000), and (3) the explosion stage (2000–present) [11]. Initially, the AI technique was used only to solve algebraic equations and prove theorems. McCarthy and Minsky attended the Dartmouth University conference on machine intelligence in the early 1950s in the United States. They were eager to learn how to make machines think like humans, how to make machines communicate with humans, and how to make machines understandable. These questions were thought to be the foundations of the AI technique. The Dartmouth University conference is also regarded as the birthplace of AI. In the industry stage, AI received a large sum of money for research purposes from the Japanese government for the first time. The main goal of donating this large sum of money is to create machines that can interact with humans through dialogue, translation, and pattern recognition. The focus of AI in this phase is *"knowledge processing"*. During the explosion stage, the world began to fill with the Internet and data, and progress was made in developing better hardware and software for computation tasks. When the algorithms reached this stage, there had already been several revisions over generations that had begun to show the amazing results at this stage. When we look back at the early inventions of the computer in the 1950s, we see that researchers went a long way toward developing an independent system with learning capabilities. The milking robot, on the other hand, is the first robotic technology that has been successfully implemented and used in agriculture. Following that, robotic floor egg collection was used in poultry farming. The seed that was planted half a century ago has grown into a full-fledged plant (computers), capable of completing tasks on its own, interacting with humans in their native languages, and recognizing movements and emotions. AI applications have established themselves in a variety of commercial and service industries. In livestock and poultry farming, for example, AI can be used remotely to monitor the animals with an HD camera that can record the animals' faces and bodies. This can be very useful in monitoring each animal's health and physical condition.

6.3.2 Background of fuzzy logic

Fuzzy logic isn't as fuzzy as you might think, and it has been working quietly behind the scenes in more places than most people realize for over 20 years. Fuzzy logic is a rule-based system that relies on an operator's practical experience to capture experienced operator knowledge. Fuzzy logic is classified as a subset of AI because it is a type of AI software. Although fuzzy logic has been known since the mid-1960s, practical applications were not demonstrated until the 1970s. Since that time, the Japanese have been the primary producers of fuzzy logic applications. Fuzzy logic has been used in cameras, washing machines, and even stock trading software. Various agricultural applications have been developed, which are discussed in Section 6.6.

6.3.3 Background of machine learning

Machine learning is an AI application. It is concerned with the techniques and methods for making computational applications more precise by modifying and adapting their actions. It gives the system the ability to automatically learn and improve based on its experience without the need for any programming. In general, the learning process is initiated by observations, data, direct experience, instructions, and so on. Machine learning techniques are typically classified into four types: (1) supervised learning, (2) unsupervised learning, (3) reinforcement learning, and (4) evolutionary learning. In supervised learning, the process begins by selecting from a pool of correct answers (training sets) to generalize and then responds to all possible inputs. Unsupervised learning, in contrast to supervised learning, attempts to identify similarities between inputs by comparing them to each other in order to classify them. In reinforcement learning, it only gets informed when it answers incorrectly to the questions, but it does not get informed when it answers correctly. As a result, in order to find the correct answers, you must investigate various options. This algorithm is a hybrid of supervised and unsupervised learning. In evolutionary learning, it interacts with the environment by producing actions and exploring the errors or rewards. Classification, regression, clustering, and association problems all can be addressed by machine learning algorithms.

6.3.4 Background of deep learning

Deep learning is a machine learning approach that is based on data representation and learning. It is a subset of machine learning that simulates neural networks in the human brain. Deep learning and machine learning techniques approach the problem in very different ways. Deep learning algorithms such as YOloNet, for example, take an image as input and output the location and names of objects. Traditional machine learning methods, such as support vector machine (SVM), require the use of a bounding box object detection technique to identify all possible objects before the Histogram of oriented Gradients (HoG) can be used as input to the learning algorithm to classify relevant objects. The study of artificial neural networks (ANN) leads to deep learning. The ANN investigates the neural networks of the brain from the perspective of information processing, developing a simple model and forming various networks based on different connection methods. As a result, deep learning is also referred to as deep neural network (DNN), which evolved from the ANN model. Convolutional neural networks (CNN's) are a type of DNN that is commonly used to evaluate visual data. To analyze data, it employs hierarchical neural networks. It analyzed data by connecting the neuron's code, which is very similar to the human brain. It processes the data through a series of layers, which then integrate with other tiers to provide more information. When we use deep learning to detect fraud, for example, it will send several signals such as IP address, credit score, and so on. The first layer examines the amount of data sent. The information is built on the sent data by the second layer. The third layer will combine the new information with the existing data, and the final layer will make a decision.

6.3.5 Background of machine vision

Machine vision serves as the machines' eyes, allowing them to see. In general, it extracts data from digital images that can be used to control a process or manufacturing activity. On the assembly line, for example, it can be used to detect colors, shapes, and sizes, as well as to monitor the position of something. It consists of a lighting system that highlights the key features of the area of interest while minimizing the other features, a digital camera for capturing images, a sensor that is generally integrated with a digital camera and is used for converting the images into digital images, a vision processing system that is used for extracting data from the digital images, and a communication system for input/output operations. The following is the workflow of machine vision techniques for agricultural product inspection:

1. First, the sensor will determine whether the product is present or not; if the product is present, the camera will record images of the product. Following that, the lighting system will highlight the product's key features. The sensor will then convert the images into digital images, which will be stored in computer memory.
2. The vision system will use computer software to perform several tasks in order to process the digital images. Initially, the software will convert the digital images to black and white. The processed images will then be checked against the operator's predefined criteria. The processed images will pass the inspection test if they pass the criteria sets. Otherwise, the inspection test will fail.

Machine vision is commonly used for quality control, robot/machine guidance, real-time process control, data collection, machine monitoring, and sorting/counting. It can inspect thousands of parts per minute in the manufacturing industry, making this technique faster and more objective.

6.4 TECHNIQUES USED IN AGRICULTURE

AI techniques enable machines to mimic human behavior. These techniques can be used to predict, learn, categorize, plan, reason, and perceive, among other things. They are primarily used in agriculture for climate detection, high yield, food safety, and crop production innovation. AI-based techniques have the potential to reduce human effort. The following sections describe the various techniques.

6.4.1 Intelligent systems: Robots, drones, expert systems

Hashimoto et al. [12] used AI systems for agriculture. They primarily created their intelligent system for three purposes: (1) AI-based agricultural applications, (2) AI-based plant production systems, and (3) AI-based agricultural robots. The authors also discussed biosystem-derived algorithms and neural network–based photosynthetic algorithms. The authors believed that their intended technique was more reliable than other techniques. Van Henten et al. [13] developed a robot for harvesting the cucumbers in the greenhouse. Autonomous vehicles, two computer vision systems, a control scheme, and other software and hardware components of robots are included. Their proposed robot also includes an end effector for delicately handling soft fruits. They used the A* algorithm to create the robot's motion planner. According to the authors, it has an 80% success rate and an average time of 45 seconds.

Munirah et al. [14] developed an expert system for diagnosing oyster mushroom disease. They created a system using rule-based and forward chaining techniques. Their proposed system detects diseases caused by bacteria, viruses, and other microorganisms. According to the authors, it provides treatment advice to users via an interactive interface. Balleda et al. [15] proposed an expert system for pest management in rice and wheat crops. Their expert system can also detect diseases caused by pesticides. The Explanation Block (EB) was used by the authors as a decision-making body. They have created an interactive user interface for any pest management-related queries. They thought it outperformed the previous systems. Spanaki et al. [16] developed AI-based drones for solving the issues of food security. Their drones were inspired by bird swarms' biomimetic behaviors. The authors believed that their proposed method would allow farmers to perform operations on inaccessible lands, increasing productivity. Gil et al. [17] developed a complex modeling system using AI techniques for improving the decision-making process in agriculture. Their proposed system is built on the Model Integration (MINT) framework and primarily contributes three features: (1) intelligent user interface, (2) semantic metadata for models, and (3) semantic data representations. The authors claimed that their system is trustworthy and precise. Facchinetti et al. [18] created a small intelligent vehicle using AI techniques to reduce pesticide spraying on fresh-cut salad in the greenhouse. The authors put their proposed method to the test in two stages of salad growth. They claimed that their proposed cuts unnecessary spraying by 55%.

The studies mentioned present various applications of AI in agriculture, including intelligent systems, robots, expert systems, drones, and modeling systems. However, there may be some gaps or limitations to consider in each study. For instance, Hashimoto et al.'s [12] system seems to have multiple purposes, but it is unclear how well each component performs individually or together, and it lacks data to support their claim of reliability. Van Henten et al.'s [13] robot has an 80% success rate, but it is unclear what constitutes "success" and how it performs compared to humans or other robots. Munirah et al.'s [14] expert system is limited to a specific crop and disease, and there is no information on its accuracy or effectiveness. Balleda et al.'s [15] expert system is limited to specific crops and pests and has no information on its accuracy or effectiveness. Spanaki et al.'s [16] drones may face regulatory or logistical challenges, and their performance compared to other methods is uncertain. Gil et al.'s [17] modeling system may be difficult to implement or scale up and lacks information on testing or validation. Finally, Facchinetti et al.'s vehicle is limited to one type of crop and growing environment, and its effectiveness in practice is unknown.

6.4.2 Fuzzy logic

Escobar [19] developed a system of fuzzy control based on fuzzy logic for climate control in the greenhouse. The users can construct and edit the elements using the fuzzy-based knowledge controller in their recommended method. A collection of rules make up the knowledge controller. According to the authors, this approach is quite dependable and useful for a variety of other things. Perini and Susi [20] developed a decision support systems (DSS) based on fuzzy logic for the pest management system. The development of this system involves two different types of dimensions: organizational dimensions and technical dimensions. The authors used web technologies to create their systems. The authors held that their system is incredibly trustworthy. Sicat et al. [21] used fuzzy logic to build the land suitability model. To categorize the suitability of the land, the authors employed the Farmer Knowledge (FK). By using a quick rural participatory technique, the farmers' knowledge was obtained. They had selected 12 FK based on its significance among all the information they had learned. In order to produce suitability maps, they have used fuzzy-AND and fuzzy-OR operators that were discovered to be true for FK. These FK-based suitability maps show the Land Resource Development Plan (LRDP) to be either in agreement or in disagreement. This model's primary objective is to offer information for the best possible land-use planning. Tremblay et al. [22] developed a system to calculate the nitrogen quantity in fertilizer based on the fuzzy inference system (FIS). They have used the soil and plant properties calculated over the three seasons: (1) 2005, (2) 2006, and (3) 2007. The authors have used the Nitrogen Sufficiency Index (NSI) to check the nitrogen status in plants. They believed that their system can give better advice for nitrogen fertilizers than an expert. Papageorgiou et al. [23] used the Fuzzy Cognitive Map (FCM) for the predictions of yield in cotton crops. The nodes in FCM represent cotton characteristics, and the edges represent the relationships between cotton properties and yield. Their proposed approach outperforms machine learning algorithm benchmarks. The authors thought it was very flexible and simple in structure. Prakash et al. [24] developed a system called "PRITHVI" based on fuzzy expert systems. This system was designed primarily for the soybean crop. They believe that this system will act as an expert, advising farmers, agriculture offices, and experts about the soybean crop. This system is capable of making decisions such as fertilizer selection, pest selection, sowing periods, and so on. The system was put through its paces in Rajasthan, India. The authors believed it produced accurate and consistent results. Tilva et al. [25] used fuzzy logic to build disease prediction systems for different weather conditions. As parameters, they used meteorological data. The authors believed that early disease detection could reduce the use of pesticides, which cause land pollution. Their proposed system can also work with very little meteorological data. Shafaei et al. [26] predicted the hydration characteristics of wheat based on the AI simulation framework called adaptive neuro-fuzzy inference system (ANFIS). The authors' experiments were carried out at five different temperatures (Celsius): (1) 30, (2) 40, (3) 50, (4) 60, and (5) 70. They compared their approach to ANN, and the results revealed that ANN is superior in terms of ease of use with simple frameworks, despite the fact that both models accurately predict hydration characteristics.

Although the studies presented above demonstrate the successful use of fuzzy logic in various agriculture-related applications, there are still some gaps in these studies. For instance, most of the studies were limited to specific crops or weather conditions, which may limit the generalizability of the proposed systems. Furthermore, the validation of the proposed systems was often carried out using limited data, which may not fully represent the diversity of situations that can occur in real-world scenarios. Additionally, the studies may have focused more on the technical aspects of the proposed systems, while paying less attention to the social and economic aspects that may affect their adoption and implementation. Therefore, there is a need for further research that addresses these gaps and provides a more comprehensive evaluation of the potential benefits and limitations of using fuzzy logic in agriculture.

6.4.3 Image processing

Sannakki et al. [27] proposed a diagnosis system for grape leaf diseases with classification by using image processing techniques and neural networks. For segmenting the grape leaf diseases, the authors used k-means clustering. The authors claimed that their proposed approach outperforms previous models because it is simple and dependable. Marcal and Cunha [28] developed an automatic agriculture spreader calibration system in real time based on an image processing technique. This calibration system follows some strict standard operating procedures. Their proposed system was tested on two different types of granules. The authors claimed that their proposed model was 75% accurate. Dhingra et al. [29] proposed a system for leaf disease detection and classification using image processing techniques. The segmentation technique with the novel fuzzy set is used by the authors to evaluate the region of interest (RoI). The authors used a variety of classifiers to demonstrate the efficacy of the proposed approach. According to the authors, the random forest algorithm outperforms the other classifiers. Their proposed method had a classification accuracy of 98.4%. Singh et al. [30] developed a system for detecting weeds and crops using image processing. Their proposed system identified the crop with an accuracy of 78.10% and the two weed species with an accuracy of 53.12% and 44.76%, respectively. According to the authors, their proposed system is a great alternative to traditional systems.

While the studies presented show promising results in the application of image processing techniques for agricultural purposes, there are still some gaps in the research. One significant gap is the lack of diversity in the crop types and geographical locations used in the studies. Most of the studies focused on specific crops or regions, which limits the generalizability of their findings to other crops or regions. Additionally, some studies did not thoroughly evaluate the robustness of their proposed systems to various environmental factors, such as changes in weather conditions, which can impact the accuracy and efficacy of the system. There is also a need for more comparative studies that compare the proposed systems to existing traditional systems to demonstrate their superiority. Finally, the studies did not provide clear information on the cost-effectiveness of implementing these systems on a larger scale, which is an important consideration for practical applications in the agricultural industry.

6.4.4 Machine learning

A component of an AI system can learn from experience without the need for programming. In general, it improves with practice by incorporating math and statistics to learn from data. It consists of various processing stages such as pre-processing, feature extraction, and segmentation. Moshou et al. [31] used the least square support vector machine (LSSVM) with sensor fusion to differentiate between healthy and water-stressed wheat canopies. The authors claimed that their proposed system has a 99% success rate. They believed that their system could distinguish between biotic and abiotic stress in a very reliable and cost-effective manner. Zhou et al. [32] used the Orientation Code Matching (OCM) for detecting disease development in the sugar beet plant. The SVM is used by the authors to classify and quantify disease pixel-by-pixel. The authors asserted that their proposed method has high precision and recall rates. Heremans et al. [33] used two types of machine-learning techniques, (1) boosted regression trees (BRT) and (2) random forest algorithm, for the prediction of yield in wheat, mainly in the winter season. The authors used meteorological variables as well as spot-vegetation Normalized Difference Vegetation Indices (NDVI) data. When RMSE and R^2 were calculated, the authors claimed that BRT outperformed the random forest algorithm. The authors also attempted to forecast early-season wheat yield. Liang et al. [34] proposed an estimation technique for the Leaf Area Index (LAI) value of crops. The authors used a variety of regression algorithms to demonstrate the relationships between simulated LAI values and simulated vegetation indices (VI) values. The authors claimed that random forest regression (RFR) outperforms other methods on a variety of datasets and VI values. Patil and Thorat [35] proposed a disease prediction system for grapes. For disease prediction, the authors used machine learning, Internet of Things (IoT), and a variety of other sensors. They also used various parameters such as temperature, humidity, moisture, and so on. Based on the hidden Markov model (HMM), their proposed system can send an SMS alert to farmers when the disease is detected. Waghmare et al. [36] proposed a grape leaf disease detection system based on leaf properties by using pattern recognition and machine learning. The multiclass SVM was used by the authors to classify the textures. Their proposed system divides diseases into two categories: mildew and black rot. The authors claimed that their proposed method is 96.6% accurate. Pantazi et al. [37] used machine learning techniques with advanced sensing techniques to develop a wheat yield prediction system. For the proposed system, they used multilayer soil data and satellite imagery. The soil parameters were estimated by the authors using online soil spectroscopy with a prototype sensor. According to the authors, their proposed system visualizes information about the factors influencing wheat yield potential. Their proposed system has an accuracy of more than 80%. Maione et al. [38] predict the geographical regions of rice crops by using various types of machine learning models. For the proposed system, the authors used the SVM, random forest algorithm, and neural networks. The authors claimed that all three machine learning models achieve an accuracy of more than 90%. Stas et al. [39] used two types of machine learning techniques, (1) BRT and (2) SVM, for the prediction of yield in wheat, mainly in the winter season. The authors tested their proposed method in Henan, China. They employed three types of NDVI-related predictors: (1) single NDVI, (2) incremental NDVI, and (3) targeted NDVI. When RMSE was considered, the authors claimed that BRT outperformed SVM, Morellos et al. [40] used machine learning methods with multivariate methods for predicting the content of nitrogen, organic compound, and moisture in the soil. According to the authors, machine learning methods outperform the multivariate method on all three criteria. Su et al. [41] proposed a prediction model for rice crops based on support vector machine-based open crop model (SBOCM) which was developed by combining developmental stage and yield prediction models. The authors used meteorological data to test their approach over a year at various scale ranges. According to the authors, their proposed approach is superior in terms of data acquisition, effective for multiscale factor integration, and parametrically simple. Behera et al. [42] used the machine learning technique with fuzzy logic for the detection of any deformity found in oranges. The computer vision technique is used to detect the deformity. Their proposed method also detects any flaw marks that may appear on the orange's surface. They calculated the accuracy using multiclass SVM with k-means clustering. For disease classification, their proposed model achieves an accuracy of 90%. The authors used fuzzy logic to assess the severity of the disease. Duarte-Carvajalino et al. [43] used various types of machine learning algorithms for predicting the "*Phytophthora infestans*" in potato crops. The authors captured the images using a unmanned aerial vehicle (UAV) for training purposes. They believed that the random forest algorithm, deep-CNN, and multilayer perceptron (MLP) all could accurately predict the disease. Islam et al. [44] used machine learning algorithms for detecting weeds in crops using images captured by UAV. The authors employed three models: (1) SVM, (2) random forest algorithm, and (3) K-nearest neighbor (KNN). The authors put their proposed method to the test on chili crops in Australia. They claimed that all three models achieve an accuracy of more than 90%. Raimundo et al. [45] used machine learning techniques to predict weather conditions. The authors attempted to create a smart irrigation system by forecasting weather conditions. The authors claimed that their proposed method can predict temperature, precipitation, wind speed, and other variables. They primarily employed three types of machine learning models: (1) linear regression, (2) decision trees, and (3) random forest. Out of these three, random forest, outperforms the other two. Patel et al. [46] used machine learning techniques for predicting suitable cropland and prediction of yield in crops. The authors also predicted based on geographical and climatic conditions. The authors employed the random forest algorithm and the gradient boosting method. According to the authors, their proposed model produces good results.

The studies discussed in the given passage highlight the potential of machine learning algorithms and sensor fusion techniques for various applications in agriculture. However, there are still several research gaps that need to be addressed. First, most studies have only tested their proposed systems on limited datasets, which limits the generalizability of their findings to other datasets. Comparative analysis between different machine learning algorithms or sensor fusion techniques is also limited, which could provide insights into the suitability of various algorithms for different applications. Additionally, most studies have focused on a single crop, which limits the generalizability of their findings to other crops. Future studies should explore the application of these techniques to other crops and investigate whether the same techniques are equally effective. Furthermore, some studies propose systems for yield prediction or disease detection, but they do not consider how farmers could use this information to make informed decisions. Future studies should focus on integrating these systems with on-farm decision-making processes to improve the efficiency of farming practices. Finally, there is a lack of attention to privacy and data security concerns raised by the use of advanced sensing techniques and IoT devices in generating a large amount of data. Studies should address these concerns and propose solutions to ensure the safe and secure use of data.

6.4.5 Deep learning

Deep learning is a subset of machine learning that uses neural networks to classify information. Deep learning models are commonly used in agricultural activities such as irrigation, fertilizer, remote sensing applications, and so on. Deep learning techniques are further classified into the following three categories.

6.4.5.1 ANN

Song and He [47] proposed a crop diagnosis system based on ANN. The authors hoped that it would assist farmers who do not know how to diagnose crops. They put their proposed method to the test on six crop symptoms. The authors claimed that it has an error rate of less than 8% and is far more reliable than the traditional diagnosis system. Zhao et al. [48] proposed a prediction system for soil textures based on soil attributes by using ANN. For training the model, they used the Levenberg–Marquardt optimization algorithm in the system. According to the authors, it achieved an accuracy of 88% for clay content and 81% for sand content. They also talked about the model's future prospects. Arif et al. [49] proposed a moisture estimation technique for the paddy field by using ANN. They used meteorological data to accomplish this. They primarily used two types of input parameters: evapotranspiration (ETo) and precipitation. They put their technique to the test in a variety of weather conditions and paddy cultivation seasons. The authors believed that this system was extremely reliable in terms of producing results. Ravichandran and Koteeshwari [50] proposed a crop yield prediction system based on ANN which can be monitored through a smartphone. They used the Delta-bar-Delta, Almeida, and Rprop algorithms to train this system. Several parameters, such as pH value, temperature, rainfall, and so on, were fed into the system, and the desired output was obtained. In comparison to the other systems, the authors believed that this system was very portable. Their proposed model achieves 90% accuracy.

The studies mentioned above showcase the application of ANN in crop diagnosis, soil texture prediction, moisture estimation, and crop yield prediction. However, there are some research gaps that need to be addressed in these studies. First, most of the studies focus on the application of ANN in crop-related issues, but they do not explore other machine learning techniques that could be more suitable for specific problems. Therefore, further research could be conducted to compare the performance of ANN with other machine learning techniques in crop-related issues. Second, although some studies have achieved high accuracy rates, the training and testing data used in these studies are limited to a specific region and crop type. As such, there is a need for more extensive datasets from different regions and crop types to test the performance and generalize the results of the proposed models. Third, most of the studies focused on predicting or diagnosing crop-related issues, but there is a lack of studies that explore the implementation of ANN in the optimization of crop management practices. Therefore, future research could be directed toward exploring the potential application of ANN in decision-making processes related to crop management practices such as irrigation, fertilization, and pest control. Finally, the proposed models in these studies are mostly based on historical data and may not account for unforeseen environmental factors such as natural disasters or climate change. Therefore, future studies could focus on developing models that can adapt to changing environmental conditions and incorporate real-time data to improve accuracy and effectiveness.

6.4.5.2 CNN

Mohanty et al. [51] proposed a smartphone-assisted disease diagnosis system based on deep learning methods. The authors used both healthy and infected plant leaves under controlled conditions. The authors used CNN to train the model to identify crop species and diseases. The authors claimed that their proposed method is 99.35% accurate. Yalcin and Razavi [52] used CNN to identify plant species based on the images collected from the agro-stations. The images were extracted using CNN by the authors. The authors claimed that their proposed method is more effective than the SVM classifier. Yalcin [53] used deep learning methods for plant phenology recognition. The authors collected visual data at the Turkey agro-station every half hour. The images were extracted using CNN by the authors. The authors compared their proposed method to manual and machine learning methods. Chen et al. [54] used deep learning models for counting apples and oranges. The authors extracted the images using a blob detector based on CNN. They have used the counting algorithm to count the fruits. The authors compared their proposed method to manual fruit counting methods. The authors believed that their proposed approach performs better with fewer data and can count the fruits in a short period of time. Amara et al. [55] used deep learning methods for identifying the disease in banana leaves. For the proposed approach, the authors used CNN's LeNet architecture. The authors tested and evaluated their proposed approach under a variety of complex conditions, including varying resolution, size, pose, complex background, and so on. The authors claimed that their proposed method has a 96% accuracy rate. Pound et al. [56] used CNN methods for the identification and localization of root and shoot. The authors created an automatic trait recognition model. According to the authors, their proposed model can easily identify 12 out of 14 traits. According to the authors, their proposed model outperforms previous studies. Their proposed model has a 97% accuracy. Uzal et al. [57] estimated the number of seeds in soybean pods based on deep learning methods. Using CNN methods, the authors improved the generalization capability. The authors tested their proposed method on different seasons and achieved an accuracy of more than 80%. When compared to other studies in the literature, the authors believed that their proposed approach was superior. Francis and Deisy [58] used CNN methods for developing a system to identify diseases based on the leaf image dataset. In the proposed system, the authors used the multi-space image reconstruction method. They extract the image's high-level and semantic features and reconstruct it with convolutional layers. They employed the softmax classifier for classification. The authors claimed that their proposed system is trustworthy and precise.

While the studies mentioned above have made significant progress in using deep learning methods for crop diagnosis and identification, there are still some research gaps that need to be addressed. One of the gaps is the need for more diverse datasets. Most studies use controlled conditions and limited datasets, which may not reflect the complexity and variability of real-world farming situations. Additionally, there is a need for more research on the generalization capabilities of the models. While many studies claim high accuracy rates, it is important to ensure that these models can perform well in different environments and situations. Furthermore, there is a need to explore the potential of combining multiple deep learning methods for more accurate and robust crop diagnosis and identification. Finally, there is a need for more research on the integration of these technologies with practical farming operations. It is important to understand how these systems can be effectively integrated into the daily activities of farmers and how they can improve their overall productivity and efficiency. Addressing these research gaps can contribute to the development of more effective and practical deep learning–based systems for crop diagnosis and identification.

6.4.5.3 Deep-CNN

Hall et al. [59] used deep-CNN with data augmentation techniques for the leaf classification system. The authors used five data augmentation techniques: (1) rotation, (2) translation, (3) shading, (4) scaling, and (5) occlusion. The Flavia dataset was used to test the authors' proposed approach. The authors claimed that their proposed method is 97.3% accurate. Sladojevic et al. [60] used deep-CNN for detecting plant diseases based on leaf images. Their proposed method can detect 13 different types of plant diseases. For their proposed approach, the authors used the deep learning framework "Caffe". The authors claimed that their proposed method is 96.3% accurate. Grinblat et al, [61] used deep-CNN for plant identification based on leaf vein patterns. For the evaluation, the authors used three types of legume species: (1) white bean, (2) red bean, and (3) soybean. The authors claimed that their proposed model outperformed the other plant identification approaches in terms of accuracy. Sa et al. [62] used deep-CNN for fruit detections. They also used a transfer learning approach with faster region-based CNN. The authors employed two modalities: (1) red, green, and blue (RGB) and (2) near-infrared (NIR). The authors used both modalities to investigate early and late fusion. The authors claimed that their proposed model is faster and more reliable than other detection methods. Ha et al. [63] used deep-CNN for detecting the Fusarium wilt in radish. They used k-means clustering and softmax clustering to divide the radish field into three regions: (1) radish, (2) bare ground, and (3) mulching film. The UMV was used by the authors to capture the infected radish. The authors claimed that their proposed method identified the three regions with 97.4% accuracy and Fusarium wilt in radish with 93.3% accuracy. Their proposed method outperforms existing machine learning models. Fuentes et al. [64] used deep learning meta architectures with deep features extractors for detecting the disease in the tomato plant and pest recognition. The authors used three deep learning meta architectures: (1) faster region-based CNN, (2) region-based fully convolutional networks (R-FCN), and (3) single shot multibox detector (SSD). They also used two kinds of deep feature extractors: (1) VGGNet and (2) ResNet. The authors trained their model using two datasets: the tomato dataset and the pests dataset. The authors claimed that their proposed method can detect nine different types of diseases and pests in complex environments. Lu et al. [65] used deep-CNN for detecting the disease in rice crops. The authors used 500 images of healthy and infected rice crops in their study. Under a tenfold cross-validation strategy, their proposed model achieves an accuracy of 95.84%. According to the authors, their proposed model is feasible and effective. Mehdipour Ghazi et al. [66] used deep-CNN with transfer learning to identify plant species. The authors employed three deep learning frameworks: GoogLeNet, AlexNet, and VGGNet. Transfer learning was also used to fine-tune the deep learning frameworks. To reduce the possibility of overfitting, the authors used four types of data augmentation techniques: (1) rotation, (2) translation, (3) reflection, and (4) scaling. The authors claimed that their proposed method achieves an accuracy of 80%. Picon et al. [67] used the deep-CNN-based algorithm for the detection of multi-plant diseases in real conditions. The authors used seven mobile devices to identify three wheat diseases: septoria, tan spot, and rust, over four seasons. According to the authors, their proposed approach outperforms previous works in the literature. Farooq et al. [68] used deep-CNN with several varieties of sensors for the classification of weeds. For their proposed approach, the authors used three types of parameters: (1) patch size, (2) spatial resolution, and (3) the number of bands. They compared their proposed strategy to HoG. In comparison to HoG, the authors claimed that their proposed approach is more powerful and effective. Sethy et al. [69] proposed a rice disease detection system based on deep-CNN. This system primarily predicts four types of rice diseases: bacterial blight, blast, brown spot, and tungro. The performance of the 11 CNN in the transfer learning approach is evaluated by the authors. The deep feature is also combined with SVM by the authors. When they compared their F1 score, they believed it outperformed the other image classification models.

The aforementioned studies have used deep-CNN for various plant-related applications, including leaf classification, disease detection, plant identification, fruit detection, and weed classification. Overall, the studies show promising results in terms of accuracy and performance. However, some research gaps are present in these studies. For example, the studies may have used limited datasets or may not have thoroughly evaluated the performance of their models in real-world conditions. Additionally, some studies did not compare their proposed approaches with other state-of-the-art methods. Furthermore, the studies may have used different deep learning frameworks, data augmentation techniques, and parameters, making it difficult to compare their results. Therefore, future studies could focus on addressing these research gaps by using larger datasets, evaluating the performance of their models in real-world conditions, comparing their proposed approaches with other state-of-the-art methods, and standardizing the deep learning frameworks, data augmentation techniques, and parameters used for the experiments.

6.4.6 Machine vision

Machine vision systems have piqued the interest of many people because they have the potential to replace manual methods. As a result, they are widely used or accepted in a variety of applications for quality inspection of agricultural products. Jiang et al. [70] proposed a navigation agriculture robot by using a machine vision technique based on a crop row detection system. Their models are divided into four sections: (1) image processing technique was used to acquire the binarization image; (2) binarization image was divided into several parts to obtain information; (3) vertical projection approach was used to estimate crop row positions, and (4) Hough transform was used to identify crop row. The authors claimed that their proposed method is fast, determining the row in 70 ms. Guevara-Hernández and Gomez-Gil [71] used the machine vision technique for the classification of wheat and barley grains. Using a feature vector, the authors optimize the classification process. For object classification, the authors used discriminant analysis (DA) and KNN. The authors believed that their proposed method has high classification accuracy while also lowering computational costs. Wu et al. [72] used machine vision technology based on shape parameters for the classification of single cereal grains. The authors imaged cereal grains with a camera. They obtained the shape features using image processing techniques. Using the Bayesian classifier, the authors extracted 13 different types of shape parameters such as area, perimeter, length, and so on. According to the authors, the Bayesian classifier achieved an accuracy of 92.22% on training data and 90% on testing data. Ebrahimi et al. [73] proposed an automatic wheat purity measuring and grading device based on machine vision technology with neural networks. The authors used four different grades for the grading device and eight different types of wheat seeds to determine purity. They combined the Imperialist Competitive Algorithm (ICA) and the ANN for two purposes: (1) setting the best characteristics parameters and (2) creating robust classification models. The authors claimed that their proposed approach outperforms the benchmark datasets. Amatya et al. [74] proposed an automatic harvesting system based on machine vision techniques. They expected it to reduce harvest labor. The cherry field was used for evaluation and testing. The authors used the Bayesian classifier to divide the pixel images into four categories: (1) branch, (2) cherry, (3) leaf, and (4) background. They had an 89.6% classification accuracy. The authors thought their proposed method outperformed the other traditional method. Chung et al. [75] used machine vision techniques for detecting the Bakanae disease in rice seedlings. Their proposed method can be used to study the color characteristics of three-week-old rice seedlings. Using SVM, the authors distinguished between infected and healthy seedlings. The authors also used a genetic algorithm to select significant attributes. Their proposed method achieves an accuracy of 87.9%. Pulido-Rojas et al. [76] proposed a weed detection system under controlled lighting conditions by using the machine vision technique. Their proposed method used an image filter to extract area and color features. They had also put in place an object labeling system. The authors calculated sensitivity, specificity, and negative prediction values to assess the performance of their proposed model. Sabzi et al. [77] used machine vision technology based on ANN-Harmony Search for segmenting different plants under several conditions such as different growth stages, different lighting conditions, etc. Their proposed model consists of two steps: (1) specify the camera state, and (2) apply an appropriate threshold. The authors extracted 126 features from six different color spaces. For classification, they used the metaheuristic and statistical classifiers. The authors claimed that their proposed technique outperforms the others due to its high accuracy and speed. Radcliff et al. [78] used the machine vision technique for the orchard navigation. Their proposed model includes two control elements: (1) tree canopy and (2) sky. From the controlling features, they had created an upward-facing camera. The image processing algorithm was used by the authors to navigate through the orchard. The authors believed that their proposed method would have a lower error rate. Gongal et al. [79] used machine vision technology for estimating the size of an apple in tree canopies. The authors use sensor fusion with 2D and 3D cameras to estimate the size of apples. According to the authors, their proposed model outperforms previous studies because it is effective and reliable. Su et al. [80] used machine vision technology for potato quality grading. The authors used a depth camera to capture images of potatoes. They calculated the deformity in potatoes by measuring the length, width, thickness, and bump. The authors created a virtual–reality model rebuilding algorithm for tracing and checking quality. They believed that their proposed model could identify normal and deformed potatoes with an accuracy of 90% and quality by appearance with an accuracy of 88%. Sultan Mahmud et al. [81] used machine vision technology based on an artificial cloud lighting system for detecting powdery mildew diseases in strawberries. The authors create the proposed system by combining various components such as custom software written in C#, two types of cameras, and so on. The authors claimed that their proposed model can detect the disease in real time. Habib et al. [82] used the machine vision technique for identifying the disease in papaya. The authors identified the disease using a digital camera. The authors used a k-means clustering algorithm to classify the disease-affected region, and SVM to classify the disease. Their proposed model achieved a 90% accuracy rate. Zhou et al. [83] proposed a sugarcane cutting system based on the machine vision technique. Their proposed model was divided into three parts: (1) mechanical, (2) electrical, and (3) visual processing. The authors also used the programmable logic controller (PLC) high-speed counter. According to the authors, their proposed model can obtain a single bud segment of sugarcane seeds. Their proposed model has a 93% accuracy. Dhakshina Kumar et al. [84] used machine vision technology with an SVM classifier for grading and sorting the tomato. Their proposed model consisted of four parts: (1) they used binary classification to distinguish tomato species from other species, (2) they determined whether the tomato was ripe or not, (3) Gabor wavelet transform was used to identify the infected region in the tomato, and (4) defects were determined. The authors calculated sensitivity, specificity, and negative prediction values to assess the performance of their proposed model. Lu et al. [85] used machine vision technology with the YOLOv3 algorithm to develop a fruit grading system. The authors combined the YOLOv3 algorithm with hand-engineered features to calculate fruit maturity. Their proposed model is composed of three components: (1) transmission unit, (2) image acquisition unit, and (3) actuator unit. Under various conditions, the authors claimed that their proposed model achieves an accuracy of 94.78% with a detection time of 0.042 s. McGuinness et al. [86] developed three types of algorithms based on machine vision techniques for measuring the root collar diameter, seedling height, and root spread. They also used image processing techniques to remove noise. According to the authors, their proposed algorithm is fast. Opiyo et al. [87] developed an orchard navigation robot based on machine vision techniques. In the proposed robot, the authors used the medial-axis technique, principal component analysis (PCA), k-means clustering, and a fuzzy logic controller. According to the authors, the robot's performance is quite satisfactory. Neethi et al. [88] used machine vision techniques for estimating the yield of mangoes. In the proposed approach, the authors used image processing techniques, de-noising methods, thresholding methods, and segmentation methods. They claimed that their proposed method produces positive results.

While machine vision systems offer many potential benefits, they also have several limitations and challenges that must be addressed. These include limited accuracy, dependence on lighting conditions, limited flexibility, high cost, limited ability to handle complex objects, dependence on high-quality data, and difficulty in handling multiple objects. These limitations can reduce the overall effectiveness of machine vision systems and may limit their applicability in certain environments or applications. Therefore, ongoing research and development in the field of machine vision is essential to address these challenges and improve the accuracy and usefulness of machine vision systems. Additionally, careful consideration of the limitations of machine vision systems is necessary when implementing them in various applications to ensure that they meet the required performance standards.

6.5 CONCLUSION

This chapter provides a thorough examination of the published works that have employed AI techniques in agriculture. In this chapter, we present 77 papers from 2001 to 2021 that deal with the concept of AI techniques used in agriculture. The methodology is used to select and evaluate the papers. To assist the researchers, we have provided a gentle introduction to the techniques. Despite the fact that AI has made tremendous advances in agriculture, its growth remains below average when compared to other fields. In the preceding texts, we discussed six types of AI-based techniques. According to our review, the most commonly used AI technique is for crop pest and disease identification. Researchers believe that there are numerous challenges associated with using AI, such as a limitation on response time and accuracy, a limitation on data availability, a limitation on implementation method, and a limitation on flexibility. The technique of decreasing human interventions calls for more monitoring of agriculture. The food production is rising steadily, and without the use of current agricultural techniques, it will be extremely difficult to meet this demand. Analyzing agriculture is of utmost importance because it aids in lowering labor costs and raising output. AI has been used to assist farmers with crop selection and fertilizer selection. The machine connects among itself to determine which crop is appropriate for collecting and also the fertilizers which support the substantial growth with the aid of the dataset that the operator has acquired and supplied to the machine. Deep learning is widely applicable, and its use in business has advanced significantly. Deep learning has an edge over machine learning and gives machine learning more depth. Farmers can be guaranteed higher crops and appropriate field preservation through a variety of important strategies. As sustenance is a human's most basic requirement, this ultimately contributes to the world's high economy. In the contemporary world, traditional agricultural practices have negligible impact. The two biggest issues farmers face while utilizing the conventional method are weather and water constraints. Agriculture digitization is a result of the numerous flaws in this approach and the urgent need to conserve farmland.

REFERENCES

1. Arnal Barbedo, J.G.: Digital image processing techniques for detecting, quantifying and classifying plant diseases. In: SpringerPlus, 2, pp. 1–12 (2013). https://doi.org/10.1186/2193-1801-2-660
2. Zareiforoush, H., Minaei, S., Alizadeh, M.R., Banakar, A.: Potential applications of computer vision in quality inspection of rice: A review. In: Food Engineering Reviews, 7, pp. 321–345 (2015). https://link.springer.com/article/10.1007/s12393-014-9101-z
3. Vithu, P., Moses, J.A.: Machine vision system for food grain quality evaluation: A review. In: Trends in Food Science & Technology, 56, pp. 13–20 (2016).
4. Shah, J.P., Prajapati, H.B., Dabhi, V.K.: A survey on detection and classification of rice plant diseases. In: 2016 IEEE International Conference on Current Trends in Advanced Computing, ICCTAC 2016. Institute of Electrical and Electronics Engineers Inc. (2016).
5. Barbedo, J.G.A.: A review on the main challenges in automatic plant disease identification based on visible range images. In: Biosystems Engineering, 144, pp. 52–60 (2016).
6. Kamilaris, A., Prenafeta-Boldú, F.X.: Deep learning in agriculture: A survey. In: Computers and Electronics in Agriculture, 147, pp. 70–90 (2018).
7. Patrício, D.I., Rieder, R.: Computer vision and artificial intelligence in precision agriculture for grain crops: A systematic review. In: Computers and Electronics in Agriculture, 153, pp. 69–81 (2018).
8. Chlingaryan, A., Sukkarieh, S., Whelan, B.: Machine learning approaches for crop yield prediction and nitrogen status estimation in precision agriculture: A review. In: Computers and Electronics in Agriculture, 151, pp. 61–69 (2018).
9. Zamora-Sequeira, R., Starbird-Pérez, R., Rojas-Carillo, O., Vargas-Villalobos, S.: What are the main sensor methods for quantifying pesticides in agricultural activities? A review. In: Molecules, 24(14), p. 2659 (2019). https://www.mdpi.com/1420-3049/24/14/2659/htm

10. Fue, K., Porter, W., Barnes, E., Rains, G.: An extensive review of mobile agricultural robotics for field operations: Focus on cotton harvesting. In: AgriEngineering, 2, pp. 150–174 (2020). https://doi.org/10.3390/agriengineering2010010

11. Lu, Y.: Artificial intelligence: A survey on evolution, models, applications and future trends. In: Journal of Management Analytics, 6, pp. 1–29 (2019). https://doi.org/10.1080/23270012.2019.1570365

12. Hashimoto, Y., Murase, H., Morimoto, T., Torii, T.: Intelligent systems for agriculture in Japan. In: IEEE Control Systems Magazine, 21, pp. 71–85 (2001). https://doi.org/10.1109/37.954520

13. Van Henten, E.J., Hemming, J., Van Tuijl, B.A.J., Kornet, J.G., Meuleman, J., Bontsema, J., Van Os, E.A.: An autonomous robot for harvesting cucumbers in greenhouses. In: Autonomous Robots, 13, pp. 241–258 (2002). https://doi.org/10.1023/A:1020568125418

14. Munirah, Y.M., Rozlini, M., Siti Mariam, Y.: An expert system development: Its application on diagnosing oyster mushroom diseases, In: International Conference on Control, Automation and Systems, pp. 329–332 (2013).

15. Balleda, K., Satyanvesh, D., Sampath, N.V.S.S.P., Varma, K.T.N., Baruah, P.K.: Agpest: An efficient rule-based expert system to prevent pest diseases of rice & wheat crops. In: 2014 IEEE 8th International Conference on Intelligent Systems and Control: Green Challenges and Smart Solutions, ISCO 2014 – Proceedings, pp. 262–268. Institute of Electrical and Electronics Engineers Inc. (2014).

16. Spanaki, K., Karafili, E., Sivarajah, U., Despoudi, S., Irani, Z.: Artificial intelligence and food security: Swarm intelligence of AgriTech drones for smart AgriFood operations. In: Production Planning and Control, 33(16), pp. 1498–1516 (2021). https://doi.org/10.1080/09537287.2021.1882688

17. Gil, Y., Garijo, D., Khider, D., Knoblock, C.A., Ratnakar, V., Osorio, M., Vargas, H., Pham, M., Pujara, J., Shbita, B., Vu, B., Chiang, Y.Y., Feldman, D., Lin, Y., Song, H., Kumar, V., Khandelwal, A., Steinbach, M., Tayal, K., Xu, S., Pierce, S.A., Pearson, L., Hardesty-Lewis, D., Deelman, E., Silva, R.F.D., Mayani, R., Kemanian, A.R., Shi, Y., Leonard, L., Peckham, S., Stoica, M., Cobourn, K., Zhang, Z., Duffy, C., Shu, L.: Artificial intelligence for modeling complex systems: Taming the complexity of expert models to improve decision making. In: ACM Transactions on Interactive Intelligent Systems, 11, p. 11 (2021). https://doi.org/10.1145/3453172

18. Facchinetti, D., Santoro, S., Galli, L.E., Fontana, G., Fedeli, L., Parisi, S., Bonacchi, L.B., Šušnjar, S., Salvai, F., Coppola, G., Matteucci, M., Pessina, D.: Reduction of pesticide use in fresh-cut salad production through artificial intelligence. In: Applied Sciences (Switzerland), 11, pp. 1–17 (2021). https://doi.org/10.3390/app11051992

19. Escobar, C.: Fuzzy control in agriculture: Simulation Software. In: Marín, J., Koncar, V. (eds.), Industrial Simulation Conference 2004 (ISC 2004), Málaga, Spain, June 2004, pp. 45–49 (2004)

20. Perini, A., Susi, A.: Developing a decision support system for integrated production in agriculture. In: Environmental Modelling and Software, 19, pp. 821–829 (2004).

21. Sicat, R.S., Carranza, E.J.M., Nidumolu, U.B.: Fuzzy modeling of farmers' knowledge for land suitability classification. In: Agricultural Systems, 83, pp. 49–75 (2005). https://doi.org/10.1016/j.agsy.2004.03.002

22. Tremblay, N., Bouroubi, M.Y., Panneton, B., Guillaume, S., Vigneault, P., Bélec, C.: Development and validation of fuzzy logic inference to determine optimum rates of N for corn on the basis of field and crop features. In: Precision Agriculture, 11, pp. 621–635 (2010). https://doi.org/10.1007/s11119-010-9188-z
23. Papageorgiou, E.I., Markinos, A.T., Gemtos, T.A.: Fuzzy cognitive map based approach for predicting yield in cotton crop production as a basis for decision support system in precision agriculture application. In: Applied Soft Computing Journal, 11, pp. 3643–3657 (2011). https://doi.org/10.1016/j.asoc.2011.01.036
24. Prakash, C.P, Singh Rathor, A., Thakur, G.S.M.: Fuzzy based agriculture expert system for soyabean RAMAN: A robotic assistive bio-mechanical study on posture deviations on elderly and remedies view project and stock portfolio selection view project. In: International Conference on Computing Sciences (2013). https://doi.org/10.13140/2.1.1765.0567
25. Tilva, V., Patel, J., Bhatt, C.: Weather based plant diseases forecasting using fuzzy logic. In: 2013 Nirma University International Conference on Engineering, NUiCONE 2013. IEEE Computer Society (2013).
26. Shafaei, S.M., Nourmohamadi-Moghadami, A., Kamgar, S.: Development of artificial intelligence based systems for prediction of hydration characteristics of wheat. In: Computers and Electronics in Agriculture, 128, pp. 34–45 (2016). https://doi.org/10.1016/j.compag.2016.08.014
27. Sannakki, S.S., Rajpurohit, V.S., Nargund, V.B., Kulkarni, P.: Diagnosis and classification of grape leaf diseases using neural networks. In: 2013 4th International Conference on Computing, Communications and Networking Technologies, ICCCNT 2013 (2013).
28. Marcal, A.R.S., Cunha, M.: Development of an image-based system to assess agricultural fertilizer spreader pattern. In: Computers and Electronics in Agriculture, 162, pp. 380–388 (2019). https://doi.org/10.1016/j.compag.2019.04.031
29. Dhingra, G., Kumar, V., Joshi, H.D.: A novel computer vision based neutrosophic approach for leaf disease identification and classification. In: Measurement: Journal of the International Measurement Confederation, 135, pp. 782–794 (2019). https://doi.org/10.1016/j.measurement.2018.12.027
30. Singh, K., Rawat, R., Ashu, A.: Image segmentation in agriculture crop and weed detection using image processing and deep learning techniques. In: International Journal of Research in Engineering, Science and Management, 4, pp. 235–238 (2021).
31. Moshou, D., Pantazi, X.E., Kateris, D., Gravalos, I.: Water stress detection based on optical multisensor fusion with a least squares support vector machine classifier. In: Biosystems Engineering, 117, pp. 15–22 (2014). https://doi.org/10.1016/j.biosystemseng.2013.07.008
32. Zhou, R., Kaneko, S., Tanaka, F., Kayamori, M., Shimizu, M.: Disease detection of cercospora leaf spot in sugar beet by robust template matching. In: Computers and Electronics in Agriculture, 108, pp. 58–70 (2014). https://doi.org/10.1016/j.compag.2014.07.004
33. Heremans, S., Dong, Q., Zhang, B., Bydekerke, L., Van Orshoven, J.: Potential of ensemble tree methods for early-season prediction of winter wheat yield from short time series of remotely sensed normalized difference vegetation index and in situ meteorological data. In: Journal of Applied Remote Sensing, 9, p. 097095 (2015). https://doi.org/10.1117/1.jrs.9.097095

34. Liang, L., Di, L., Zhang, L., Deng, M., Qin, Z., Zhao, S., Lin, H.: Estimation of crop LAI using hyperspectral vegetation indices and a hybrid inversion method. In: Remote Sensing of Environment, 165, pp. 123–134 (2015). https://doi.org/10.1016/j.rse.2015.04.032

35. Patil, S.S., Thorat, S.A.: Early detection of grapes diseases using machine learning and IoT. In: Proceedings – 2016 2nd International Conference on Cognitive Computing and Information Processing, CCIP 2016. Institute of Electrical and Electronics Engineers Inc. (2016).

36. Waghmare, H., Kokare, R., Dandawate, Y.: Detection and classification of diseases of grape plant using opposite colour local binary pattern feature and machine learning for automated decision support system. In: 3rd International Conference on Signal Processing and Integrated Networks, SPIN 2016, pp. 513–518. Institute of Electrical and Electronics Engineers Inc. (2016).

37. Pantazi, X.E., Moshou, D., Alexandridis, T., Whetton, R.L., Mouazen, A.M.: Wheat yield prediction using machine learning and advanced sensing techniques. In: Computers and Electronics in Agriculture, 121, pp. 57–65 (2016). https://doi.org/10.1016/j.compag.2015.11.018

38. Maione, C., Batista, B.L., Campiglia, A.D., Barbosa, F., Barbosa, R.M.: Classification of geographic origin of rice by data mining and inductively coupled plasma mass spectrometry. In: Computers and Electronics in Agriculture, 121, pp. 101–107 (2016). https://doi.org/10.1016/j.compag.2015.11.009

39. Stas, M., Van Orshoven, J., Dong, Q., Heremans, S., Zhang, B.: A comparison of machine learning algorithms for regional wheat yield prediction using NDVI time series of SPOT-VGT. In: 2016 5th International Conference on Agro-Geoinformatics, Agro-Geoinformatics. Institute of Electrical and Electronics Engineers Inc. (2016).

40. Morellos, A., Pantazi, X.E., Moshou, D., Alexandridis, T., Whetton, R., Tziotzios, G., Wiebensohn, J., Bill, R., Mouazen, A.M.: Machine learning based prediction of soil total nitrogen, organic carbon and moisture content by using VIS-NIR spectroscopy. In: Biosystems Engineering, 152, pp. 104–116 (2016). https://doi.org/10.1016/j.biosystemseng.2016.04.018

41. Su, Y.-X., Xu, H., Yan, L.-J.: Support vector machine-based open crop model (SBOCM): Case of rice production in China. In: Saudi Journal of Biological Sciences, 24, pp. 537–547 (2017). https://doi.org/10.1016/j.sjbs.2017.01.024

42. Behera, S.K., Jena, L., Rath, A.K., Sethy, P.K.: Disease classification and grading of orange using machine learning and fuzzy logic. In: Proceedings of the 2018 IEEE International Conference on Communication and Signal Processing, ICCSP 2018, pp. 678–682. Institute of Electrical and Electronics Engineers Inc. (2018).

43. Duarte-Carvajalino, J.M., Alzate, D.F., Ramirez, A.A., Santa-Sepulveda, J.D., Fajardo-Rojas, A.E., Soto-Suárez, M.: Evaluating late blight severity in potato crops using unmanned aerial vehicles and machine learning algorithms. In: Remote Sensing, 10, p. 1513 (2018). https://doi.org/10.3390/rs10101513

44. Islam, N., Rashid, M.M., Wibowo, S., Xu, C.Y., Morshed, A., Wasimi, S.A., Moore, S., Rahman, S.M.: Early weed detection using image processing and machine learning techniques in an Australian chilli farm. In: Agriculture (Switzerland), 11, p. 387 (2021). https://doi.org/10.3390/agriculture11050387

45. Raimundo, F., Gloria, A., Sebastiao, P.: Prediction of weather forecast for smart agriculture supported by machine learning. In: 2021 IEEE World AI IoT Congress, AIIoT 2021, pp. 160–164. Institute of Electrical and Electronics Engineers Inc. (2021).

46. Patel, M.N.C., Kruthi, M.N., Shirisha, K.S., Karthik, H.C., Lahari, M.J.: A machine learning approach for crop prediction and crop yield prediction. In: International Journal of Research in Engineering, Science and Management, 4, pp. 110–113 (2021)

47. Song, H., He, Y.: Crop nutrition diagnosis expert system based on artificial neural networks. In: Proceedings – 3rd International Conference on Information Technology and Applications, ICITA 2005, pp. 357–362 (2005).

48. Zhao, Z., Chow, T.L., Rees, H.W., Yang, Q., Xing, Z., Meng, F.R.: Predict soil texture distributions using an artificial neural network model. In: Computers and Electronics in Agriculture, 65, pp. 36–48 (2009). https://doi.org/10.1016/j.compag.2008.07.008

49. Arif, C., Mizoguchi, M., Mizoguchi, M., Doi, R.: Estimation of soil moisture in paddy field using artificial neural networks. In: International Journal of Advanced Research in Artificial Intelligence, 1 (2012). https://doi.org/10.14569/ijarai.2012.010104

50. Ravichandran, G., Koteeshwari, R.S.: Agricultural crop predictor and advisor using ANN for smartphones. In: 1st International Conference on Emerging Trends in Engineering, Technology and Science, ICETETS 2016 – Proceedings. Institute of Electrical and Electronics Engineers Inc. (2016).

51. Mohanty, S.P., Hughes, D.P., Salathé, M.: Using deep learning for image-based plant disease detection. In: Frontiers in Plant Science, 7, p. 1419 (2016). https://doi.org/10.3389/fpls.2016.01419

52. Yalcin, H., Razavi, S.: Plant classification using convolutional neural networks. In: 2016 5th International Conference on Agro-Geoinformatics, Agro-Geoinformatics 2016. Institute of Electrical and Electronics Engineers Inc. (2016).

53. Yalcin, H.: Plant phenology recognition using deep learning: Deep-Pheno. In: 2017 6th International Conference on Agro-Geoinformatics, Agro-Geoinformatics. Institute of Electrical and Electronics Engineers Inc. (2017).

54. Chen, S.W., Shivakumar, S.S., Dcunha, S., Das, J., Okon, E., Qu, C., Taylor, C.J., Kumar, V.: Counting apples and oranges with deep learning: A data-driven approach. In: IEEE Robotics and Automation Letters, 2, pp. 781–788 (2017). https://doi.org/10.1109/LRA.2017.2651944

55. Amara, J., Bouaziz, B., Algergawy, A.: A deep learning-based approach for banana leaf diseases classification. In: Lecture Notes in Informatics (LNI), Proceedings – Series of the Gesellschaft fur Informatik (GI), pp. 79–88 (2017).

56. Pound, M.P., Atkinson, J.A., Townsend, A.J., Wilson, M.H., Griffiths, M., Jackson, A.S., Bulat, A., Tzimiropoulos, G., Wells, D.M., Murchie, E.H., Pridmore, T.P., French, A.P.: Deep machine learning provides state-of-the-art performance in image-based plant phenotyping. In: GigaScience, 6, pp. 1–10 (2017). https://doi.org/10.1093/gigascience/gix083

57. Uzal, L.C., Grinblat, G.L., Namías, R., Larese, M.G., Bianchi, J.S., Morandi, E.N., Granitto, P.M.: Seed-per-pod estimation for plant breeding using deep learning. In: Computers and Electronics in Agriculture, 150, pp. 196–204 (2018). https://doi.org/10.1016/j.compag.2018.04.024

58. Francis, M., Deisy, C.: Mathematical and visual understanding of a deep learning model towards m-agriculture for disease diagnosis. In: Archives of Computational Methods in Engineering, 28, pp. 1129–1145 (2021). https://doi.org/10.1007/s11831-020-09407-3

59. Hall, D., McCool, C., Dayoub, F., Sünderhauf, N., Upcroft, B.: Evaluation of features for leaf classification in challenging conditions. In: Proceedings – 2015 IEEE Winter Conference on Applications of Computer Vision, WACV 2015, pp. 797–804. Institute of Electrical and Electronics Engineers Inc. (2015).

60. Sladojevic, S., Arsenovic, M., Anderla, A., Culibrk, D., Stefanovic, D.: Deep neural networks based recognition of plant diseases by leaf image classification. In: Computational Intelligence and Neuroscience, 2016, pp. 1–11 (2016). https://doi.org/10.1155/2016/3289801

61. Grinblat, G.L., Uzal, L.C., Larese, M.G., Granitto, P.M.: Deep learning for plant identification using vein morphological patterns. In: Computers and Electronics in Agriculture, 127, pp. 418–424 (2016). https://doi.org/10.1016/j.compag.2016.07.003

62. Sa, I., Ge, Z., Dayoub, F., Upcroft, B., Perez, T., McCool, C.: DeepFruits: A fruit detection system using deep neural networks. In: Sensors (Switzerland), 16, p. 1222 (2016). https://doi.org/10.3390/s16081222

63. Ha, J.G., Moon, H., Kwak, J.T., Hassan, S.I., Dang, M., Lee, O.N., Park, H.Y.: Deep convolutional neural network for classifying Fusarium wilt of radish from unmanned aerial vehicles. In: Journal of Applied Remote Sensing. 11, p. 1 (2017). https://doi.org/10.1117/1.jrs.11.042621

64. Fuentes, A., Yoon, S., Kim, S.C., Park, D.S.: A robust deep-learning-based detector for real-time tomato plant diseases and pests recognition. In: Sensors (Switzerland), 17, p. 2022 (2017). https://doi.org/10.3390/s17092022

65. Lu, Y., Yi, S., Zeng, N., Liu, Y., Zhang, Y.: Identification of rice diseases using deep convolutional neural networks. In: Neurocomputing, 267, pp. 378–384 (2017). https://doi.org/10.1016/j.neucom.2017.06.023

66. Mehdipour Ghazi, M., Yanikoglu, B., Aptoula, E.: Plant identification using deep neural networks via optimization of transfer learning parameters. In: Neurocomputing, 235, pp. 228–235 (2017). https://doi.org/10.1016/j.neucom.2017.01.018

67. Picon, A., Alvarez-Gila, A., Seitz, M., Ortiz-Barredo, A., Echazarra, J., Johannes, A.: Deep convolutional neural networks for mobile capture device-based crop disease classification in the wild. In: Computers and Electronics in Agriculture, 161, pp. 280–290 (2019). https://doi.org/10.1016/j.compag.2018.04.002

68. Farooq, A., Hu, J., Jia, X.: Analysis of spectral bands and spatial resolutions for weed classification via deep convolutional neural network. In: IEEE Geoscience and Remote Sensing Letters, 16, pp. 183–187 (2019). https://doi.org/10.1109/LGRS.2018.2869879

69. Sethy, P.K., Barpanda, N.K., Rath, A.K., Behera, S.K.: Deep feature based rice leaf disease identification using support vector machine. In: Computers and Electronics in Agriculture. 175, p. 105527 (2020). https://doi.org/10.1016/j.compag.2020.105527

70. Jiang, G.Q., Zhao, C.J., Si, Y.S.: A machine vision based crop rows detection for agricultural robots. In: 2010 International Conference on Wavelet Analysis and Pattern Recognition, ICWAPR 2010, pp. 114–118 (2010).

71. Guevara-Hernandez, F., Gomez-Gil, J.: A machine vision system for classification of wheat and barley grain kernels. In: Spanish Journal of Agricultural Research, 9, p. 672 (2011). https://doi.org/10.5424/sjar/20110903-140-10
72. Wu, L.L., Wu, J., Wen, Y., Xiong, L., Zheng, Y.: Classification of single cereal grain kernel using shape parameters based on machine vision. In: Advanced Materials Research, 605–607, pp. 2179–2182 (2013).
73. Ebrahimi, E., Mollazade, K., Babaei, S.: Toward an automatic wheat purity measuring device: A machine vision-based neural networks-assisted imperialist competitive algorithm approach. In: Measurement: Journal of the International Measurement Confederation, 55, pp. 196–205 (2014). https://doi.org/10.1016/j.measurement.2014.05.003
74. Amatya, S., Karkee, M., Gongal, A., Zhang, Q., Whiting, M.D.: Detection of cherry tree branches with full foliage in planar architecture for automated sweet-cherry harvesting. In: Biosystems Engineering, 146, pp. 3–15 (2016). https://doi.org/10.1016/j.biosystemseng.2015.10.003
75. Chung, C.L., Huang, K.J., Chen, S.Y., Lai, M.H., Chen, Y.C., Kuo, Y.F.: Detecting Bakanae disease in rice seedlings by machine vision. In: Computers and Electronics in Agriculture. 121, pp. 404–411 (2016). https://doi.org/10.1016/j.compag.2016.01.008
76. Pulido-Rojas, C.A., Molina-Villa, M.A., Solaque-Guzmán, L.E.: Machine vision system for weed detection using image filtering in vegetables crops. In: Revista Facultad de Ingenieria. 2016, pp. 124–130 (2016). https://doi.org/10.17533/udea.redin.n80a13
77. Sabzi, S., Abbaspour-Gilandeh, Y., Javadikia, H.: Machine vision system for the automatic segmentation of plants under different lighting conditions. In: Biosystems Engineering, 161, pp. 157–173 (2017). https://doi.org/10.1016/j.biosystemseng.2017.06.021
78. Radcliffe, J., Cox, J., Bulanon, D.M.: Machine vision for orchard navigation. In: Computers in Industry, 98, pp. 165–171 (2018). https://doi.org/10.1016/j.compind.2018.03.008
79. Gongal, A., Karkee, M., Amatya, S.: Apple fruit size estimation using a 3D machine vision system. In: Information Processing in Agriculture, 5, pp. 498–503 (2018). https://doi.org/10.1016/j.inpa.2018.06.002
80. Su, Q., Kondo, N., Li, M., Sun, H., Al Riza, D.F., Habaragamuwa, H.: Potato quality grading based on machine vision and 3D shape analysis. In: Computers and Electronics in Agriculture, 152, pp. 261–268 (2018). https://doi.org/10.1016/j.compag.2018.07.012
81. Sultan Mahmud, M., Zaman, Q.U., Esau, T.J., Price, G.W., Prithiviraj, B.: Development of an artificial cloud lighting condition system using machine vision for strawberry powdery mildew disease detection. In: Computers and Electronics in Agriculture, 158, pp. 219–225 (2019). https://doi.org/10.1016/j.compag.2019.02.007
82. Habib, M.T., Majumder, A., Jakaria, A.Z.M., Akter, M., Uddin, M.S., Ahmed, F.: Machine vision based papaya disease recognition. In: Journal of King Saud University: Computer and Information Sciences, 32, pp. 300–309 (2020). https://doi.org/10.1016/j.jksuci.2018.06.006
83. Zhou, D., Fan, Y., Deng, G., He, F., Wang, M.: A new design of sugarcane seed cutting systems based on machine vision. In: Computers and Electronics in Agriculture, 175, p. 105611 (2020). https://doi.org/10.1016/j.compag.2020.105611

84. Dhakshina Kumar, S., Esakkirajan, S., Bama, S., Keerthiveena, B.: A micro-controller based machine vision approach for tomato grading and sorting using SVM classifier. In: Microprocessors and Microsystems, 76, p. 103090 (2020). https://doi.org/10.1016/j.micpro.2020.103090

85. Lu, Z., Zhao, M., Luo, J., Wang, G., Wang, D.: Design of a winter-jujube grading robot based on machine vision. In: Computers and Electronics in Agriculture, 186, p. 106170 (2021). https://doi.org/10.1016/j.compag.2021.106170

86. McGuinness, B., Duke, M., Au, C.K., Lim, S.H.: Measuring radiata pine seedling morphological features using a machine vision system. In: Computers and Electronics in Agriculture. 189, p. 106355 (2021). https://doi.org/10.1016/j.compag.2021.106355

87. Opiyo, S., Okinda, C., Zhou, J., Mwangi, E., Makange, N.: Medial axis-based machine-vision system for orchard robot navigation. In: Computers and Electronics in Agriculture, 185, p. 106153 (2021). https://doi.org/10.1016/j.compag.2021.106153

88. Neethi, M.V., Kiran, A.G., Tiwari, H.: Yield estimation in mango orchards using machine vision. In: AIP Conference Proceedings. p. 050004. AIP Publishing LLC (2021)

Chapter 7

Prediction of vitiligo skin disease spreading rate by image processing

Durai Selvaraj, Mahaboob Mohamed Iqbal, and Mukkoti Maruthi Venkata Chalapathi

7.1 INTRODUCTION

One of the crucial aspects of digital image processing that is frequently employed for picture analysis and interpretation is image classification. There are several uses for digital picture classification in various fields, such as remote sensing and area monitoring. Similar demands for digital image processing exist in the field of medical sciences to automate processes. Since the skin covers the majority of the body, it has a higher likelihood of being impacted by various diseases than any other region of the body. There are numerous forms of skin diseases, many of which can be seriously damaging and others which are not. Due to the ease with which skin diseases can develop while a person is being observed, it is crucial for doctors to have early detection and prevention of skin diseases. Many issues are tackled utilizing image processing in the expanding field of digital image processing. In this study, the disease vitiligo is chosen to be detected using photographs of the human body. Utilizing a convolution neural network (CNN) approach, vitiligo is detected. A CNN isa sort of artificial neural algorithm. CNN employs supervised learning, where it is trained using pre-existing data.

Even though the present medical field is very much advanced, identification and classification of most diseases are largely based on physical examination. Many of the diseases are identified and cured by physical examination, but the identification accuracy is not up to the mark. Hence in the proposed system, the identification and classification are completely dependent on the deep learning–based approach to solve the problem of classifying vitiligo using CNNs. By using the CNN model, we can achieve an accuracy level of 95% and an error of 1.06%in vitiligo disease classification.

The main objective of the "prediction of vitiligo skin disease spreading rate by image processing" is to predict and classify the vitiligo skin disease spreading rate by image processing using CNN algorithm with the help of pretrained models. In medical field, especially doctors can use this for determining the spreading rate. Even patients and others can use it to identify the disease and spreading rate. It makes easier for victims to identify the disease in advance and take the precautionary steps to prevent the disease from spreading further more.

DOI: 10.1201/9781003433941-7

Allugunti [1] proposed a convolutional neural network (CNN) model for the diagnosis of skin cancer was created, constructed, and evaluated using a well-known melanoma dataset. The recommended method, which is a two-stage learning platform, has impressive projected accuracy at each level, as seen by its overall accuracy of 88.83%. This applies to all methods of classification, not only DT, RF, and GBT. It is fair to see the suggested method, which is based on CNN, as a successful multiclass classification method. Our CNN classifier outperforms cutting-edge machine learning methods in terms of melanoma classification accuracy while significantly reducing the amount of computing labor due to its modular and hierarchical structure. Balakrishnan et al. [2] done research with an emphasis on disorders including vitiligo, Down syndrome, hyperthyroidism, leprosy, and beta-thalassemia, this study attempts to forecast Illnesses using 2D face photos. The work tackles the difficulties of gathering complicated, costly, and time-consuming disease-specific picture datasets, achieving over 90% accuracy in facial recognition.

He, X et al. [3] used two datasets, Skin-10 with 10,218 photos over 10 common classes and Skin-100 with 19,807 images across 100 classes, we assess CNN-based methods for classifying skin diseases. The accuracy of Skin-100 is surprisingly lower than that of Skin-10. Using a combination of CNN models in an ensemble approach, we obtain the greatest accuracy of 79.01% for Skin-10 and 53.54% for Skin-100. Low et al. [4] demonstrated that segmenting vitiligo is possible using a U-Net with a contracting pathway based on InceptionResnetV2 with watershed post-processing. They have calculated the time required to segment increasingly more complicated lesions as well as the potential variance across reviewers. Maduranga, M. W. P., and Dilshan Nandasena [5] proposed mobile AI software that uses CNNs on the HAM10000 dataset to accurately diagnose skin diseases. Dermatologists and patients alike can benefit from the app's ability to quickly and precisely analyse impacted regions. It reduces the computational burden by nearly half while achieving 85% accuracy by utilizing MobileNet in conjunction with transfer learning. This method has the potential to help general practitioners diagnose skin diseases more quickly and accurately using cell phones.

Omotosho, Lawrence, et al. [6] system's validation accuracy on the test set reached 99.44%, and it obtained an astounding 98.44% network accuracy. Subsequent testing revealed a 97.8% identification accuracy and a 2.2% rejection rate. Swapna [7] done the research on the current diagnostic system for skin diseases which involves physical contact with the patient's body. However, this traditional approach has limitations in terms of accuracy. For instance, computer-aided diagnosis methods that rely on identifying burns and injuries as skin diseases may not be reliable enough. Using CNN, Resnet, Alexnet, and Inceptionv3, it has been determined whether it is feasible to create a categorization system for all skin diseases. On training data, CNN outperformed, but not on testing data. A training set's accuracy can be improved by giving it greater variance and by expanding its size. Additionally, it was discovered that Resnet performed more accurately in the identification of skin illnesses when compared to other networks.

Thurnhofer-Hemsi et al. [8] used a novel method utilizing deep CNNs was employed to classify skin lesions, involving an ensemble of networks for enhanced accuracy. The approach incorporates multiple shifted copies of the test input image, each controlled by a different network in the ensemble, to create a regular lattice of shift vectors. Yanlinget al. [9] proposed an automatic segmentation method for vitiligo lesions to objectively assess disease severity. Their approach combines a novel face vitiligo segmentation algorithm with the vitiligo segmentation network FCN-UTA, leveraging both vitiligo face image synthesis and segmentation techniques.

Silverberg, N [10] give a summary of autoimmune skin responses, emphasizing vitiligo and alopecia areata as notable cases. The intricacy of autoimmune reactions is deliberated, and the genetic processes implicated—such as single-gene illnesses and multifactorial genes—are emphasized. Shiu, Jessica, et al. [11] used noninvasive multiphoton microscopy (MPM) imaging and single-cell RNA-Seq (scRNA-Seq) to investigate the persistence of white patches in stable vitiligo patients. They identified keratinocyte subpopulations in vitiligo skin, noting shifts towards oxidative phosphorylation compared to nonlesional skin. Analysis of cell-to-cell communication networks revealed a subset of keratinocytes secreting CXCL9 and CXCL10, potentially perpetuating vitiligo. Yang, Ting-Ting et al. [12] examined how various instruments for assessing health-related quality of life (QoL) represent the burden of vitiligo. Our goal in this study is to assess, with the resources at our disposal, how vitiligo affects quality of life.

7.1.1 Existing system

As input, the system will take a dataset of picture data. Qualities of the images are increased. A training file is formed from the input image dataset. Then CNN is used to classify both the newly constructed training file collection and the freshly created test input images. Hence melanomas are detected. The input can be given from both the clinical-based images and the images extracted from the Internet. Then the CNN model is trained using the large datasets of image collected from various resources. Training the given CNN model on large datasets can help improve the accuracy percentage of the CNN model and decreases the error rate parallel. A pre-trained CNN model can also be used to classify the vitiligo lesions, where the model is already trained using the datasets and is available readily.

Advantages

1. The modular and hierarchical structure of the proposed CNN classifier outperforms the cutting-edge machine learning methods in terms of melanoma classification accuracy.

2. It significantly minimizes the amount of computational effort that is required.
3. The percentage of error is also decreased in classifying the images.

Disadvantages

1. In order to obtain the maximum accuracy for the proposed system, a large quantity of dataset is required for training.
2. Obtaining those large datasets may require a large amount of time and money.
3. It may either take a more amount of time for classifying the images which are captured not up to the mark or is taken under low-light conditions.

7.2 LITERATURE REVIEW

Wang, Jingying, et al. [13] provided thorough description of the function of damage associated molecular patterns (DAMPs) in the pathophysiology of vitiligo in their article. Mehmood et al. [14] offers a way to use a clustering algorithm to divide up skin lesions. The outcomes of skin lesion segmentation using the suggested approach were compared to annotated images. The results show that the proposed work might be used in real-time, and the computation time is reasonable. Guo Let al. [15] generated two large datasets consisting of cured images of vitiligo lesions from the individuals of Chinese descent with Fitzpatrick skin types III or IV. One dataset comprised 2,720 images for lesion localization inquiry, while the other included 1,262 images for lesion segmentation examination. Additionally, a second test set of 145 images of vitiligo lesions on individuals with Fitzpatrick skin types I, II, or V was created. The hybrid model was developed in three stages, which included training and validating the YOLO v3 (You Only Look Once, v3) architecture to classify and localize vitiligo lesions with sensitivity and error rate serving as the main performance metrics.

Zhang L et al. [16] utilized two datasets consisting of images of vitiligo and other depigmented or hypopigmented lesions: a Chinese internal dataset (2,876 photographs) and a worldwide public dataset (1,341 images). Three CNN models were trained on these datasets, and their performance was compared to that of 14 human raters from four groups: dermatology residents, intermediate raters (5–10 years), expert raters, and general practitioners. Performance was evaluated using measures such as the F1 score, area under the receiver operating characteristic curve, specificity, and sensitivity.

Allugunti [1] work is broken up into two phases: system development and application development. The system development approach uses the (MobileNet V2) model to identify the three categories of skin conditions, while the application development uses Tensor Flow Lite to deploy the MobileNet V2 model on a smartphone and display the results.

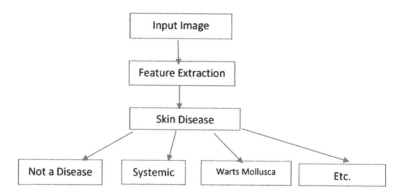

Figure 7.1 The structure of the system for detecting and classifying skin diseases.

The initial component of the system was a smartphone that was used to photograph the patient's skin lesion. To prepare for the deep learning process, the image data is pre-processed. The resizing, augmentation, data splitting, and normalization all are part of the pre-processing image. The photos have been reduced in size to $224 \times 224 \times 3$. In order to create efficient and accurate skin lesion classification systems, data augmentation techniques like rotate and flip are used to increase the number of training images.

Low et al. [4] used dataset is built up with308 red, green, and blue (RGB) photographs of vitiligo lesions. Skin color and anatomical position of the lesions vary greatly. The photos were captured by doctors in a variety of lighting conditions, including UV or natural light, and from various angles. They then use the semi-autonomous Watershed GUI and human adjustments to produce the ground truth segmentation result. Each ground truth output image is a binary mask of the lesion, where vitiligo is represented by white and healthy skin by zero (black) and the environment by 255 (black). The dataset is divided so that 60% of it is used to train the model (188 images), 20% to validate the model (66 images), and the remaining 20% to test the model on unobserved data.

Swapna [7] proposed system is a web application that assists in the preliminary diagnosis of skin diseases by allowing the user to upload an image of the affected skin area, which is then analyzed using a deep learning–based method. This system utilizes computational techniques to process and classify the image data based on various features. The system also provides suggestions related to the disease. The architecture of the skin disease detection and classification system is depicted in Figure 7.1.

7.3 PROPOSED SYSTEM

The objective of the proposed work is to help doctors and patients for knowing the spread rate of vitiligo skin disease. In this work, the dataset from Kaggle

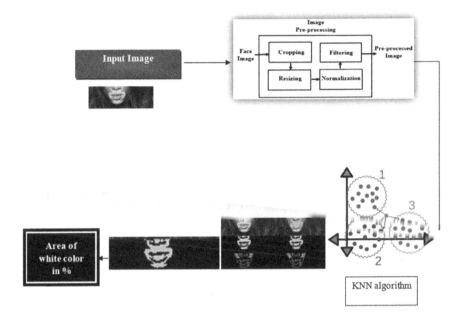

Figure 7.2 Architecture of the proposed system.

have been utilized. The ultimate aim of this work is to find the area of white patches which affect the skin color. Between the visits to the doctor for consultation, the proposed work needs to know the area of white patches for the previous and current visit. Figure 7.2 shows the architecture of the proposed system.

7.3.1 Dataset

The data of 368 images of vitiligo-affected people are collected from Kaggle, which we can freely access it. The sample collected images are shown in Figure 7.3.

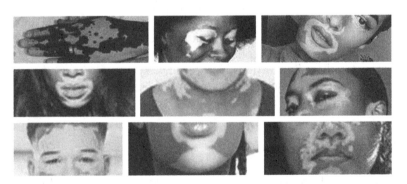

Figure 7.3 Sample images of vitiligo-affected people.

7.3.2 Image pre-processing

The color image must be transformed into grayscale and then into black and white in order to extract the features. An *m* by *n* × 3 numeric array represents the True color image. Grayscale images, however, are returned as a *m*×*n* numeric array. After the RGB image has been transformed to grayscale, the unsharp masking approach is used to sharpen the grayscale input image. The unsharp masking method was inspired by a technology used in the publishing industry to sharpen an image by eliminating its blurry (unsharp) counterpart. Do not be misled by this filter's name; it is merely an operator for sharpening images.

The grayscale image is then converted to binary (black and white)image. The adaptive method we used to obtain the binary image converts the original picture into a binary image using a threshold. When adaptive, the local first-order picture statistics around each pixel are used to calculate a locally adaptable image threshold. The adaptthresh function selects the threshold based on the first-order statistics of the local mean intensity surrounding each pixel. To transform the grayscale image into a binary image, use the threshold along with the imbinarize function. The behavior of imbinarize for the "adaptive" approach is undefinable if the picture contains Infs or NaNs. It is possible that Infs and NaNs would not always propagate in the same area as those pixels.

7.3.3 K-means clustering algorithm

To divide an unlabeled dataset into different clusters, the unsupervised learning algorithm K-means clustering is used. The number of predefined clusters to be generated is determined by the value of *K*. For instance, if *K* is set to 2, two clusters will be formed, and if *K* is set to 3, three clusters will be formed, and so on. For our proposed work, we have used the *k*-value as 4 for better clustering. Figure 7.4 shows the work flow of K-means clustering algorithm. Figure 7.5 shows the output image after applied K-means clustering algorithm. The final image of vitiligo-affected area images are shown in Figure 7.6.

7.3.4 Calculated area of the affected place

Table 7.1 shows the area of the affected place of an image. In the table, nnz refers to the number of non-zero elements in the image.total_pxrefers to the total pixel in the image. Since it is a binary image, only the white color area is having non-zero values. To calculate the area of affected skin, the ratio between nnz and total_px is given. From this table, we can find the area of affected skin by giving the captured image and also accurately measure the area. So between the visits to doctors, we can calculate the spreading rate.

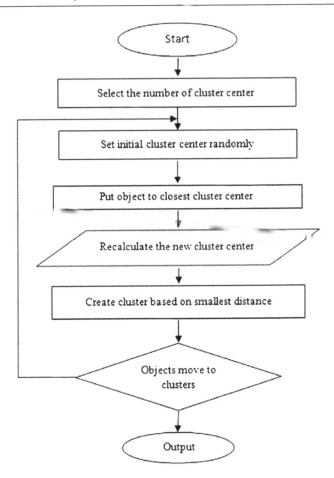

Figure 7.4 Workflow of K-means clustering algorithm.

7.4 CONCLUSION

The classification of the vitiligo skin disease and its rate of spread both are effectively based on CNNs. To categorize and forecast the rate at which the skin condition vitiligo would spread, some pre-trained models of CNNs are employed. Hence, by using this pre-trained models of CNN, we can identify skin diseases in advance and take precautionary steps for preventing the disease. These pre-trained models can be used to identify more ailments, such as infections, sunburns, and rashes. These can also be implemented using smartphones so that everyone can access detection of diseases in advance. Hence you can conclude that this study helps in achieving classification and assessing the spreading rate of vitiligo skin disease more efficiently. The proposed system is more accurate than any other physical examination in classifying, identifying, and finding the spreading rate of the vitiligo skin disease.

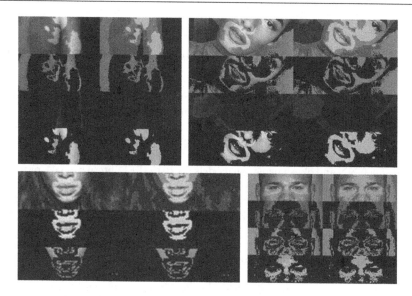

Figure 7.5 Output image after applied K-means clustering algorithm.

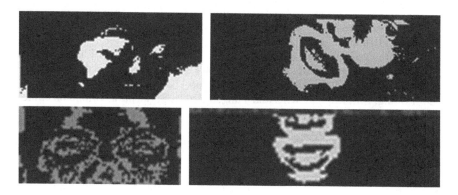

Figure 7.6 Vitiligo-affected area from the image.

Table 7.1 Area of affected place of an image

Figure label	nnz	total_px	Area of affected skin %
1	1,312	7,800	16.82051
2	3,106	14,454	21.48886
3	388	3,120	12.4359
4	3,300	26,751	12.33599
5	863	3,116	27.69576

REFERENCES

1. Allugunti, V.R., 2022. A machine learning model for skin disease classification using convolution neural network. International Journal of Computing, Programming and Database Management, 3(1), pp. 141–147.
2. Balakrishnan, D., Dhanunjai, M.S., Pranitha, S.N. and Haritha, N., 2022. Detection of diseases using facial features with deep transfer learning. International Journal of Health Sciences, (I), p. 430125.
3. He, X., Wang, S., Shi, S., Tang, Z., Wang, Y., Zhao, Z., Dai, J., Ni, R., Zhang, X., Liu, X. and Wu, Z., 2019. Computer aided clinical skin disease diagnosis using CNN and object detection models. In 2019 IEEE International Conference on Big Data (Big Data) (pp. 4839–4844). IEEE.
4. Low, M., Huang, V. and Raina, P., 2020. Automating Vitiligo skin lesion segmentation using convolutional neural networks. In 2020 IEEE 17th International Symposium on Biomedical Imaging (ISBI) (pp. 1 4) IEEE.
5. Maduranga, M.W.P. and Nandasena, D., 2022. Mobile-based skin disease diagnosis system using convolutional neural networks (CNN). IJ Image Graphics Signal Process, 3, 47–57.
6. Omotosho, L., Sotonwa, K., Adegoke, B., Oyeniran, O and Oyeniyi, J, 2022. An automated skin disease diagnostic system based on deep learning model. Journal of Engineering Studies and Research, 27(3), pp. 43–50. doi: 10.29081/jesr.v27i3.287
7. Swapna, T., 2021. Detection and classification of skin diseases using deep learning. The International Journal of Analytical and Experimental Modal Analysis, XIII(VIII), 2021, pp. 1096–1101.
8. Thurnhofer-Hemsi, K., López-Rubio, E., Domínguez, E. and Elizondo, D.A., 2021. Skin lesion classification by ensembles of deep convolutional networks and regularly spaced shifting. IEEE Access, 9, pp.112193–112205.
9. Yanling, L.I., Kong, A.W.K. and Thng, S., 2021. Segmenting vitiligo on clinical face images using CNN trained on synthetic and internet images. IEEE Journal of Biomedical and Health Informatics, 25(8), pp. 3082–3093.
10. Silverberg, N., 2022. The genetics of pediatric cutaneous autoimmunity: The sister diseases vitiligo and alopecia areata. Clinics in Dermatology, 40, pp. 363–373.
11. Shiu, J., Zhang, L., Lentsch, G., Flesher, J.L., Jin, S., Polleys, C., Jo, S.J., Mizzoni, C., Mobasher, P., Kwan, J. and Rius-Diaz, F., 2022. Multimodal analyses of vitiligo skin identify tissue characteristics of stable disease. JCI Insight, 7(13), e154585.
12. Yang, T.-T., Lee, C.-H. and Lan, C.-C.E., 2022. Impact of vitiligo on life quality of patients: Assessment of currently available tools. International Journal of Environmental Research and Public Health, 19(22), p. 14943.
13. Wang, J., Pan,Y., Wei,G., Mao,H., Liu,R. and He,Y., 2022. Damage-associated molecular patterns in vitiligo: Igniter fuse from oxidative stress to melanocyte loss. Redox Report, 27(1), pp. 193–199.
14. Mehmood, N., Khan, S.J. and Rashid, M., 2022. K-means clustering-based color segmentation on vitiligo skin lesion. 2022 International Conference on Emerging Trends in Smart Technologies (ICETST) (pp. 1–5). doi: 10.1109/ICETST55735.2022.9922940

15. Guo, L., Yang, Y., Ding, H., Zheng, H., Yang, H., Xie, J., Li, Y., Lin, T. and Ge, Y., A deep learning-based hybrid artificial intelligence model for the detection and severity assessment of vitiligo lesions 2022. A deep learning-based hybrid artificial intelligence model for the detection and severity assessment of vitiligo lesions. Annals of Translational Medicine, 10(10), p. 590. doi: 10.21037/atm-22-1738

16. Zhang, L., Mishra, S., Zhang, T., Zhang, Y., Zhang, D., Lv, Y., Lv, M., Guan, N., Hu, X.S., Chen, D.Z. and Han, X., 2021. Design and assessment of convolutional neural network based methods for vitiligo diagnosis. Frontiers in Medicine (Lausanne), 8, p. 754202. doi: 10.3389/fmed.2021.754202

Chapter 8

A comparative analysis of different approaches to lexical and semantic document similarity

Pratik Kanani, Devang Shah, Riya Bihani, Khushi Chavan, Aniket Kore, and Nilesh Patil

8.1 INTRODUCTION

With the rapid expansion of the Internet and social media, a significant amount of information has been produced, which users can easily access. Moreover, according to Magara et al. [1], with the easy accessibility of information due to the Internet, it is much easier to download and modify the information as per one's requirements. Although technology offers many advantages, its main drawback is that it often leads to plagiarism, which occurs when someone uses someone else's work without giving proper credit. Plagiarism is a common problem, and it can happen inadvertently when a document is unintentionally similar to an existing one. For example, an academic paper may be flagged for plagiarism if it contains passages that are similar to previously published work. Foltýnek et al. [2] frequently undervalue instances of plagiarism while occasionally exaggerating the negative effects of non-plagiarized content. However, plagiarism should be taken seriously as it undermines academic integrity and can have negative consequences for the individual and the academic community.

One way to detect potential instances of plagiarism is by performing a document similarity check. While it is not the same as plagiarism detection, a document similarity check can be a useful tool to highlight areas where the content appears to be similar or identical to other works, which may warrant further investigation. As noted by Qurashi et al. [3], since the number and size of text documents are increasing exponentially, there is a growing need for new automated systems for document analysis.

A similarity (or distance) measure is the quintessential way to calculate the similarity between two text documents and is widely used in various machine learning (ML) methods, including clustering and classification, as mentioned by Oghbaie et al. [4]. There are various software tools available, like Turnitin and Viper, as mentioned by Desai et al. [5], which carry out plagiarism detection by comparing the suspicious paper against a set of reference papers that is stored in a database. Additionally, document similarity checks can be used by teachers to verify students' work to ensure that no one copies it and to recommend similar books and articles.

DOI: 10.1201/9781003433941-8

This chapter compares various different models for document similarity check and suggests a more accurate model for the same. The models considered for this chapter were built using unsupervised learning methods because the dataset used was unlabeled. The dataset was obtained through web scraping, which involved extracting five distinct domain topics from the Springer website. The first step is to perform text pre-processing, which involves identifying and resolving any irregularities or inconsistencies in the data. After completing this step, the pre-processed data is utilized to implement various models considered in this chapter, which include TF-IDF vectorization, LDA topic modeling, BERT sentence transformer encodings, GloVe word embeddings, and Doc2Vec embeddings. Subsequently, two different text similarity metrics are evaluated: the Jaccard and Cosine similarity metrics [3], which are used to analyze the results. The top-k most similar papers are displayed along with a match percentage. Execution time, correctness of results, and semantics of similar documents are factors considered to make a statistical comparison between different approaches. One limitation of implementing document similarity checking is the potential trade-off between performance and efficiency, as the tool may not be able to scan all documents over the Internet very quickly. This constraint needs to be considered while using the tool to compare documents.

8.2 LITERATURE REVIEW

The purpose of the paper by Qurashi et al. [3] was to assess the various methods for precisely calculating text similarity between documents. Lexical and semantic similarity are the two categories of similarity, according to the study. Lexical similarity evaluates the surface closeness or sequence of strings that are similar to each other, but measurements of semantic similarity depend on the context of words. This study evaluated the Jaccard and Cosine similarity metrics, which are separate similarity measures. While the Jaccard similarity measure focused on lexical similarity, the Cosine similarity metric used Word2Vec to convert sentences into vectors and compare the cosine angle between these vectors. Based on the data, it was shown that the Cosine similarity metric outperformed the Jaccard similarity metric in terms of accuracy.

Wang et al. [6] integrated the concepts obtained by Word2Vec word vector conversion technology along with the LDA model and trained the model using the principle of importance sampling. In order to uncover the hidden subject information, latent Dirichlet allocation (LDA), a Bayesian topic model with three tiers, employs the unsupervised learning technique. The distance between each topic in the document vector and the model was then determined using cosine similarity. The paper concludes by claiming that the recall rate and accuracy have improved because of the use of this approach.

Hussein [7] outlined a content-based paradigm for document similarity analysis and visualization. Simple string-matching techniques were first utilized. The advent of document modeling techniques like the TF-IDF model then helped to mostly fix lexical and syntactic issues. Latent semantic analysis was then used to look at the underlying connections between the documents and their various *n*-gram phrases. The latent semantics from the given text were extrapolated using singular value decomposition (SVD). The comparison in literal terms could be calculated using the provided methodology. The results for the *n*-gram sizes differed every time. It was determined that an *n*-gram of 3 produced the best results.

The challenges of determining similarity between document pairings with dissimilar lengths were addressed by Gong et al. [8]. The problem arose from the fact that it is challenging to compare the rich details of a lengthy paper with a concise summary. Similar to the modeling assumption in LDA, the paper developed an embedding-based hidden topic model to extract topics and gauge their relevance. However, in contrast to LDA, a set of vectors were the themes rather than words or the distribution of words. As much information from the document and the summary as possible was captured using the various hidden topic vectors, which were then used to create a common ground to score the relevance of the pair using cosine similarity. The Word Movers' Distance (WMD) and Doc2Vec baseline approaches were included in the paper for comparison with their model. As a result, the proposed model did better than the baselines.

Wang and Dong [9] studied different methods for calculating text similarity. It provided a full description of the semantic similarity measurements as well as various text distance for similarity measurement techniques. Length distance, distribution distance, and semantic distance are the three categories into which text distance can be divided. These are divided further into numerous categories, including cosine distance and Euclidean distance. The four distinct categories of text representation are string-based, corpus-based, semantic text matching, and graphical representation. The article concludes by expressing that while each method has benefits and drawbacks, the popular text representation and suitable text spacing have generally produced positive outcomes.

8.3 RESEARCH GAPS

As seen above, there have been many different approaches for measuring the similarity between documents. It makes choosing the most appropriate algorithm for the similarity measurement difficult. This chapter focuses on the comparison of these different algorithms and the similarity metrics. It helps in determining the most efficient algorithm based on both performance and time for certain circumstances.

8.4 EVALUATION FRAMEWORKS

Figure 8.1 shows the workflow of the proposed approach. Gathering conference papers and preparing a dataset is the initial step for document similarity. For this, web scraping is used. The dataset consists of 1,000+ conference papers split across five different domains. Necessary pre-processing is performed on the text to make it standard and avoid any misinterpretations. Converting a document into a mathematical object (i.e., vector or embedding) and defining a similarity measure are the two steps required for machines to predict source–target similarities.

8.4.1 Dataset

Due to lack of labeled and reliable data, this chapter addresses unsupervised learning techniques. Similar documents are computed dynamically. So, a corpus is prepared before carrying out the experiments. Web scraping serves as a convenient way of extracting the texts. Using Beautiful Soup, we request and extract the DOM of each link. We then retrieve information using classname and tags. For the literature works needed for this chapter, a variety of Springer links (https://link.springer.com) are used. A number of entities were retrieved which included the article title, author, publishing date, conference, journal, paper abstract, and paper keywords. Due to the fact that abstracts are a shortened version of the complete work, this work will mostly use them as objective for similarity measurement. Research works from five different

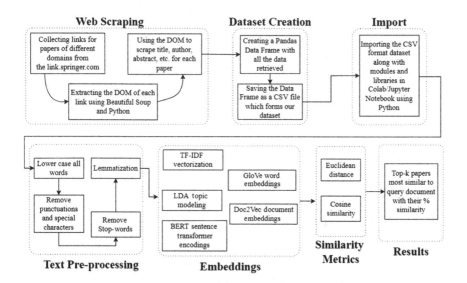

Figure 8.1 Proposed workflow for calculating document similarities.

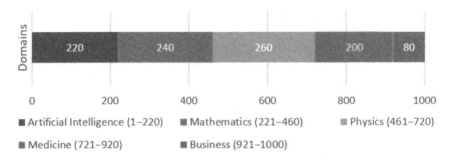

Figure 8.2 Domains considered for the dataset creation and their document IDs.

disciplines were extracted, as displayed in Figure 8.2, showcasing the breadth of our data collection. Artificial Intelligence (220 papers: 1–220), Mathematics (240 papers: 221–460), Physics (260 papers: 461–720), Medicine (200 papers: 721–920), and Business (80 papers: 921–1000) were the domains considered.

8.4.2 Text pre-processing

It is a common natural language processing (NLP) practice to perform text pre-processing. In order to create a cleaning function, a large number of samples are examined, and rules are added until a reasonable level of cleanliness is observed. Initially, all the text is transformed to the same case (lower case) to avoid any disambiguation. Following this, punctuation marks are removed using the Regex library. The removal of punctuation marks, which are used to divide text into sentences, paragraphs, and phrases, serves to be an important step as our document similarity approach relies on the frequency of words and phrases in each document. Stop-words are common terms that do not add anything to the context of any data. We were able to focus more on the crucial content by getting rid of these phrases and the supporting details from the text. By eliminating these phrases, no harm is done to our algorithms. Moreover, it reduces dataset size, which reduces algorithm runtime. The NLTK library offers a simple method for stop-word elimination. To find the part of speech of a specific word, use the WordNet Lemmatizer of the NLTK library; it does not categorize phrases.

8.5 REVIEW

8.5.1 Text representations

To represent text as vectors, we use word embeddings. Similarly, to represent documents for analyzing text as vectors, we use document embeddings. It is necessary to create numerical representation of the data so that it can be acted on by mathematical and statistical models, Embeddings are a form of real-valued vectors. Words close to each other in vector space are considered to be similar. Only using similarity metrics will provide lexical similarity. But this chapter focuses on semantic similarity, so text representation plays an important role here. The following are the algorithms reviewed to convert data into its numerical representation.

8.5.1.1 Bag of words method

The primary tenet of the BOW method is to ignore the sequence of words in the document and instead describe the document as a collection of words.

TF-IDF: This combines inverse document frequency with term frequency. It is used to calculate a quantitative digest of every paper abstract. Every word in the text is given a weight, which is determined by taking into account both the frequency of that word in the current document and the frequency of documents that contain that word across the whole corpus of documents. The quickest and easiest way to transform text into mathematical vectors is via TF-IDF. The TF-IDF algorithm also takes into account the relative weights assigned to each term in a corpus of documents. The pre-processed text is fitted and transformed on a TF-IDF vectorizer of Sklearn with max features parameter set to 64 so as to limit the size of the sparse matrix. Also, the resultant vectors are changed to an array using numpy. TF-IDF score calculation is as follows:

$$tf(w, d) = Freq(w, d) \tag{8.1}$$

$$idf(w, D) = \log\left(\frac{|D|}{N(w)}\right) \tag{8.2}$$

$$tfidf(w, d, D) = tf(w, d) \times idf(w, D) \tag{8.3}$$

Freq(w, d) shows how frequently a word appears in the document, *D* shows the number of documents, and $N(w)$ is the total number of words in the document.

8.5.1.2 Matrix factorization methods

These techniques break down big matrices that include statistical data about a corpus using low-rank approximations.

LDA: A series of observations are explained by unobserved groups using word-context matrix factorization algorithms based on latent Dirichlet allocation, and each group explains why some portions of the data are similar. Topic modeling is the foundation of LDA. A dictionary is created when the documents are converted into tokens. After that, the corpus is turned into a matrix and given to the Gensim library's LDA model for training. Refer

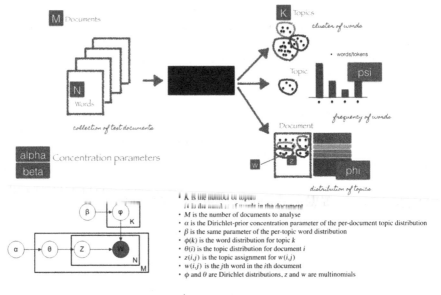

Figure 8.3 Topic modeling using LDA by Christine Doig [10].

Figure 8.3 for understanding LDA algorithm. In order to achieve a higher coherence value, the "number of topics" parameter is adjusted to 10.

8.5.1.3 Shallow window-based techniques

Shallow window-based techniques bring related words closer together in space and captures the semantic distance between words due to word independence.

GloVe: A generative statistical model called Global Vectors for Word Representation was developed. Words with greater distance are given less weight. It uses global word frequency data that models the interaction between words in context to explain the semantic information of words. Pre-trained word embeddings have advantages like faster training and better performance. Glove.6B 100-dimensions pre-trained word vectors consisting of 6B word vectors were used. We then calculated document embeddings using the created embedding matrix. When creating the vectors, it takes into account word pair to word pair relationships.

Doc2Vec: All of the techniques that have been mentioned so far represent whole documents using word embeddings or vectors. Instead of averaging word vectors to create a document vector, it would be preferable to represent the complete document as a vector. Here, the unsupervised learning technique Doc2vec is helpful. See Figure 8.4 for the architecture of the Doc2vec model. In order to predict other words in the paragraph, the Distributed Bag of Words (PV-DBOW) model suggests training the paragraph vectors using them as the input to a straightforward classification task. This means that in

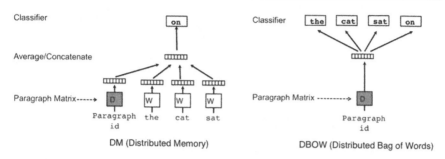

Figure 8.4 Architecture of Doc2Vec, as given by Le and Mikolov [11].

actuality, the cosine distance between the document embedding and the word embeddings it includes should be minimized. The Distributed Memory model (PV-DM) approaches the issue differently. To anticipate a target word, a context window is employed as the input source. In order to train the Gensim's doc2vec model, all input documents were converted to Tagged Document format, which basically provides a unique identifier to each document. Then, the vocab is built and the model is initiated with default parameters. Furthermore, the model iterated over the corpus 100 times. Though the doc2vec model needs long queries as input, it does take care of semantics of the words well.

BERT: The transformer-based design of the Bidirectional Encoder Representation from Transformers uses an attention model to produce embeddings. Since it is a bidirectional model, which means that during training it takes into account the context from both the left and right of the vocabulary to extract patterns or representations, the semantics of the document are well taken care of. Figure 8.5 shows the architecture of the BERT model. Our

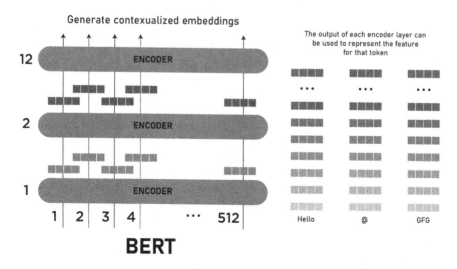

Figure 8.5 Architecture of BERT, as given in explanation of BERT model – NLP [12].

method involved using a pre-trained BERT model from Hugging Face, which had a hidden size of 768 and had 12 transformer blocks, 12 attention heads, 110 million parameters, and transformer blocks.

Now that we have created the vectors, embeddings, or topic models, we can fit them on a similarity metric to calculate similarities.

8.5.2 Similarity metrics

Vectors in geometrical representations have both magnitude and direction. This means that we can measure either the angle or the distance between two vectors and infer if the two vectors are similar or not. Similarity metrics are based on this principle. The Sklearn package plays an integral role in the implementation of similarity metrics. The following are the metrics used to calculate similarities.

8.5.2.1 Euclidean distance

Measuring the distance between two vectors is the simplest method for determining similarity. Using the Pythagorean theorem, we calculate the distance between the two points in Euclidean distance. More similarity exists between two vectors when the Euclidean distance between them is smaller. Its formula is given as follows:

$$d(a,b) = d(b,a) = \sqrt{\sum_{i=1}^{n}(b_i - a_i)^2} \tag{8.4}$$

One drawback is the lack of orientation considered in the calculation, i.e., it is based solely on magnitude. Euclidean distance works well on low-dimensional data and when the magnitude of the vectors is important to be measured. Methods like kNN and HDBSCAN show great results if Euclidean distance is used on low-dimensional data.

8.5.2.2 Cosine similarity

This method provides accurate results by taking care of the magnitude and direction. The cosine similarity method is used to calculate the cosine of the angles between two vectors. The cosine similarity value usually falls between –1 and +1. The vectors under evaluation are very similar, as indicated by the value of +1. The vectors under examination are said to be highly opposing or different if the value is –1. The following formula determines the cosine similarity between vectors A and B:

$$\cos(\theta) = \frac{A \cdot B}{\|A\| \cdot \|B\|} = \frac{\sum_{i=1}^{n} A_i B_i}{\sqrt{\sum_{i=1}^{n} A_i^2}\sqrt{\sum_{i=1}^{n} B_i^2}} \tag{8.5}$$

The numerator denotes the scalar product of the vectors and the denominator denotes the magnitude of these vectors. Cosine similarity works well on high-dimensional data and when the magnitude of the vectors is not of importance. The metric is widely used for text analysis when the data is represented by word counts. It could be used in the case where documents have uneven lengths and the magnitude of the count is of less importance.

8.6 COMPUTATIONAL BENCHMARKS

Benchmarks for computational performance were determined during model training and evaluation. The User CPU time for each algorithm is shown in the results section. It shows how each model has performed overall. All experiments were run more than once before the results were reported, and the data were then averaged to improve generality. On pristine Google Collaboratory Notebook instances, the algorithms were executed. The VM instance for a collaborative contains two virtual CPUs (n1-highmem-2 instance), a two-core Intel Xeon processor running at 2.20 GHz, 13 GB of RAM, and 33 GB of disk space. The psutil software calculated the CPU requirements. The time package was used to perform the time measurements. Typically, we have applied the default hyperparameters described in the cited studies. However, a few hyperparameters were adjusted for fairness.

8.7 RESULTS AND DISCUSSION

To ascertain which algorithm and similarity metric offers the best results, experiments were carried out. Depending on the type of dataset and the experimental circumstances, the experiments may be subjective. Algorithms – TF-IDF, GloVe, LDA, Doc2Vec, and BERT – are evaluated for accuracy and performance using a dataset containing papers from five different fields (AI, mathematics, physics, medicine, and business). The technique locates the top-k most comparable papers in the dataset after receiving a query document or paper abstract as input. A query document from the dataset's AI domain was chosen for comparison purposes, as depicted in Figure 8.6. The top similar

Query Document: It is always a known fact that the role of data and its purity is very crucial in the data mining. The key role of data in the data mining is related to from decision-making. It is a well-known fact that if data are impure, then result will be a false picture. This crucial stage is also known as the ambiguities in datasets. Anomalous or irregular value in database is solitary of the biggest problems faced in data analysis and in data mining applications. Data pre-processing for the data mining is a key phase which is a crucial stage place where ambiguities of database can be reduced or removed. The present study proposed an algorithm which tries to solve the problem related to anomalous and irregular values, i.e., outliers, inliers, and missing values from a real-world imbalanced database. The study projected is based on the fragmented central affinity approach for reducing ambiguities in dataset.

Figure 8.6 Input query document (Document id: 2, domain: artificial intelligence).

Table 8.1 Execution time of algorithms for different dataset sizes

Algorithms	Time (s) to process 1,000 papers	Time (s) to process 500 papers	Time (s) to process 250 papers
TF-IDF	0.2235	0.1431	0.0730
GloVe	17.8824	9.3412	4.9702
LDA	2.1089	1.1194	0.6915
Doc2Vec	146.5204	82.9238	50.2240
BERT	346.9195	187.4460	107.4118

papers should ideally come from the same field, in this case AI. The results from each model for the unsupervised method of calculating document similarity were compared through observation and comprehension. For performance evaluation, the time required by each algorithm to compute top-k most similar papers is computed (see Table 8.1). Refer computational benchmark's section above for details about the experimental setup. The TF-IDF method, which is the fastest of all, is taken into account first. Although TF-IDF is based on information retrieval rather than semantic analysis or content optimization, the predictions appear to be correct, as illustrated in Figure 8.7. It is clear from Figure 8.10 that Doc2Vec model anticipated that a manuscript in a different domain would be highly comparable. Although the dataset contained the same publication as the query document, LDA and Doc2Vec algorithms were unable to offer a 100% match, as seen in Figure 8.9 and 8.10.

Document #2: It is always a known fact that the role of data and its purity is very crucial in data mining. The key role of data in data mining is related to from decision-making. It is a well-known fact that if data are impure, then the result will be a false picture. This crucial stage is also known as the ambiguities in datasets. Anomalous or irregular value in database is solitary of the biggest problems faced in data analysis and in data mining...
Cosine Similarity: 100.0000000000000%

Document #59: The contemporary technology landscape is big data oriented and driven by analytics. The paradigm shift fueled by rapid data generation and higher storage capabilities has resulted in a massive transition across data storage technologies. Traditional database management systems being used in record-based transactional applications are paving the way for new rapid engagement-based data stores leading the newer...
Cosine Similarity: 72.66783350871377%

Document #212: Many use cases give the impression that fundamental spatial data themes could help to bridge the gap of data silos and even approach a common conscious dataspace. Starting from the fundamental data themes of UNGGIM, we evaluate the minimal consensus for spatial data quality and create evidence for a missing common spatial data space by pragmatic examples from a data provider viewpoint. By the hand of given examples...
Cosine Similarity: 71.86154589630873%

Figure 8.7 Results of TFIDF: top-3 similar document ids – 2 (artificial intelligence), 59 (artificial intelligence), 212 (artificial intelligence).

Document #2: It is always a known fact that the role of data and its purity is very crucial in data mining. The key role of data in data mining is related to from decision-making. It is a well-known fact that if data are impure, then the result will be a false picture. This crucial stage is also known as the ambiguities in datasets. Anomalous or irregular value in database is solitary of the biggest problems faced in data analysis and in data mining...

Cosine Similarity: 100.0000000000000%

Document #59: The contemporary technology landscape is big data oriented and driven by analytics. The paradigm shift fueled by rapid data generation and higher storage capabilities has resulted in a massive transition across data storage technologies. Traditional database management systems being used in record-based transactional applications are paving the way for new rapid engagement-based data stores leading the newer...

Cosine Similarity: 70.26545880524057%

Document #17: While the processor is momentarily disabled or busy performing other orders in parallel, the Direct Memory Access (DMA) technology allows direct access to peripherals and memory. DMA gets control of the buses to transfer the data directly to the I/O devices. DMA completes the data transfer to all peripherals without the interference of the processor. The DMA controller supports eight channels with 32-bit data...

Cosine Similarity: 62.013735934901746%

Figure 8.8 Results of GloVe: top-3 similar document ids – 2 (artificial intelligence), 59 (artificial intelligence), 17(artificial intelligence).

The finest outcomes are produced using the cutting-edge transformer-based BERT model. Its intricacy in terms of time is its only downside, as illustrated in Figure 8.11. Also Figure 8.8 shows that GloVe delivers positive outcomes and is reasonably priced. There needs to be a trade-off between model correctness and performance based on individual problem statements. BERT and GloVe can be used in this way.

Document #1: Due to advancements in technologies and to achieve high efficiency, the world is shifting from 4G to a 5G network. The advantages of 5G network are enormous in every field and thus are catching speed to be a better version of what exists in today's world. The features like increased bandwidth availability, massive network capacity, and ultralow latency are keeping 5G out of the box and giving raw network engineers to explore...

Cosine Similarity: 87.42260932922363%

Document #8: The authors provide a crisp yet in-depth summary of the relevance of artificial intelligence in the hospitality and tourism industry. Focusing on artificial intelligence, the chapter draws the attention of the reader toward its usage and role in the lives of the customers and service providers in the hospitality sector. It also focuses on the costs involved in the incorporation of artificial intelligence in the hospitality industry. So...

Cosine Similarity: 84.14265513420105%

Document #2: It is always a known fact that the role of data and its purity is very crucial in data mining. The key role of data in data mining is related to from decision-making. It is a well-known fact that if data are impure, then the result will be a false picture. This crucial stage is also known as the ambiguities in datasets. Anomalous or irregular value in database is solitary of the biggest problems faced in data analysis and in data mining...

Cosine Similarity: 84.01463031768799%

Figure 8.9 Results of LDA: top-3 similar document ids – 1 (artificial intelligence), 8 (artificial intelligence), 2 (artificial intelligence).

Document #2: It is always a known fact that the role of data and its purity is very crucial in data mining. The key role of data in data mining is related to from decision-making. It is a well-known fact that if data are impure, then the result will be a false picture. This crucial stage is also known as the ambiguities in datasets. Anomalous or irregular value in database is solitary of the biggest problems faced in data analysis and in data mining...

Cosine Similarity: 99.56004639981611%

Document #136: We survey some foundational results on querying graph-structured data. We focus on general- purpose navigational query languages, such as regular path queries and its extensions with conjunctions, inverses, and path comparisons. We study complexity, expressive power, and static analysis. The course material should be useful to anyone with an interest in query languages for graph-structured data, and more...

Cosine Similarity: 60.641775330989866%

Document #249: We present a method for constructing differential and integral spline quasi-interpolants defined on uniform partition of the real line. It is based on an expression to the quasi-interpolation error for an enough regular function and involves the errors for the non-reproduced monomials. From it, a minimization problem is proposed whose solution is calculated progressively It is characterized in terms of some splines which...

Cosine Similarity: 59.13394796642738%

Figure 8.10 Results of Doc2Vec: top-3 similar document ids – 2 (artificial intelligence), 136 (artificial intelligence), 249 (mathematics).

Document #2: It is always a known fact that the role of data and its purity is very crucial in data mining. The key role of data in data mining is related to from decision-making. It is a well-known fact that if data are impure, then the result will be a false picture. This crucial stage is also known as the ambiguities in datasets. Anomalous or irregular value in database is solitary of the biggest problems faced in data analysis and in data mining...

Cosine Similarity: 100.0%

Document #171: The treatment of records with several discrete missing values present in the databases is still a delicate problem. Indeed, these records can bias the results of data mining algorithms, thus invalidating the results. In this paper, we present an extension of the Hybrid Method for Efficient Imputation of Discrete Missing Attributes (HMID) to effectively handle these records. The method consists of partitioning the database...

Cosine Similarity: 86.10889911651611%

Document #117: The traffic matrix (TM) is an important type of information in network management, which is needed in network load balancing and routing configuration. Due to technical and cost reasons, it is difficult to directly measure the matrix, but we can use prediction instead of direct measurement. The long short-term memory (LSTM) model in deep learning is very suitable for time series forecasting problems...

Cosine Similarity: 85.35273671150208%

Figure 8.11 Results of BERT: top-3 similar document ids – 2 (artificial intelligence), 171 (artificial intelligence), 117 (artificial intelligence).

8.8 CONCLUSION

This study contains a thorough analysis of the many document similarity calculation systems that have been suggested, developed, and used. It helps in locating a more efficient, exact solution that is tailored to your particular issue. On the basis of their execution time and error-free output, the proposed results undoubtedly draw a conclusion for all algorithms taken into consideration. The approaches in this work are a good solution for search engine and plagiarism-type situations where cost-effectiveness needs to be improved along with accuracy and are constructed by forming a combination of text representation techniques and similarity metrics offered by Sklearn. Modern deep learning models exist addressing these issues, but because of their complexity, computing demands, and power requirements, their practical uses may be limited. The successful adoption of such technologies would invalidate copyright violations. The system can also be expanded to include fields like education, SEO, content development, and so forth. The accuracy of the document similarity algorithms and models could also be improved and expanded to include a huge number of papers and researches prior to publication.

REFERENCES

1. Magara, M. B., Ojo, S. O., and Zuva, T., 2018. A comparative analysis of text similarity measures and algorithms in research paper recommender systems. *Conference on Information Communications Technology and Society (ICTAS)*, pp. 1–5. doi: 10.1109/ICTAS.2018.8368766
2. Foltýnek, T., Dlabolová, D., Anohina-Naumeca, A., Razı, S., Kravjar, J., Kamzola, L., Guerrero-Dib, J., Çelik, Ö., and Weber-Wulff, D., 2020. Testing of support tools for plagiarism detection. *CoRR*, abs/2002.04279. https://arxiv.org/abs/2002.04279
3. Qurashi, A. W., Holmes, V., and Johnson, A., 2020. Document processing: Methods for semantic text similarity analysis. In 2020 International Conference on INnovations in Intelligent SysTems and Applications (INISTA). doi: 10.1109/INISTA49547.2020.9194665
4. Oghbaie, M. and Mohammadi Zanjireh, M., 2018. Pairwise document similarity measure based on present term set. Journal of Big Data, 5, p. 52. doi: 10.1186/s40537-018-0163-2
5. Desai, T., Deshmukh, U., Gandhi, M., and Kurup, L., 2016. A hybrid approach for detection of plagiarism using natural language processing. In Proceedings of the Second International Conference on Information and Communication Technology for Competitive Strategies (ICTCS'16). Association for Computing Machinery, New York, NY, Article 6, pp. 1–6. doi: 10.1145/2905055.2905061
6. Wang, X., Dong, X. and Chen, S., 2020. Text duplicated-checking algorithm implementation based on natural language semantic analysis. In *2020 IEEE 5th Information Technology and Mechatronics Engineering Conference (ITOEC)*, pp. 732–735. doi: 10.1109/ITOEC49072.2020.9141886
7. Hussein, A. S., 2016. Visualizing document similarity using *n*-grams and latent semantic analysis. In *2016 SAI Computing Conference (SAI)*, pp. 269–279. doi: 10.1109/SAI.2016.7555994
8. Gong, H., Sakakini, T., Bhat, S., and Xiong, J., July 2018. Document similarity for texts of varying lengths via hidden topics. In Proceedings of the 56th Annual Meeting of the Association for Computational Linguistics (Volume 1: Long Papers), pp. 2341–2351, Melbourne, Australia: Association for Computational Linguistics. doi: 10.18653/v1/P18-1218

9. Wang, J. and Dong, Y., 2020. Measurement of text similarity: A survey. *Information*, 11(9), p. 421. doi: 10.3390/info11090421

10. Doig, C., 2015. Introduction to topic modeling in python. https://github.com/chdoig/pytexas2015-topic-modeling

11. Le, Q. V. and Mikolov, T., 2014. Distributed representations of sentences and documents. *CoRR*, abs/1405.4053. http://arxiv.org/abs/1405.4053

12. pawangfg., 2022. Explanation of BERT model – NLP. https://www.geeksforgeeks.org/explanation-of-bert-model-nlp/

Chapter 9

Artificial intelligence in banking and financial services

Naga Simhadri Apparao Polireddi

9.1 INTRODUCTION

Artificial intelligence (AI) has emerged as a disruptive technology with significant potential to revolutionize banking and financial services. The banking and financial services industry is highly regulated and complex, which requires a significant amount of time and resources to manage [1]. AI-powered chatbots and virtual assistants are rapidly transforming the banking and financial services industry, offering a cost-effective and efficient way to handle customer queries, complaints, and inquiries. These chatbots and virtual assistants use natural language processing (NLP) and machine learning (ML) algorithms to understand customer requests, offer personalized solutions, and perform tasks like money transfers, balance inquiries, and account opening [2]. These applications not only reduce wait times but also improve the overall customer experience by offering personalized and targeted solutions. Second, AI-based chatbots can handle a high volume of customer requests simultaneously, providing a seamless and frictionless customer experience. In addition, they are available 24/7, eliminating the need for customers to wait for business hours to get their queries resolved. Third, they can reduce operational costs for banks, as they require less staff to handle customer inquiries. This chapter aims to explore, analyze, understand, and compare the existing ML and NLP techniques that enhance the operational capability of the AI-based chatbots in the banking and financial services [3–5].

9.1.1 Overview of automation in banking and financial services

AI has become a buzzword in the banking and financial services industry, with the potential to transform how banks and financial institutions interact with customers, manage risk, and make decisions. From chatbots and virtual assistants to fraud detection and credit risk analysis, AI applications are already being deployed in various areas of the industry. One of the key areas where AI is being used in banking and financial services is customer service. Chatbots and virtual assistants are increasingly being used by banks and financial institutions to

DOI: 10.1201/9781003433941-9

handle customer queries and provide personalized solutions. These applications use ML and NLP techniques to understand customer requests and provide quick and efficient responses, reducing wait times and improving the overall customer experience [6]. AI is also being used to enhance risk management in banking and financial services. ML algorithms are able to work with large amounts of application data to check the patterns and anomalies, enabling banks and financial institutions to detect fraud and prevent financial crimes. AI applications can also analyze credit risk by assessing credit scores, payment history, and other relevant data to make more accurate lending decisions. Another area where AI is being used in banking and financial services is investment management. AI applications can analyze financial data and market trends to make investment decisions, offering a more data-driven approach to portfolio management [7, 8]. AI-powered robo-advisors are also becoming increasingly popular, providing customers with personalized investment advice based on their risk appetite and investment goals.

9.1.2 Benefits of AI in banking and financial services

The advantage of AI in banking and financial services offers several benefits for banks, financial institutions, and customers alike. These benefits include the following:

Improved customer experience: AI-powered chatbots and virtual assistants offer a more personalized and efficient way for customers to interact with banks and financial institutions, reducing wait times and providing targeted solutions.

Cost-savings: The use of AI can reduce operational costs for banks and financial institutions by automating repetitive tasks and reducing the need for human intervention.

Enhanced risk management: AI can help banks and financial institutions identify and prevent financial crimes, such as fraud, money laundering, and cyberattacks, reducing financial losses and reputational damage.

Data-driven decision-making: AI applications can analyze large amounts of data and identify patterns and trends, providing banks and financial institutions with insights to make more informed decisions.

Increased efficiency: AI-powered applications can handle a high volume of requests simultaneously, providing a seamless and frictionless customer experience while also reducing wait times.

9.1.3 Challenges of AI in banking and financial services

While the use of AI in banking and financial services offers significant benefits, it also raises several challenges and concerns:

Data privacy and security: This is a major challenge in the use of AI in banking and financial services. As AI applications rely heavily on data, financial institutions need to ensure that they protect customer data and maintain data privacy. Financial institutions need to adhere to regulatory guidelines and laws regarding the protection of customer data. AI-based systems should also be designed to prevent data breaches and minimize the risks of cyberattacks. One major concern is the unauthorized access of sensitive data. Financial institutions need to implement stringent data security protocols to ensure that customer data is secure. This includes using strong encryption techniques, access controls, and other security measures to prevent unauthorized access. AI models require a large amount of data to train and improve their accuracy, and financial institutions need to ensure that they have the appropriate infrastructure to handle and store this data securely. They also need to establish policies and procedures to ensure that data is not misused, and they need to have the capability to identify and respond to potential data breaches [9–11].

Ethical concerns: Another challenge in the use of AI in banking and financial services is ethical concerns. AI-based systems can make decisions that affect customers' lives, and there is a risk of bias in these decisions. Financial institutions need to ensure that their AI models are fair and unbiased and that they do not discriminate against any group of customers. They need to ensure that the AI models are transparent and that customers can understand the decisions made by the AI models.

Regulatory compliance: Regulatory compliance is another challenge in the use of AI in banking and financial services [12]. Financial institutions need to ensure that their AI models comply with regulatory guidelines and laws. Regulatory agencies are increasingly scrutinizing the use of AI in banking and financial services, and financial institutions need to ensure that they comply with all relevant regulations and guidelines.

9.1.3.1 Human–machine collaboration

One challenge in the use of AI in banking and financial services is human–machine collaboration. While AI-based systems can handle a large volume of customer requests, they cannot replace human interaction entirely. Financial institutions need to ensure that there is a balance between human and machine interaction, and they need to train their staff to work effectively with AI-based systems [13]. Hence, while the use of AI in banking and financial services offers significant benefits, financial institutions need to address the challenges and concerns associated with the use of AI. They need to ensure that they protect customer data and maintain data privacy, address ethical concerns, comply with regulatory guidelines, and establish effective human–machine collaboration. By addressing these challenges, financial institutions can harness the full potential of AI and provide customers with better services while improving operational efficiency.

9.2 OVERVIEW OF AI AND CHATBOTS IN BANKING AND FINANCIAL SERVICES

This section will provide an overview of AI and chatbots in the banking and financial services industry. It will discuss the history and evolution of chatbots and their current state in the banking and financial services industry. It will also provide a detailed overview of how chatbots and AI are transforming the banking and financial services industry. Chatbots have been around for decades, but their use in the banking and financial services industry has only recently gained momentum. In the past, chatbots were simple programs that responded to basic commands or questions. However, advances in NLP and ML have enabled chatbots to understand and respond to more complex queries [14]. Chatbots have become a key component of the digital transformation of the banking and financial services industry. They have the potential to automate repetitive tasks, provide 24/7 customer service, and offer personalized experiences. In addition, chatbots can help reduce operational costs for banks by reducing the need for customer service staff.

AI-powered chatbots use advanced ML and NLP algorithms to understand customer queries, analyze data, and offer personalized solutions. They can perform a wide range of tasks, including account opening, balance inquiries, and money transfers. These chatbots can also learn from past interactions and improve their responses over time. The adoption of chatbots in the banking and financial services industry has been driven by several factors. First, customers are increasingly using digital channels to interact with their banks, and chatbots offer a convenient and fast way to get information and resolve issues. Second, chatbots can help banks reduce costs and improve efficiency by automating customer service tasks. Third, the availability of large amounts of customer data has enabled banks to use AI to offer more personalized experiences [15]. Chatbots are being used by banks and financial institutions in various ways. Some banks use chatbots to provide basic customer service, while others use them to offer more complex services, such as financial advice or investment management. Some banks are also using chatbots to provide personalized marketing and promotions to customers. Despite the many benefits of chatbots in the banking and financial services industry, their adoption is not without challenges [16]. One of the key challenges is data privacy and security. Banks have access to sensitive customer data, and there is a risk that this data could be compromised if chatbots are not properly secured. Another challenge is ensuring that chatbots are accurate and provide reliable information. Chatbots need to be trained on large amounts of data to improve their accuracy, and banks need to ensure that the data used to train chatbots is accurate and unbiased. Finally, chatbots need to be designed with the customer in mind. They need to be easy to use, provide relevant information, and offer a seamless customer experience. If chatbots are not designed with the customer in mind, they may fail to gain traction and be seen as a nuisance by customers. Hence, chatbots and AI are transforming the banking and financial services industry. They offer a convenient and cost-effective way for banks to interact with customers, automate tasks, and offer personalized experiences. However, their adoption is not without challenges, and banks need to ensure that chatbots are properly secured, accurate, and designed with the customer in mind.

9.2.1 ML techniques for chatbots in banking and financial services

This section will discuss the various ML techniques that are being used to enhance the operational capability of chatbots in the banking and financial services industry. It will provide a detailed discussion of the various ML algorithms and techniques that are being used to improve chatbot performance. ML is a subfield of AI that involves the development of algorithms and models that enable machines to learn from data without being explicitly programmed. In the context of chatbots in the banking and financial services industry, ML algorithms and techniques are being used to enhance the operational capability of chatbots by enabling them to learn from past interactions and improve their responses over time. In this section, we will discuss some of the most commonly used ML techniques in the context of chatbots in the banking and financial services industry.

NLP: It is a branch of AI that deals with the interaction between computers and humans using natural language. NLP techniques are used in chatbots to enable them to understand the natural language of customers and respond in a manner that is appropriate and relevant. NLP algorithms analyze the input text and identify the intent of the user, extract relevant entities, and generate appropriate responses. Some common NLP techniques used in chatbots include sentiment analysis, entity recognition, and intent recognition [17].

Supervised learning: Supervised learning is a type of ML technique that involves training a model on a labeled dataset. In the context of chatbots, supervised learning algorithms are used to train chatbots on a dataset of labeled customer queries and corresponding responses. This enables the chatbot to learn from past interactions and improve its response accuracy over time. Common supervised learning algorithms used in chatbots include decision trees, support vector machines (SVMs), and neural networks.

Unsupervised learning: Unsupervised learning is a type of ML technique that involves training a model on an unlabeled dataset. In the context of chatbots, unsupervised learning algorithms are used to identify patterns and relationships in customer data that can be used to improve chatbot performance. Common unsupervised learning algorithms used in chatbots include clustering and association rule mining.

Reinforcement learning: Reinforcement learning is a type of ML technique that involves training a model to make decisions based on rewards and punishments. In the context of chatbots, reinforcement learning algorithms are used to train chatbots to make decisions based on the feedback received from customers. This enables the chatbot to learn from past interactions and improve its response accuracy over time. Common reinforcement learning algorithms used in chatbots include Q-learning and policy gradient methods.

Deep learning: Deep learning is a subfield of ML that involves the development of neural networks with multiple layers. In the context of chatbots, deep learning algorithms are used to enable chatbots to understand and respond to complex customer queries. Deep learning algorithms are particularly effective in situations where the input data is unstructured, such as in the case of natural language queries. Common deep learning algorithms used in chatbots include recurrent neural networks (RNNs) and convolutional neural networks (CNNs).

Transfer learning: This is a type of ML technique that involves transferring knowledge from one domain to another. In the context of chatbots, transfer learning algorithms are used to enable chatbots to learn from past interactions in a different domain and apply that knowledge to a new domain. This enables chatbots to improve their response accuracy in a new domain with less training data. Common transfer learning algorithms used in chatbots include pretrained language models such as BERT and GPT-3. Overall, the use of ML algorithms and techniques is essential in enhancing the operational capability of chatbots in the banking and financial services industry. By enabling chatbots to learn from past interactions, ML algorithms and techniques can help improve chatbot performance, reduce response times, and enhance the overall customer experience.

9.2.2 Natural language processing techniques for chatbots in banking and financial services

This section will provide an in-depth discussion of NLP techniques for chatbots in the banking and financial services industry. It will discuss the different types of NLP techniques and how they are being used to improve chatbot performance. NLP is a critical component of chatbot technology, particularly in the banking and financial services industry, where precise communication and understanding of customer needs are paramount [18]. Natural language understanding is the key component where 142 NLP and 143 natural language understanding user requests are done [19]. User query/message will be provided to the 144 NLP units as input. This unit's job is to prepare and clean 145 input text data, which includes 146 text pre-processing steps [20]. NLP enables chatbots to understand and respond to customer queries in natural language, resulting in a more human-like interaction. There are various NLP techniques used in chatbot development, including the following:

Named entity recognition (NER): This is a technique that involves identifying and extracting entities from text, such as names of people, places, organizations, and dates. In the banking and financial services industry, NER is used to extract relevant information from customer queries, such as account numbers, transaction dates, and payment amounts.

Sentiment analysis: Sentiment analysis is a technique used to determine the tone of a customer's query or feedback, whether it is positive, negative, or neutral. This technique is important for chatbots to understand customer satisfaction levels and take appropriate actions to address any issues.

Intent recognition: Intent recognition is the process of understanding the intention behind a customer's query. For instance, a customer may ask about the status of a transaction or request to transfer money between accounts. Intent recognition helps chatbots to identify the customer's intention and provide an appropriate response.

Language translation: In the banking and financial services industry, chatbots must be able to communicate with customers in different languages. Language translation is an NLP technique used to translate customer queries and responses into different languages, allowing chatbots to serve a wider range of customers.

Question answering: Question answering is an NLP technique used to generate responses to customer queries. Chatbots use ML algorithms to analyze customer queries and provide relevant responses based on the context and intent of the query.

In addition to these techniques, other NLP techniques such as tokenization, part-of-speech tagging, and dependency parsing are also used to improve chatbot performance in the banking and financial services industry. The use of NLP techniques in chatbots has significantly improved the customer experience in the banking and financial services industry. Chatbots can now understand and respond to customer queries in a more human-like manner, resulting in improved customer satisfaction and loyalty. Moreover, NLP techniques have made chatbots more efficient, enabling them to handle a high volume of customer requests simultaneously, providing a seamless and frictionless customer experience.

9.2.3 Chatbot use cases in banking and financial services

This section will provide a detailed overview of chatbot use cases in the banking and financial services industry. It will discuss the different types of chatbots and how they are being used to improve customer experience, reduce operational costs, and increase efficiency. Chatbots have become an increasingly popular tool in the banking and financial services industry. They are being used to provide customers with quick and convenient access to information, as well as to automate various processes. One type of chatbot commonly used in this industry is the customer service chatbot. This type of chatbot is designed to assist customers with their queries and concerns. It can answer frequently asked questions, provide account information, and even help customers with transactions such as transferring funds or paying bills.

Another type of chatbot used in banking and financial services is the transactional chatbot. This type of chatbot is used to automate transactions, such as transferring money between accounts or paying bills. It is designed to streamline the process and reduce the time and effort required by customers. Chatbots can also be used for more complex tasks, such as providing financial advice and investment recommendations. These chatbots are typically powered by AI and ML algorithms, which enable them to analyze customer data and provide personalized recommendations. In addition to improving customer experience, chatbots can also help banks and financial services companies to reduce operational costs and increase efficiency. By automating repetitive tasks and reducing the need for human intervention, chatbots can help organizations to save time and money. Overall, chatbots are becoming an increasingly important tool for banks and financial services companies. They offer a range of benefits, from improving customer experience to reducing costs and increasing efficiency. As technology continues to evolve, it is likely that chatbots will become even more sophisticated and widespread in the industry.

9.2.4 Advantages and challenges of chatbots in banking and financial services

This section will discuss the advantages and challenges of chatbots in the banking and financial services industry. It will provide a detailed discussion of the benefits that chatbots bring to the industry, including improved customer experience, increased efficiency, and reduced operational costs. It will also discuss the challenges that chatbots face, including the need for continuous training and development, data privacy and security concerns, and the potential for bias and discrimination.

Improved customer experience: Chatbots can provide customers with a fast and convenient way to access information, such as account balances and transaction history. They can also answer customer queries 24/7, which improves customer satisfaction and reduces wait times. In addition, chatbots can offer personalized recommendations and advice, which can help customers make informed financial decisions.

Increased efficiency: Chatbots can automate routine tasks, such as processing transactions and answering common customer queries, which reduces the need for human intervention. This can save time and resources, and also reduce the likelihood of errors. Chatbots can also handle multiple queries simultaneously, which increases efficiency and reduces wait times.

Reduced operational costs: Chatbots can be less expensive than hiring additional staff to handle routine tasks. They can also work round the clock without the need for breaks, which further reduces costs. Chatbots can also help organizations to scale their operations more easily, as they can handle increasing volumes of queries without requiring additional resources.

9.2.5 Future trends in chatbots and AI in banking and financial services

This section will discuss the future trends in chatbots and AI in the banking and financial services industry. It will discuss the emerging technologies and trends that are expected to transform the industry, including voice-activated chatbots, augmented reality, and blockchain technology.

Personalization: Personalization is key to delivering a better customer experience, and chatbots are playing a critical role in this. Banks and financial institutions are using chatbots to offer personalized recommendations, advice, and product suggestions based on the customer's past behavior, preferences, and spending habits. This helps customers make better financial decisions and increases engagement and loyalty.

Voice-enabled chatbots: As more customers use voice assistants like Amazon's Alexa, Google Assistant, and Apple's Siri, banks and financial institutions are exploring voice-enabled chatbots. Voice-enabled chatbots provide a more conversational and natural experience, enabling customers to interact with the chatbot using voice commands. This trend is expected to grow as more customers become comfortable with voice assistants and demand a more natural and conversational experience.

Fraud detection: Chatbots can also help in fraud detection and prevention. Banks and financial institutions are using chatbots to monitor transactions and detect unusual activity. The chatbot can notify the customer of the suspicious activity and take action, such as blocking the transaction or freezing the account. This helps prevent fraud and provides customers with peace of mind.

Chatbots for customer service: Chatbots are increasingly being used for customer service, allowing customers to get quick answers to their questions and resolve issues without having to wait on hold or speak with a human agent. Banks and financial institutions are using chatbots to provide 24/7 customer support, handle routine inquiries, and escalate complex issues to human agents. This improves customer satisfaction and reduces the workload on human agents.

Chatbots for sales: Chatbots can also be used for sales, offering personalized product recommendations and guiding customers through the sales process. Banks and financial institutions are using chatbots to cross-sell and upsell products and services, increasing revenue and customer engagement.

Predictive analytics: Predictive analytics is another area where chatbots and AI can help in banking and financial services. By analyzing customer data and behavior, chatbots can predict future behavior and recommend products and services that meet the customer's needs. This helps banks and financial institutions personalize their offerings and improve customer satisfaction.

Blockchain and cryptocurrency: Chatbots and AI can also help in the blockchain and cryptocurrency space. Banks and financial institutions are exploring the use of chatbots and AI to automate cryptocurrency trading, monitor blockchain transactions, and offer personalized investment advice. This trend is expected to grow as blockchain and cryptocurrency become more mainstream.

Hence, chatbots and AI are transforming the banking and financial services industry, offering personalized experiences, improved customer service, fraud detection, and predictive analytics. As technology continues to advance, we can expect to see more innovative applications of chatbots and AI in banking and financial services.

9.2.6 Case studies of chatbots in banking and financial services

This section will provide case studies of chatbots in the banking and financial services industry. It will discuss the different types of chatbots and how they are being used by banks and financial institutions to improve customer experience and reduce operational costs. Chatbots have become increasingly popular in the banking and financial services industry due to their ability to provide quick and efficient customer service. In this chapter, we will explore some case studies of chatbots in banking and financial services:

Bank of America's Erica: Bank of America's Erica is a virtual assistant that uses AI and NLP to provide customers with personalized financial guidance. Erica can help customers with tasks such as checking their account balance, transferring funds, paying bills, and finding nearby ATMs. Erica can also offer personalized insights, such as ways to save money or pay off debt faster. Since its launch in 2018, Erica has helped Bank of America's mobile banking user base grow to over 29 million.

Capital One's Eno: Capital One's Eno is a chatbot that helps customers manage their credit card accounts. Eno can help customers with tasks such as checking their balance, paying their bill, and disputing a charge.

Eno can also provide personalized alerts, such as when a customer's balance is low or when a payment is due. Eno has been successful in reducing the amount of time customers spend on the phone with customer service representatives.

HDFC Bank's EVA: HDFC Bank's EVA is a chatbot that uses AI and NLP to provide customers with personalized banking services. EVA can help customers with tasks such as checking their account balance, transferring funds, and paying bills. EVA can also provide personalized recommendations, such as investment advice or loan options. Since its launch, EVA has helped HDFC Bank increase its customer engagement and satisfaction.

Ally Bank's Ally Assist: Ally Bank's Ally Assist is a virtual assistant that uses AI to provide customers with personalized financial guidance. Ally Assist can help customers with tasks such as checking their account balance, transferring funds, and finding nearby ATMs. Ally Assist can also provide personalized insights, such as ways to save money or pay off debt faster. Since its launch, Ally Assist has helped Ally Bank increase its customer engagement and satisfaction.

HSBC's Amy: HSBC's Amy is a chatbot that uses AI and NLP to provide customers with personalized banking services. Amy can help customers with tasks such as checking their account balance, transferring funds, and paying bills. Amy can also provide personalized recommendations, such as investment advice or loan options. Since its launch, Amy has helped HSBC increase its customer engagement and satisfaction.

With this, we can say that chatbots are becoming increasingly popular in the banking and financial services industry due to their ability to provide quick and efficient customer service. These case studies highlight some of the successful implementations of chatbots in the industry, providing personalized financial guidance, reducing customer service call volume, and increasing customer engagement and satisfaction.

9.2.7 Ethical considerations in chatbots and AI in banking and financial services

This section will explore the ethical considerations in chatbots and AI in the banking and financial services industry. It will discuss the potential ethical issues that arise with the use of chatbots and AI, including privacy concerns, bias and discrimination, and the potential for job displacement. It will also provide recommendations for addressing these ethical considerations and ensuring the responsible use of chatbots and AI in the industry.

Chatbots and AI have revolutionized the banking and financial services industry, offering faster and more efficient services to customers. However, the use of these technologies also raises ethical considerations that need to be addressed to ensure that the benefits of the technology do not come at the expense of ethical concerns. In this chapter, we will explore some ethical considerations in chatbots and AI in banking and financial services:

Transparency: One of the primary ethical considerations in chatbots and AI in banking and financial services is transparency. Customers need to know when they are interacting with a chatbot and when they are interacting with a human representative. Chatbots should disclose that they are not humans and inform customers of the limitations of their capabilities. The use of clear and concise language in chatbot interactions can help promote transparency.

Bias: Chatbots and AI in banking and financial services can unintentionally perpetuate bias if they are not designed to be unbiased. For example, a chatbot that uses historical data to make loan approval decisions may inadvertently discriminate against certain demographics. To address this, companies should ensure that chatbots and AI are trained on unbiased data and regularly audited for bias.

Privacy: Chatbots and AI in banking and financial services may collect and store sensitive customer information. It is essential that companies ensure that customer data is protected and only used for legitimate purposes. Companies must be transparent about how they collect, use, and store customer data and obtain explicit consent from customers for data collection and usage.

Security: Chatbots and AI in banking and financial services can be vulnerable to security breaches, potentially leading to the theft of sensitive customer information. Companies should implement appropriate security measures to protect chatbots and AI from cyber threats. These measures should include regular security assessments and the use of encryption and other data protection technologies.

Accountability: Companies must be accountable for the actions of their chatbots and AI in banking and financial services. Chatbots and AI should be designed with built-in accountability mechanisms, such as audit trails and log files. Companies should also establish protocols for dealing with situations where chatbots and AI make mistakes or cause harm to customers.

Human oversight: Chatbots and AI should not be a replacement for human employees in banking and financial services. While chatbots and AI can handle routine tasks, human oversight is necessary for complex or sensitive situations. Companies should ensure that human employees are available to intervene when necessary and that customers have the option to speak to a human representative if they prefer.

Hence, ethical considerations are essential in the development and deployment of chatbots and AI in banking and financial services. Companies must prioritize transparency, avoid bias, protect privacy and security, establish accountability, and provide human oversight. By addressing these ethical considerations, chatbots and AI can enhance customer service while upholding ethical standards.

9.3 CONCLUSION

In conclusion, chatbots and AI have emerged as disruptive technologies that have the potential to transform the banking and financial services industry. They offer a cost-effective and efficient way to handle customer queries, complaints, and inquiries, while also improving the overall customer experience. The use of ML and NLP techniques has enhanced the operational capability of chatbots, enabling them to handle a high volume of customer requests simultaneously and provide personalized and targeted solutions. However, the use of chatbots and AI also raises ethical considerations, including privacy concerns, bias and discrimination, and the potential for job displacement. It is important for the industry to address these considerations and ensure the responsible use of chatbots and AI. Regulatory frameworks can also play a crucial role in ensuring the responsible use of chatbots and AI in the industry. Overall, the future of chatbots and AI in banking and financial services is promising, with emerging technologies and trends expected to transform the industry in the coming years.

REFERENCES

1. A. K. Tiwari and D. Saxena, "Application of artificial intelligence in Indian banks," 2021 International Conference on Computational Performance Evaluation (ComPE), Shillong, India, 2021, pp. 545–548. doi: 10.1109/ComPE53109.2021.9751981
2. Financial Stability Board, "Artificial Intelligence and Machine Learning in Financial Services," 2017. www.fsb.org/wp-content/uploads/P011117.pdf
3. A. Lui and G. W. Lamb, "Artificial intelligence and augmented intelligence collaboration: Regaining trust and confidence in the financial sector," Inf. Commun. Technol. Law, vol. 27, no. 3, pp. 267–283, 2018.
4. M. Daks, "Banking on technology: Artificial intelligence helping banks get smarter," NJBIZ, vol. 31, no. 7, p. 10, 2018.
5. A. K. Singh, P. M. Sharma, M. Bhatt, A. Choudhary, S. Sharma, and S. Sadhukhan, "Comparative analysis on artificial intelligence technologies and its application in FinTech," 2022 International Conference on Augmented Intelligence and Sustainable Systems (ICAISS), Trichy, India, 2022, pp. 570–574. doi: 10.1109/ICAISS55157.2022.10010573
6. X. Hu and K. Wang, "Bank financial innovation and computer information security management based on artificial intelligence," 2020 2nd International Conference on Machine Learning, Big Data and Business Intelligence (MLBDBI), Taiyuan, China, 2020, pp. 572–575. doi: 10.1109/MLBDBI51377.2020.00120
7. Z. Qihai, H. Tao, and W. Tao, "Analysis of business intelligence and its derivative: Financial intelligence," 2008 International Symposium on Electronic Commerce and Security, Guangzhou, China, 2008, pp. 997–1000. doi: 10.1109/ISECS.2008.28

8. R. Dhaigude and N. Lawande, "Impact of artificial intelligence on credit scores in lending process," 2022 Interdisciplinary Research in Technology and Management (IRTM), Kolkata, India, 2022, pp. 1–5. doi: 10.1109/IRTM54583.2022.9791511

9. M. Sigova, V. Dolbezhkin, and A. Koltsov, "Objective contradictions in the integration of social networks, payments services and distributed ledger technology," 2019 International Conference on Artificial Intelligence: Applications and Innovations (IC-AIAI), Belgrade, Serbia, 2019, pp. 12–124. doi: 10.1109/IC-AIAI48757.2019.00009

10. H. X. Tang and Y. D. Feng, "An ontology-based model for personalized financial planning product design," 2011 2nd International Conference on Artificial Intelligence, Management Science and Electronic Commerce (AIMSEC), Deng Feng, China, 2011, pp. 117–120. doi: 10.1109/AIMSEC.2011.6010372

11. A. Mehrotra, "Artificial intelligence in financial services: Need to blend automation with human touch," 2019 International Conference on Automation, Computational and Technology Management (ICACTM), London, UK, 2019, pp. 342–347. doi: 10.1109/ICACTM.2019.8776741

12. M. Swapna, "Ethics of using artificial intelligence in financial banking industry," 2018. https://medium.com/datadriveninvestor/ethics-of-using-ai-in-the-financial-banking-industry-fa93203f6f25

13. I. Samuel, F. A. Ogunkeye, A. Olajube, and A. Awelewa, "Development of a voice chatbot for payment using Amazon Lex Service with Eyowo as the payment platform," 2020 International Conference on Decision Aid Sciences and Application (DASA), Sakheer, Bahrain, 2020, pp. 104–108. doi: 10.1109/DASA51403.2020.9317214

14. P. A. Angga, W. E. Fachri, A. Elevanita, and R. D. Agushinta, "Design of chatbot with 3D avatar voice interface and facial expression," 2015 International Conference on Science in Information Technology (ICSITech), 2015, pp. 326–330.

15. J. Zamora, "I'm sorry Dave I'm afraid I can't do that: Chatbot perception and expectations," Proceedings of the 5th International Conference on Human Agent Interaction, pp. 253–260, 2017.

16. M. Ganesan, D. C., H. B., K. A.S. and L. B., "A Survey on Chatbots Using Artificial Intelligence," 2020 International Conference on System, Computation, Automation and Networking (ICSCAN), Pondicherry, India, 2020, pp. 1–5. doi: 10.1109/ICSCAN49426.2020.9262366.

17. M. Anusuya and S. Katti, "Speech recognition by machine: A review," International Journal of Computer Science and Information Security, vol. 6, no. 01/13, 2010.

18. M. A. Tehrani, A. A. Amidian, J. Muhammadi, and H. Rabiee, "A survey of system platforms for mobile payment," 2010 International Conference on Management of e-Commerce and e-Government, pp. 376–381, 2010.

19. P. Kulkarni, A. Mahabaleshwarkar, M. Kulkarni, N. Sirsikar, and K. Gadgil, "Conversational AI: An overview of methodologies, applications & future scope," Proceedings of the 5th International Conference on Computing, Communication, Control and Automation (ICCUBEA), 2019, p. 7.

20. S. Kusal, S. Patil, K. Kotecha, R. Aluvalu, and V. Varadarajan, "AI based emotion detection for textual big data: Techniques and contribution," Big Data Cogn. Comput., vol. 5, no. 3, p. 43, 2021, doi: 10.3390/bdcc5030043

Chapter 10

Healthcare applications of federated deep learning for cybersecurity in the Internet of Things

Praneeth Kanagala

10.1 INTRODUCTION

In recent times, due to the huge development of the bitcoin system, block chain technology usage is highly improved and has attracted greater attention [1]. Block chain technology is performed based on the cryptography-linked techniques to create various linked information blocks and each block is enclosed with the significant data to verify its authority and to create the subsequent blocks [2]. Moreover, block chain is worked as a distributed database because of this condition; it attains important features such as privacy protection, non-tamperability, and decentralization that are helped to secure data sharing [3]. Also, it contributes data integrity and transparency to the information system; thus, it is applied in various significant applications such as identity management, game systems, industries, supply chains, tracing food, etc. [4]. In addition, the electricity industry, the Internet of cars, and the healthcare industry all make considerable use of the growing block chain technology [5]. Block chain in the healthcare system is carried out as supreme transformation. Normally, the patient data is straightforward, but sometimes this will be more complicated to manage the unstructured data of patients [6]. This medical data is gathered from various users and it is accessed or manipulated for significant usage via different users. Due to the critical importance, the data of patients should be carried out as secured, reliable, and protected [7]. Thus, the recent blockchain technology execution is considered for the access of entire data regulation, transaction, and storage [8]. However, it has carried out transaction numbers, block, or address numbers. Thus, secured data sharing is a major challenge because the security of medical images stored in digital media is important [9, 10]. The medical images have been large in size as well as in number. Cybersecurity encloses robbing patient data, electronic health records, medical components, Ransomware attacks, and hospital infrastructure [11, 12]. Consequently, blockchain system has certain characteristic issues while it is utilized to support a huge amount of customers which are creating a huge size of data like from the Internet of Things (IoT) [13].

DOI: 10.1201/9781003433941-10

10.1.1 Background

Using a distributed learning strategy, parallel learning models can be trained on-premises. Pushing the same data onto parallel nodes (data-parallel) or pushing the same data onto all nodes, where they train separate parts of a machine learning (ML) model (model-parallel), are two strategies used to implement parallelism. However, when dealing with huge datasets, model partitioning becomes more difficult, and heterogeneous computing and storage systems present new issues [14]. Non-independent and identically distributed (non-IID) data presents a further difficulty because it necessitates unified feature learning and optimization [15]. With two methods, centralized FL (CFL) and distributed FL (DFL), federated learning (FL) ensures local learning in IoMT while still respecting data homogeneity and privacy concerns.

While CFL uses cloud-based aggregation and may be applied to broad models, DFL places emphasis on edge-based aggregation and makes the distribution of users a primary criterion. Edge-cloud-based aggregation describes situations in which a unified blend of CFL and DFL approach (hybrid FL) is achievable. In CFL, each medical center contributes to the global model by training its own model using locally collected data and sending it to the rest of the network. Due to the fact that transmitting the data to a global server is unneeded to acquire the result, CFL reduces the latency of the system. Instead, local model parameters are kept up-to-date by healthcare institutions via global updates. When using CFL, however, healthcare nodes (or remote sites) must rely on a central server (a CC server) to accurately transmit the global parameters under which the local training would occur [16]. As a result, a malevolent adversary may poison the global server or the local updates, resulting in erroneous CFL model training [17].

To solve these problems in CFL, where a centralized model is unnecessary and peer learning is used instead, DFL models were developed. Single-hop neighbors gain insight into local changes, which are broadcast to other nodes to enhance global updates. Thus, DFL has intrinsic potential in a wide range of applications, including transportation networks [18], unmanned aerial vehicles [19], the IoT [20], and monetary systems. It is challenging to get clinical datasets from the far-flung hospitals and medical institutions due to the lack of availability and restricted access to patients' sensitive medical information. This means that DFL protects the privacy of the training data while enabling a large number of agents to jointly develop a single prediction model. The HIPPA act forbids the exchange of patient-level data with third parties such as insurance companies and healthcare facilities, therefore most practical EHR solutions are decentralized.

10.1.2 Overview of deep learning (DL) for cybersecurity in the IoT

The IoT is the interconnection of computing devices in control systems through the use of network protocols and sensing technologies such as sensors, laser scanners, radio frequency identification, etc. In recent years, the

IoT has been utilized by a wide variety of industries, including transportation, manufacturing, drone healthcare, crowdsourcing, cyber-physical systems, agriculture, and many more [1]. Due to the exponential growth of IoT, there are now millions of embedded physical devices, all of which are linked together and expose data that could compromise users' security and privacy. IoT devices have a huge attack surface that is actively exploited by hackers [2] because they lack effective security defense solutions.

Modern ML's [3] ability to extract relevant and complicated data models from massive datasets in a centralized location is attracting more attention than ever before. The training data in conventional ML systems is stored in one convenient location, without resolving issues of privacy and lowering the cost of data transmission. When combined with additional security measures, such as blockchain and authentication [4, 5], ML algorithms can help intrusion detection systems identify malicious from benign behavior [6, 7].

10.1.2.1 Centralized learning

ML for IoT applications has traditionally been carried out by transmitting data from each linked IoT device to a single, centralized cloud server. A centralized learning model can instantly apply the results of generalization from one set of networked IoT devices to any other set of IoT devices that are relevant to the task at hand. Centralized learning was the norm until recently, but it has drawbacks in the areas of privacy, latency, bandwidth, and connectivity.

10.1.2.2 Federated learning

Safely constructing ML models using data acquired across several devices is the goal of federated learning. IoT devices may now update their models with local IoT data by employing a novel technique called federated learning. By transmitting their locally trained models to a centralized server, IoT devices can have their results combined (weights averaged, for example) into a single, more accurate global model. The adoption of federated learning presents both practical and technological obstacles, and the distribution of data is an integral part of addressing these issues.

10.1.3 Benefits of DL approach for healthcare application

DL, sometimes called hierarchical learning or deep structured learning, is a form of ML that analyzes data through numerous layers of algorithms and a hierarchical structure. Each layer of a DL model receives data and processes it before using the results from the previous layer to make its own decisions. Because they are able to "learn" from their past mistakes and improve their ability to draw connections and correlations, DL models become more precise as more data is processed.

DL is inspired by the interconnected neural networks of vertebrate brains. Like electrical signals that go between the cells of living organisms, the nodes of a network are activated when they receive stimuli from the neurons in the layers below them.

The healthcare sector can reap several rewards from the application of DL. Examples include the following:

- For patients with comparable symptoms or conditions, DL can understand the significant correlations in concerned data and store knowledge about previous customers.
- When a risk score is needed for administration other than discharge, we can use DL to build a model based on any accessible data
- In order to confidently and roughly allocate resources, DL offers accurate and timely risk scores.
- The use of DL techniques can help reduce expenses and boost productivity.
- Interacting with the training data, DL algorithms improve in precision and accuracy, providing for previously unattainable insights into care processes, variability, and diagnostics.
- Energy efficiency and processing speed of graphics processing units, or GPUs, both are improving.
- As DL algorithms become more affordable, they are being used to fuel a surge in innovation.
- More healthcare data than ever before can be used by trained algorithms, thanks to electronic health records (EHR) and other digitalization efforts.
- DL, which finds patterns by linking the tools, is making diagnostics faster and more precise.
- Whether or not skin lesions are malignant can be determined by DL just as accurately as by a dermatologist with a board certification.

10.1.4 Benefits of AI DL

DL, in its simplest definition, is a type of ML that can address problems that traditional ML methods cannot. DL makes use of neural networks to expedite computation and generate reliable outcomes. Examples of excellent applications of DL include natural language processing (NLP), audio recognition, and face recognition. Facebook, for instance, will suggest tagging concerned friend when this will upload a group photo together. Facebook's facial recognition technology uses DL methods in artificial intelligence (AI). Using DL, computers can understand and transcribe human speech. When combined with the IoT, DL has the potential to usher in a wave of revolutionary developments.

10.1.4.1 Application of DL in healthcare

Many recent DL news stories have highlighted experimental or exploratory work that has yet to be commercialized. However, DL is gradually being integrated into cutting-edge technologies that have significant practical value in the clinical setting. Some of the most fascinating examples of health IT in action include fresh patient-facing applications and some surprisingly well-established tactics for improving the user experience.

10.1.4.1.1 Drug development

In the medical field, DL is helpful for finding new treatments and creating new drugs. The software analyzes the patient's records to determine the best course of treatment. Additionally, data is gleaned from patient's symptoms and diagnostic tests with the help of this technology.

10.1.4.1.2 Imaging in medicine

Diseases like heart disease, cancer, and brain tumors can be diagnosed with the help of medical imaging therapies like MRI, CT, and ECG. Therefore, DL aids physicians in conducting accurate diagnoses and providing optimal care.

10.1.4.1.3 Insurance swindle

Potential instances of medical insurance fraud are researched using DL. It is able to predict when claims of fraud will be lodged using predictive analytics. The insurance industry can reach out to its target clientele with discounts and offers by educating them thoroughly.

10.1.4.1.4 Alzheimer's disease

Alzheimer's disease is a huge obstacle for the healthcare system. In order to detect Alzheimer's disease in its early stages, a DL algorithm is applied.

10.1.4.1.5 Personalized medical treatments

Healthcare providers can use DL algorithms to deliver individualized care for patients by analyzing data from the patients' medical records, symptoms, and diagnostic tests. For the most frequent medical procedures, NLP can extract useful information from the free-text medical data.

10.1.4.1.6 Responding to patient's queries

DL chatbots can help doctors and people alike spot patterns in their patients' symptoms.

10.1.4.1.7 Audit of prescriptions

Potential diagnostic or prescription errors can be uncovered by using DL algorithms to compare prescriptions with patient health records.

10.1.4.1.8 Studying mental health

Researchers are enhancing mental healthcare by utilizing DL models. Researchers are using deep neural networks to probe the brains of people with mental illness and other conditions. The team found that trained DL models could beat baseline ML algorithms in a number of scenarios. For instance, DL systems can be trained to locate relevant brain biomarkers. Another effort plans to use ML to create an affordable digital clinical decision-support system for mental health.

In recent years, there has been a trend toward using DL, the cutting-edge AI approach, to analyze biomedical data. DL is being used in computational medicine. While DL serves an important purpose in computational medicine, it is challenging to use to its full potential due to the fact that biomedical data are not as clean, easily analyzed, and easily accessible as data from other sectors.

10.1.5 Challenges of DL for cybersecurity in the IoT for healthcare application

1. Privacy and security-preserving services
2. Dynamic and low-cost scheduling
3. Full use of system resources

The UDEC model uses deep reinforcement learning to ensure the security of vital user data at the edge nodes, where it is generated in response to service requests. Their results demonstrate the UDEC model's efficacy in reducing energy consumption.

10.1.5.1 Security and privacy challenges

Recent research has shown that even while federated learning claims to keep local user data private, analyzing the global model can nevertheless identify the involvement of specific participants. Some methods, such as differential privacy, have been developed to address this issue, but they either hinder model performance or necessitate extra conditions that are not feasible for IoT networks (such as lots of processing power). That is why IoT networks and apps need federated techniques that are easy to build, deliver great speed, and protect privacy without requiring excessive computing cost.

10.1.5.2 IoT Network settings challenges

Users and aggregators will be sharing parameters via the IoT network; thus, it is important to design a dependable federated DL system. Bandwidth, interference, and noise are only a few examples of the network issues that can limit communication routes and processing capability. As a result, due to the client access and restricted network stability, there are significant research problems involved with establishing a federated DL system for cybersecurity in IoT applications.

10.1.5.3 Data-related challenges

Problems with data-generating bias (including but not limited to cognition, sampling, reporting, and confirmation) pose a serious obstacle to the advancement of ML research. In FL, however, the situation is more convoluted because information is shared between more than one entity. For instance, if data amounts from IoT devices change, the FL-based system may prioritize the collective efforts of the devices' users. There is a risk that IoT networks with slower devices or networks will be underrepresented in global model updates if these updates are dependent on network latency.

10.1.5.4 FL platforms challenges

Collaboration's outstanding performance in the correct domains makes FL a real possibility for many IoT-based applications. The construction of a specialist IoT framework based on FL is still an important topic of research that must account for the underlying IoT architecture, despite the fact that there are a number of emerging frameworks for FL in general.

10.2 OVERVIEW OF HEALTHCARE KEY STUDIES ON FEDERATED DL FOR CYBERSECURITY IN THE IoT

10.2.1 General overview

Recently, DL and ML have seen widespread application in the healthcare industry, particularly in smart health-monitoring networks and related services. Different types of IoMT devices and sensors produced health data, which was analyzed using DL and ML. The cloud network and cloud services have been storing and managing these health records. These complicated health data are analyzed using ML and DL to complete multiobjective tasks. By the year 2020, Ali et al. estimated that there will be approximately 50 billion medical devices in use, each posing unique security risks. In addition to detecting cyber risks, he claims that large data collection is another application of DL/ML.

When applied to problem recognition, DL is useful, and data-driven performance improves results across the board. The algorithms for learning are straightforward, meaning they are simple to understand and implement. ML is nonlinear, but traditional DL can still generate rapid and powerful results in areas like language acquisition and accountability for accurate patient records. Like the patients' actual conditions in real time, it is possible to learn data and information about them, including in the form of photographs and texts. New healthcare applications rely on DL models, which are complex and resource-heavy. Training and evaluating these elaborate neural networks takes a long time. The longer the time it takes to make a prediction and the more complex the network, the more accurate the prediction must be. This is a major problem for healthcare and other IoT applications where instant feedback is essential. Potential improvements to the value control engineering system can be delivered via DL. Beneficial tools for comprehending the domain are a responsibility of ML. Opportunities for studying dynamic systems, adapting to new settings, and recognizing data in various formats are made possible by ML. By studying a patient's DNA, clinicians can use DL to diagnose genetic disorders, including Turner's syndrome, hemophilia, and sickle cell anemia, and develop effective therapies for these conditions. By analyzing patient data, both normal and pathological patterns may be identified, allowing doctors to more accurately diagnose patients using DL and ML.

AI or ML is used to recognize and diagnose patients' conditions in real time. The raw data or historical data of patients can be used by DL to reconstruct the patients' conditions in real time. This versatility allows its application in domains as diverse as the healthcare system and the protection of the cybercrime industry. Nevertheless, it is increasingly desired that elderly people endure hardships alone, making it an integral part of the healthcare system for both young and old. Taking everything into account, DL is a must for progress.

In the present day, cardiovascular disease has a steadily rising mortality rate. DL is used for data collecting from patients who are either too young or too old to appreciate wearing wearable gadgets that help them identify or recognize their real-time status. A computational learning system, SHM, the IoT, and knowledgeable doctors who can detect their patients' real-time condition and have the proper information or prediction of future condition can significantly reduce the prevalence of acute diseases like diabetes, Alzheimer's disease, genetic diseases, cancer, and respiratory malady in the current healthcare system.

Approximately 30% of the population suffers from cardiovascular disorders, according to medical studies. Health-monitoring devices, the IoT, and AI come together to form smart health monitoring, which we might describe as using computational learning or robotic learning. The function of the SHM in contemporary medicine is essential. Thanks to AI's implementation, ML algorithms and software are now used in healthcare systems. The data employed in ML forms the basis for AI's findings. The game essentially solves this problem for us. Since it is an ANN used for visualizing images like ultrasound, MRI, CT scan, and X-ray, convolutional neural network (CNN) learning is crucial to the operation of DL models.

There are many ways in which DL and ML have contributed to the evolution of other sectors, including but not limited to industry, businesses, educational institutions, and healthcare systems. Automatically identifying cancer cells is a major area of application for DL. While ML relies on humans to complete its many possible problem-solving tasks, DL uses ML to complete its many possible actions on its own. When compared to ML, DL provides an automatic solution to the entire issue. When it comes to cardiac illness diagnosis, elderly patients and those in a coma can all benefit more from DL than youngsters.

10.2.2 Secure Internet of Healthcare Things

As more complex diseases and symptoms, like COVID-19, are discovered and introduced, health management has become a pressing issue and powerful challenge.

A federated learning approach was used to train and maintain this DL-based clinical decision support tool. The proposed solution prioritized a method to protect patient privacy while also counteracting the risk of cyberattacks during large-scale clinical data mining. The suggested method is based on a federated learning model that allows each local neural network to be trained using rich clinical data without requiring the sharing of sensitive patient information.

In order to lessen the amount of power required for federated learning, a new technique was developed. This system divides the model into three parts, with the most computationally intensive part being transferred to a server in the cloud.

10.2.3 Secure cloud computing

A growing number of clients are hesitant of entrusting their data to traditional ML training models, which store and distribute data in a centralized cloud environment for reasons of privacy or peer rivalry. One solution presented is federated learning, a distributed platform for training ML models in which multiple clients work together without needing to combine their datasets. When it came to cloud security, HFWP was a federated learning technique that put an emphasis on privacy. The HFWP technique is secure against both colluding parties and an honest but curious server because it is based on a lightweight encryption protocol. Experiments performed on two real-world datasets – the MNIST and the UCI Human Activity Recognition Datasets – show the highest accuracy compared to earlier studies in the field.

10.2.4 The IoT paradigm

The physical resource layer, the network layer, and the data application layer make up the three tiers of a typical IoT architecture.

Physical layer: In this layer, physical components like sensors and actuators are connected to a network in order to collect data in real time.

Network layer: Secure communication between network nodes is achieved by using multiple networking protocols at this level. This layer facilitates inter-device communication for the purpose of maintaining the network's safety and quality of service.

Application layer: This layer employs ML algorithms to provide application-specific services, such as those for "smart cities" and "smart healthcare". This is a critical part of the IoT infrastructure that can be breached. The IoT network's safety and dependability are guaranteed by the ML algorithm used in this layer.

A rule engine processes data from sensors and actuators that communicate with the application via device gateways. A device is a piece of hardware that can exchange data with sensors via wired or wireless means. Gateways are used for communication between devices and systems if direct connections are not possible. To rephrase, a Gateway is utilized to facilitate communication or translation between various devices and parts. The Rule engine in the IoT allows for the creation of non-programmable processing rules. Here, users can define relatively straightforward rules that direct the system to take the desired action in response to incoming events.

10.2.5 IoT-based smart environments

The purpose of an IoT-based smart environment is to improve service quality through the interconnection and communication of various IoT devices. The term "smart environment" is used in the context of the IoT to describe the degree to which interconnected objects can carry out autonomous tasks, apply knowledge, and make judgments in reaction to changes in their surroundings. The primary goal of smart environments is to supply services dependent on data gathered by sensors and analyzed by intelligent methods. As the service becomes increasingly automated, business processes become more streamlined, and smart surroundings play an increasingly important part in bringing them into the 21st century. Adoption of smart environments is influenced by a number of factors, including the number of users, scalability, and the ability to manage enormous amounts of data. These are important to keep in mind as this implements smart environment applications based on the IoT.

10.2.6 Significance of IoT security

There are numerous security concerns that must be addressed in the introduction of IoT systems. Keeping up with the ever-changing security threats posed by IoT devices is a daunting and time-consuming task. The following are examples of some of the most pressing security issues that must be resolved:

Heterogeneity: Researchers face challenges in developing a model that can accommodate the heterogeneity of IoT devices due to differences in device size, quantity, bandwidth, hardware, and software.

Volume: The IoT is able to gather information from a wide variety of sources. As a result, the IoT ecosystem generates an overwhelming amount of data that must be processed.

Susceptibility to attacks: Cookie theft, cross-site scripting, structured query language injection, session hijacking, and distributed denial of service are just some of the security attacks that can be launched against IoT devices.

Latency and reliability: Most of the difficulties encountered by IoT networks revolve around latency and dependability. Most cutting-edge uses of technology, such as smart healthcare, lane detection, and traffic monitoring, necessitate a system architecture with low latency and high dependability.

Cost-effectiveness and resource utilization: In the IoT, where resources are limited, striking the right balance between low costs and efficient use of those resources is difficult.

10.2.7 Healthcare cyber-physical system (HCPS)

In healthcare, cyber-physical systems can be broken down into many layers:

- Unit-level HCPS
- Integration-level HCPS
- System-level HCPS
- Acceptance-level HCPS
- Evolutionary-level HCPS

Patients in hospital wards and intensive care units are monitored and managed using first-tier or unit-level HCPS. At this point, information is gathered from the patient's associated health actuators and sent to the intelligent systems responsible for evaluating and controlling the patient's vitals (temperature, blood pressure, heart rate, etc.). The medical staff is also connected to the HCPS network, so they can receive timely updates and advice from medical professionals.

In the second phase of HCPS, known as the integration level, hospitals work in tandem with connected homes to offer remote patient monitoring and other telehealth services. When transporting critically ill patients, hospitals can work in tandem with smart ambulances to track the patient's condition in real time and prepare for any emergency by ensuring things like beds and ventilators are readily available.

When many separate autonomous systems contribute to the HCPS in order to create a Smart City Healthcare Cyber-physical System, we will have reached the system level of HCPS. The smart grid provides power and serves as the backbone for many different cyber-physical systems in the healthcare ecosystem, which also includes smart homes, smart ambulances, smart hospital manufacturing units, and smart hospitals.

At the Acceptance HCPS level, researchers, technologists, engineers, health professionals, and academics work together to develop policies and standards that will facilitate the smooth rollout of the healthcare ecosystem.

In the future, HCPS should ideally evolve to an evolutionary level where it can self-adapt and manage itself. Components of cyber-physical systems that are capable of self-adaptation use historical data to inform their actions in the present. As a result, cyber-physical systems' dynamic environment necessitates and greatly benefits from evolutionary behavior.

The physical components and processes that make up the cyber-physical system can be in one of four states: healthy, sick, critical, or non-working. The closed-loop system as a whole can only be as healthy as its individual parts.

Sensors, actuators, and physical machines controlled by external inputs like mobile devices at the dew layer and systems at the cyber level are only few of the device kinds found in CPS. Data formats can be structured or unstructured, and as different devices employ different forms for input and output, interfaces are required to translate between formats. The efficiency and dependability of HCPS is of the utmost importance, and time is of the essence in this regard. The efficacy and dependability of the system can be compromised by even a few seconds' or microseconds' delay in the delivery of medication to patients.

The idea of a health-monitoring system (HMS) for cyber-physical systems arose from the need for ongoing monitoring and control to ensure peak performance. HMS can serve a dual purpose by both assessing the CPS's physical health and providing a proactive method of determining the CPS's probability of well-being. Passive monitoring methods include observing how components behave in simulations, whereas active monitoring techniques use responses to stimuli to identify anomalies.

REFERENCES

1. M. A. Ferrag and L. Maglaras, "DeepCoin: A novel deep learning and block-chain-based energy exchange framework for smart grids," IEEE Trans. Eng. Manage., vol. 67, no. 4, pp. 1285–1297, 2019.
2. X. Hei, X. Yin, Y. Wang, J. Ren, and L. Zhu, "A trusted feature aggregator federated learning for distributed malicious attack detection," Comput. Secur., vol. 99, p. 102033, 2020.
3. H. Wen, Y. Wu, C. Yang, H. Duan, and S. Yu, "A unified federated learning framework for wireless communications: Towards privacy, efficiency, and security," Proceedings of the IEEE Conference on Computer Communications Workshops (INFOCOM WKSHPS), July 2020, pp. 653–658.
4. M. T. Hammi, B. Hammi, P. Bellot, and A. Serhrouchni, "Bubbles of trust: A decentralized blockchain-based authentication system for IoT," Comput. Secur., vol. 78, pp. 126–142, 2018.
5. D. Puthal and P. Mohanty, "Proof of authentication: IoT-friendly blockchains," IEEE Potentials, vol. 38, no. 1, pp. 26–29, 2018.

6. M. A. Ferrag, L. Maglaras, A. Ahmim, M. Derdour, and H. Janicke, "RDTIDS: Rules and decision tree-based intrusion detection system for Internet-of-Things networks," Future Internet, vol. 12, no. 3, p. 44, 2020.

7. M. A. Ferrag, L. Maglaras, S. Moschoyiannis, and H. Janicke, "Deep learning for cyber security intrusion detection: Approaches, datasets, and comparative study," J. Inf. Secur. Appl., vol. 50, p. 102419, 2020.

8. Y. Zhang, Q. Wu, and M. Shikh-Bahaei, "Vertical federated learning based privacy-preserving cooperative sensing in cognitive radio networks," Proceedings of the IEEE Globecom Workshops (GC Wkshps), 2020, pp. 1–6.

9. B. McMahan, E. Moore, D. Ramage, S. Hampson, and B. A. Y. Arcas, "Communication-efficient learning of deep networks from decentralized data," Proceedings of the 20th International Conference on Artificial Intelligence and Statistics, pp. 1273–1282, 2017.

10. S. Khatri, H. Vachhani, S. Shah, J. Bhatia, M. Chaturvedi, S. Tanwar, and N. Kumar, "Machine learning models and techniques for VANET based traffic management: Implementation issues and challenges," Peer-to-Peer Netw. Appl., vol. 14, pp. 1778–1805, 2021.

11. G. B. Giannakis, Q. Ling, G. Mateos, I. D. Schizas, and H. Zhu, "Decentralized learning for wireless communications and networking," In Splitting Methods in Communication, Imaging, Science, and Engineering; Springer: Berlin/Heidelberg, Germany, 2016, pp. 461–497.

12. P. Bhattacharya, P. Mehta, S. Tanwar, M. S. Obaidat, and K. F. Hsiao, "HeaL: A blockchain-envisioned signcryption scheme for healthcare IoT ecosystems," Proceedings of the 2020 International Conference on Communications, Computing, Cybersecurity, and Informatics (CCCI), Sharjah, United Arab Emirates, 3–5 November 2020, pp. 1–6.

13. A. Verma, P. Bhattacharya, U. Bodkhe, A. Ladha, and S. Tanwar, "DAMS: Dynamic association for view materialization based on rule mining scheme," Lecture Notes in Electrical Engineering, vol. 701, pp. 529–544, Springer, 2021.

14. B. McMahan, E. Moore, D. Ramage, S. Hampson, and B. A. Arcas, "Communication-efficient learning of deep networks from decentralized data," Proceedings of the Artificial Intelligence and Statistics, Fort Lauderdale, FL, USA, 20–27 April 2017, pp. 1273–1282.

15. Z. Chai, H. Fayyaz, Z. Fayyaz, A. Anwar, Y. Zhou, N. Baracaldo, H. Ludwig, and Y. Cheng, "Towards taming the resource and data heterogeneity in federated learning," Proceedings of the 2019 USENIX Conference on Operational Machine Learning (OpML'19), Santa Clara, CA, USA, 20 May 2019, pp. 19–21.

16. V. K. Prasad and M. Bhavsar, "Efficient resource monitoring and prediction techniques in an IaaS level of cloud computing: Survey," Proceedings of the International Conference on Future Internet Technologies and Trends, Surat, India, 31 August–2 September 2017, pp. 47–55.

17. B. Ghimire and D. B. Rawat, "Recent advances on federated learning for cybersecurity and cybersecurity for federated learning for Internet of Things," IEEE Internet Things J., vol. 9, pp. 8229–8249, 2022.

18. V. A. Patel, P. Bhattacharya, S. Tanwar, N. K. Jadav, and R. Gupta, "BFLEdge: Blockchain based federated edge learning scheme in V2X underlying 6G communications," Proceedings of the 2022 12th International Conference on Cloud Computing, Data Science & Engineering (Confluence), Noida, India, 27–28 January 2022, pp. 146–152.

19. D. Saraswat, A. Verma, P. Bhattacharya, S. Tanwar, G. Sharma, P. N. Bokoro, and R. Sharma, "Blockchain-based federated learning in UAVs beyond 5G networks: A solution taxonomy and future directions," IEEE Access, vol. 10, pp. 33154–33182, 2022.
20. T. Alam and R. Gupta, "Federated learning and its role in the privacy preservation of IoT devices," Future Internet, vol. 14, p. 246, 2022.

Chapter 11

Prediction of suicidal risk using machine learning models

Gautam Siddharth Kashyap, Ayesha Siddiqui,
Ramsha Siddiqui, Karan Malik, Samar Wazir,
and Alexander E. I. Brownlee

11.1 INTRODUCTION

Mr. X is a military veteran who has just returned from the war. He presents himself at the military hospital claiming that he is having war nightmares and is unable to go outside and be normal around his children. Mr. X says he wants to die, his wife takes away his guns. He has no family history of suicide. For his safety, he is admitted to the hospital. With proper treatment and optimal medication, his symptoms are controlled. After getting discharged from the hospital, Mr. X discontinued his medications because they make him feel dull. Two weeks later at his follow-up appointment, he reported feeling okay, but still inner thoughts of dying rapidly increased in the coming weeks and became severe in the following months. He expresses being at the end of the rope and wanting to die. He spends most of his time thinking about how to kill himself, and one day the disaster struck when his wife was at work.

This example may be familiar to most of us, as many of us have faced or have met a person who is dealing with these symptoms. Typically, two types of prediction rules can be used for "Mr. X": (1) *Clinical prediction rules:* It is an algorithm that includes several types of combinations of symptoms, medical signs, or other possibilities. (2) *Mental health prediction rules:* These are not mathematical pattern-based tools; for example, Wells criteria (it determines the risk of pulmonary embolism) [1] and CHADS$_2$ score (it determines the risk of stroke with atrial fibrillation) [2]. Mainly clinical prediction rules are used for dealing with suicidal patients. Clinical prediction rules help the clinicians to weigh the odds and reach an average level of information to predict risks [3] rather than the mental health prediction rules which are slower to develop. Any mental healthcare provider who has lost a patient to suicide knows very well that despite all best efforts and all psychotropic medications, there is no way to predict what this veteran will

DOI: 10.1201/9781003433941-11

do next. Prediction of suicidal risk is generally evaluated and validated on the following scales [4–6]:

1. Columbia severity rating scale
2. Suicide trigger scale
3. Brown health suicide risk assessment

In the above-mentioned scales, only the Columbia Severity Rating Scale is a standardized scale that can be used for different populations ranging from children to adults.

Many studies that investigated the cause of complete suicide came to the conclusion that 60% of deaths result from the first suicide attempt. Therefore, a complicated relationship exists between the *previous suicide attempts → present suicidal ideation → lifetime suicide risk* [7–9]. No blood test can predict the suicidal risk which makes it difficult to predict that how long the patients will take to recover. The overall ability to predict the suicidal risk of patients by the mental healthcare provider is limited due to the following reasons:

1. Lack of clinical prediction rules availability
2. Individual patient's diagnostics, psychological, and medical comorbidity

At this point, the use of machine learning comes into the picture to overcome the above-mentioned limitations. For the last ten years, machine learning has played an important role in medical practice and biomedical applications as well as in the development of well-accepted clinical prediction rules [1]. Researchers believe that the prediction of suicidal risk using machine learning predictive models may be worthwhile even if they have statistical limitations because of the low cost [10].

In this chapter, we have used the following machine learning models to predict suicidal risk using existing freely available suicide datasets [11]:

1. k-Nearest neighbors
2. Linear regression
3. Decision tree
4. Random forest
5. Gradient boosting
6. Multilayer perceptrons (MLP)
7. XGBoost

The above-mentioned models are tuned in such a way that they show optimum performance on the datasets.

We will try to find the answers to the following questions in this chapter:

1. Can we improve modelling accuracy over the existing approaches?
2. Is there a perceivable difference in the suicide risk for the two studied genders – male and female?
3. Is there a specific age group that is more at risk than the others?

This chapter is structured as follows. In Section 11.2, we will go through the existing approaches proposed in the related literature that uses machine learning to predict suicide. In Section 11.3, the empirical study is conducted. In Section 11.4, the machine learning models and their results are discussed. In Section 11.5, the statistical test is conducted and we conclude the chapter in Section 11.5.

11.2 LITERATURE REVIEW

Many studies have used machine learning for risk calculation and predicting the outcomes in multiple medical and surgical specialties. However, a few studies have used machine learning to predict suicidal risk in clinical and non-clinical settings. Passos et al. [12] used outpatients with mood disorders to predict suicidal risk. The authors believe that psychosis, cocaine dependence, and PTSD are major depressive disorders. Their model has a sensitivity and specificity of 70% each to predict suicide risk. Kessler et al. [13] used machine learning to build the model STARRS (study to assess risk and resilience in service member). This model contains the records of a total of 53,769 formerly deployed soldiers and veterans who were hospitalized from 2004 to 2009. The authors believed that this model has a sensitivity and specificity of 70% each to predict suicide risk. Moreover, it can predict gender, the enrollment date in the military, previous criminal charges, and the presence of previous suicidal attempts which is the main indicator of the completed suicide. Ruderfer et al. [14] used two types of samples, (1) UK Biobank and (2) VUMC (Vanderbilt University Medical Center), for predicting the chances of attempting suicide. These samples were genotyped using microarrays. The authors used the random forest algorithm and they achieved an AUC (area under the curve) of 0.94. Baca-Garcia et al. [15] used the prediction model SNPs (single nucleotide polymorphisms) to distinguish between suicide attempters and non-attempters. They have used 277 male psychiatric patients as a sample. The authors selected 840 SNPs from the candidate genes. Using only three SNPs, the authors were able to discriminate between suicide attempters and non-attempters. Their model achieved an accuracy of 67% using SVMs (support vector machines). Kautzky et al. [16] used 225 patients from the GSRD (European Group for the Study of Resistant Depression). The authors selected 12 SNPs from the candidate genes. They explore the interactions between SNPs and clinical variability along with suicidality. Their model achieved an accuracy of 50% using the random forest algorithm and the k-means clustering algorithm. Setoyama et al. [17] performed a comprehensive metabolome analysis of 123 metabolites on three psychiatric patients who had the major depressive disorder and bipolar disorder. The experiments were performed with or without medications. To evaluate the severity of depression, the metabolic profile is used. The authors were able to discriminate patients from suicidal ideations and non-ideations. They have used random forest algorithms and achieved an AUC of 0.7. Dargél et al. [18] used 635 bipolar patients for the research of emotional hyperreactivity. The experiments were performed in the French Network of Bipolar Expert Centers. The experiment results show that those who have emotional hyperreactivity have (1) high levels of suicide attempts, (2) high systolic and diastolic blood pressure, and (3) high sensitivity C-reactive proteins. Their model achieved an accuracy of 84.9% using the random forest algorithm. Bhak et al. [19] used the random forest to classify the subjects who depended on blood-derived methylome and transcriptome. Their sample contains 56 suicide attempters, 39 major depressive disorder patients, and 87 healthy patients. The authors created the model's features that are DMS (differentially methylated regions), and DEGs (differentially expressed genes) after next-generation sequencing. They create three separate models to compare: (1) suicide attempters with major depressive disorders with an accuracy of 92.6%, (2) major depressive disorder with healthy patients with an accuracy of 87.3%, and (3) suicide attempters with healthy patients with an accuracy of 86.7%. Just et al. [20] used the fMRI (functional magnetic resonance imaging) to measure the emotional segments in the neural networks in the brain. The authors used 17 suicide ideators and 17 control subjects. The main aim of this study was to measure brain activity and to distinguish between suicide attempters and non-attempters. They also measured the location and the intensity of responses and compared the data with the known emotional states. Their model achieved an accuracy of 91% with the Gaussian naive Bayes classifier. Cáceda et al. [21] explored acute suicidal behaviors rather than personality traits. The authors compared 10 recent suicidal attempters with 9 suicide ideators, 17 depressed non-suicidal patients, and 18 healthy control patients using rs-fcMRI (resting state-functional connectivity magnetic resonance imaging). They used the leave-one-outcross-validation approach because the sample size was not large enough for the train–test data approach. Their model achieved an accuracy of 78% on SVMs. Gosnell et al. [22] used both the rs-fMRI and rs-fcMRI. Their samples contained 63 suicidal and 65 non-suicidal in-patients. They leveraged random forest classification and got a ROC (receiver operating characteristics curve) of 0.72. Weng et al. [23] used machine learning that depends on structural MRI. Their samples contained 41 depressed patients with suicidal ideations, 54 depressive patients without suicidal ideations, and 58 healthy control patients. The authors used various types of machine learning models and achieved 85% prediction accuracy. Amini et al. [24] used the sample of Hamadan province, Iran from 2008 to 2010. Their samples contain 457 suicides among a cohort of 5,414 patients with suicide attempters. Their model achieved an AUC of 0.72 on SVMs and AUC of 0.75 on ANN (artificial neural networks). DelPozo-Banos et al. [25] used the database of health routine records in Welsh from 2001 to 2015. Their samples contain 2,604 suicides and 52,080 control patients. Their model achieved an AUC of 0.72 on ANN. Choi et al. [26] used the data of South Korea from 2004 to 2013. Their samples contain 2,546 suicide among a cohort of 81,9951 patients. Their model achieved an AUC of 0.69 on SVMs and AUC of 0.68 on DNN (deep neural networks). Gradus et al. [27] used the data of the Danish health department from 1995 to 2015. Their samples contain

10,152 male patients, 3,951 female patients, 130,591 male control patients, and 134,592 female control patients. The authors have used classification trees. They achieved an AUC of 0.72 for the men and for the women, their AUC was 0.88. Kessler et al. [28] used the model STARRS. Their samples contain the records of a total of 240 suicides among a cohort of 238,888 military veterans who were hospitalized from 2004 to 2009. The authors have used the naive Bayes, random forest, SVM, and elastic net-penalized regression. Their model achieved an overall AUC of 0.59. Kessler et al. [29] used the samples from 2009 to 2011 of the military veterans which consist of 6,360 suicides among a cohort of 2,112,008. The authors have used the penalized logistic regression and Bayesian additive regression tree. Their model has a 0.3% base suicide rate. The summary of the above-mentioned literature is presented in Table 11.1.

Table 11.1 Literature summary

Study	Machine learning algorithms	Model predictions
Passos et al. [12]	RVM (relevance vector machines)	Sensitivity: 70% Specificity: 70%
Kessler et al. [13]	Elastic net-penalized regression	Sensitivity: 70% Specificity: 70%
Ruderfer et al. [14]	Random forest algorithm	AUC (area under the curve): 0.94 Sensitivity: 0.92 Specificity: 0.82
Baca-Garcia et al. [15]	SVM (support vector machines)	Accuracy: 67% Sensitivity: 0.50 Specificity: 0.82
Kautzky et al. [16]	Random forest algorithm and k-means clustering	Accuracy: 50% Sensitivity: 25%
Setoyama et al. [17]	Random forest algorithm	AUC >0.7
Dargél et al. [18]	Random forest algorithm	Accuracy: 84.9% Sensitivity: 0.787 Specificity: 0.908
Bhak et al. [19]	Random forest algorithm	(1) SA versus MDD: Accuracy: 92.6% (2) MDD versus CS: Accuracy: 87.3% Sensitivity: 59% (3) SA versus CS: Accuracy: 86.7%. Sensitivity: 67.9%
Just et al. [20]	Gaussians naive Bayes classifiers	(1) SI versus CS: Accuracy: 91% Sensitivity: 0.88 Specificity: 0.94 (2) SI attempt versus SI non-attempt: Accuracy: 91% Sensitivity: 0.88 Specificity: 1

(Continued)

Table 11.1 Literature summary *(Continued)*

Study	Machine learning algorithms	Model predictions
Cáceda et al. [21]	SVM	SA versus SI: Mean AUC: 0.9 Mean accuracy: 0.788
Gosnell et al. [22]	Random forest classification	Testing sample: ROC (receiver operating characteristics curve): 0.84 Sensitivity: 0.79 Specificity: 0.72 Independent sample: ROC: 0.72 Sensitivity: 0.81 Specificity: 0.75
Weng et al. [23]	Unsupervised neural networks, supervised extreme gradient boosting and logistic regression	Accuracy: 85% Sensitivity: 75% Specificity: 100%
Amini et al. [24]	SVM and ANN (artificial neural networks)	SVM: AUC: 0.72 Sensitivity: 53% PPV (positive predictive value): 13.1% ANN: AUC: 0.75 Sensitivity: 75% PPV: 14.7%
DelPozo-Banos et al. [25]	ANN	AUC: 0.8 Sensitivity: 64.5% PPV: 14.3%
Choi et al. [26]	SVM and DNN	SVM: AUC: 0.69 DNN: AUC: 0.68
Gradus et al. [27]	Classification trees	Men: AUC: 0.80 Sensitivity: 32% PPV: 48% Women: AUC: 0.88 Sensitivity: 54.4% PPV: 31%
Kessler et al. [28]	Naive Bayes, random forest algorithms, SVM, and elastic net-penalized regression	AUC: 0.59 Sensitivity: 22.4% PPV: 0.4%
Kessler et al. [29]	Penalized logistic regression and Bayesian additive regression tree	Sensitivity: 2.7% PPV: 8.1%

CS: control group subject; MDD: major depressive disorder; SA: suicide attempter; SI: suicide ideation group.

This chapter makes the following novel contributions with respect to existing literature:

1. Mainly the SVM and random forest algorithms are used in most of the studies. We consider a wide range of other machine learning models that can also be used to attain better accuracies.
2. None of the researchers help in improving the clinical prediction rule because the samples that they used are smaller in size and most of the models have not attained a good prediction accuracy. We focus on population-level data and achieve higher accuracy.
3. Most approaches treat this as a classification problem, but suicidal tendencies are very subjective and depend on a lot of factors. It is not necessary for them to be black and white. Hence we have considered this problem to be a regression task, with a continuous variable conveying the risk of suicide for a person, using the national data as the benchmark.

In the next section, we will see the empirical study.

11.3 EMPIRICAL STUDY

To improve the performance of machine learning models, we have used both the traditional train–test approach with 80% data used as training set and 20% used as test-set and k-fold cross-validation, with the number of folds $(k) = 10$. The two metrics are used to evaluate the various types of machine learning models' performance by calculating their accuracy and RMSE (root mean square error). Also, a statistical test is conducted to test for the following two null hypotheses: male and female suicide rates do not differ and age and suicide rates are independent of each other. The machine learning models are implemented on Google Collaboratory on a PC with AMD E1-6010 APU 1.35 GHz to 4 GB RAM.

11.3.1 Datasets description

The suicide dataset is collectively made by the WHO, World Bank, and UNDP (United Nations Development Program) and is published on Kaggle. This is a compiled dataset from 1985 to 2016.

The following observations can be made after seeing the datasets:

1. It has 27,820 instances and 12 attributes.
2. It contains six different age categories: (i) 5–14 years, (ii) 15–24 years, (iii) 25–34 years, (iv) 35–54 years, (v) 55–74 years, and (vi) 75+ years.
3. *Country, year, gender, age_group, country-year,* and *generation* are the categorical features in the datasets.

4. *Suicide_count*, *population*, *suicide_rate*, *HDI for year*, *gdp_for_year*, and *gdp_per_capita* are numerical features in the datasets.
5. These datasets contain the records of 101 countries.

11.3.2 Data pre-processing

The data that is obtained from the repository has a chance that it can contain some missing values. These chances increase when the data is related to the healthcare field. Therefore, for building the models, a proper selection of attributes is important that is free from correlated variables, biases, and unwanted noise.

For this process, we have removed all the null values from the datasets as they can tamper with the performance of the models. For example, the column HDI for the year has 19,456 null values which are 70% of the data in the datasets. Also, the country-year column is the same as the country and year columns, respectively, so removing this column does not affect the model's performance.

11.4 MODEL BUILDING AND TRAINING

We build the machine learning models from the feature-label pairs, that hold our training set. The main aim of the models is to accurately predict new and unforeseen data. Machine learning algorithms are mainly of two types: (1) supervised learning and (2) unsupervised learning. This type of work is done by supervised learning as they can be used to predict the outcomes from a certain number of features given. Supervised learning is of two types generally: (1) classification and (2) regression. In classification, the task is to predict a class label that is a choice from a predefined list of possibilities, whereas in regression the task is to predict a continuous number. The datasets that we used come under the regression problems, as the prediction (suicide rate) is a continuous number.

Since our model can differentiate between the genders as well as the various age groups, the information of any patient can be used to determine his/her likeliness to be at risk for suicide. This suicide rate differs for different countries and as a result, our model can effectively predict the risk of a person belonging to a particular age group and gender, while accounting for the country they live in.

We have used two cross-validation techniques, namely the train–test holdout and the tenfold cross-validation. The train–test holdout method was used given the considerable number of instances or rows available in the given data, to get a quick overview of the model's performance. To leverage each input in the given dataset and to get a more comprehensively trained model, we also applied the tenfold cross-validation technique. The results of both of these techniques have been presented for each model in the following section.

11.4.1 *k*-Nearest neighbors (KNN)

This is the simplest algorithm that puts all available classes and predicts the numerical target that depends on similarity measures. Given any data point, the model searches for *k* of the closest training examples to the given instance in the dataset. Since this is a classification task, the object is classified by a vote of its *k* neighbors, i.e., it is assigned the class that is most frequent in the given neighbors.

The tuning of KNN regression is generally done by the hyperparameters *n_neighbors* and *weight*. This hyperparameter is tuned using GridSearchCV. The number of neighbors is finalized to be equal to 5 with a leaf size of 30, while the Minkowski metric is used for the distance.

The results of the KNN regression are listed in Tables 11.2 and 11.3. Figure 11.1 shows the training and testing set performance of different

Table *11.2* Computation results for train–test split k-nearest neighbors (KNN)

Data	Accuracy	RMSE
Training data	1.000	0.000
Testing data	0.812	0.536

Table *11.3* Computation results for tenfold cross-validation k-nearest neighbors (KNN)

Data	Average accuracy	Average RMSE
Tenfold CV	0.01	1.197

Observations: There is an inconsistency between the training and testing set of performance for *n_neighbors* <5, which is a clear sign of overfitting.

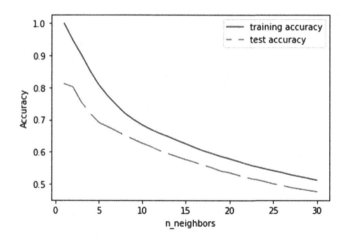

Figure *11.1* k-Nearest neighbors (KNN) model results for multiple *n_neighbors*.

Table 11.4 Computation results for train–test split-linear regression

Data	Accuracy	RMSE
Training data	0.288	1.013
Testing data	0.296	1.037

Table 11.5 Computation results for tenfold cross-validation linear regression

Data	Average accuracy	RMSE
Tenfold CV	0.230	1.021

Observations: The scores of the training and testing set are very close to each other and are quite low. This means that the model has been underfitted.

numbers of *n_neighbors* ranging from 1 to 30 with uniform *weight*. Accuracy throughout this chapter refers to the r^2 score for regression.

11.4.2 Linear regression

This is the classic regression method. It minimizes the RMSE by finding the parameters w and b on the training set. It assumes there to be a linear relationship between the inputs and the target variable. The model then attempts to form a line to the given input data that most accurately predicts the target variable. This line is further extrapolated to predict values for unseen data points.

This model does not require any tuning as there are no hyperparameters available. Therefore, an underfitting problem occurs in this model. The results of linear regression are listed in Tables 11.4 and 11.5.

11.4.3 Decision trees: Regression

They are widely used to solve classification and regression problems. Generally, it consists of if–else questions that lead to a decision. In machine learning, these if–else questions are termed possible tests. We used these possible tests to find the target variable.

The mean squared error (MSE) function is being used to measure the quality of a split. To avoid overfitting, we limit the maximum depth of the trees to 9.

The results of decision trees – regression are listed in Tables 11.6 and 11.7. Figure 11.2 shows the training and testing set performance of different numbers of *max_depth* ranging from 1 to 30.

11.4.4 Random forest: Ensemble of regression trees

Random forest is an ensemble that uses several decision trees to make a prediction. The predictions of each of the individual trees are collected and they

Table 11.6 Computation results for train–test split-decision trees: Regression

Data	Accuracy	RMSE
Training data	0.967	0.220
Testing data	0.951	0.272

Table 11.7 Computation results for tenfold cross-validation decision tree: Regression

Data	Average accuracy	RMSE
Tenfold CV	0.890	0.379

Observations: By increasing the max_depth parameter, the performance of the model gradually increased. When the max_depth >9, then overfitting occurs. Overall, this model has achieved 95.6% accuracy.

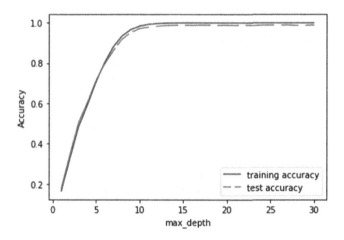

Figure 11.2 Decision trees: Regression model results for multiple max_depth.

are combined (for example, averaged) to get the final prediction of the ensemble. Each of the trees is distinct and has varying hyperparameters. Moreover, the trees are independent, i.e., they have a very low correlation and they are built-in parallel. Since a large number of trees can be used to cover up for faulty predictions from a few of the given trees, they are more effective than a single decision tree.

The number of trees has been set equal to 100, with the MSE function being used to measure the quality of a split. To avoid overfitting, we limit the maximum depth of the trees to 9.

The results of random forest – ensemble of regression trees are listed in Tables 11.8 and 11.9. Figure 11.3 shows the training and testing set performance of different numbers of *max_depth* ranging from 1 to 30.

Table 11.8 Computation results for train–test split-random forest:
Ensemble of regression trees

Data	Accuracy	RMSE
Training data	0.987	0.139
Testing data	0.980	0.176

Table 11.9 Computation results for tenfold cross-validation random
forest

Data	Average accuracy	RMSE
Tenfold CV	0.929	0.300

Observations: This model achieved an accuracy of 99.4% without tuning any
parameters. But this might be due to the overfitting. Therefore, by tuning the
hyperparameters – n_estimators and max_depth – using GridSearchCV, the
model achieved an accuracy of 98% which is still better than the previous model.

11.4.5 Gradient boosting: Ensemble of regression trees

Gradient boosted trees is another ensemble method, just like the random for-
ests, that combines several weak learners (i.e., decision trees) to create the
final model. Unlike the random forest, this works by building the trees in a
serial manner, where every tree corrects the mistake of the previous trees.
Since these trees complement each other, GBT usually outperforms random
forest on proper tuning. However, they are more prone to overfitting and are
often difficult to tune properly.

We have set the value of n_estimators = 100, with a learning rate of 0.5.
The least-squares regression is selected as the loss function to be optimized.

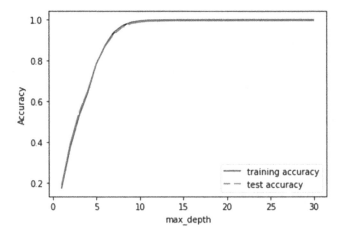

Figure 11.3 Random forest: Ensemble of regression trees model results for multiple max_depth.

Table 11.10 Computation results for the gradient boosting: Ensemble of regression trees

Data	Accuracy	RMSE
Training data	0.988	0.130
Testing data	0.983	0.159

Table 11.11 Computation results for tenfold cross-validation gradient boosting: Ensemble of regression trees

Data	Average accuracy	RMSE
Tenfold CV	0.956	0.231

Observations: This model achieved an accuracy of 94.3% without tuning the parameters. This model did not show signs of overfitting. The tuned parameters are *learning_rate*, *n_estimators*, and *max_depth*. But the model performance did not change after tuning the parameters. Therefore, only *learning_rate* and *max_depth* are tuned and the default value is taken for *n_estimators*. Now, this model achieved an accuracy of 99.2%.

The Friedman MSE (friedman_mse) function is being used to measure the quality of a split. The maximum depth for each tree is equal to 3 to avoid overfitting.

The results of gradient boosting – ensemble of regression trees are listed in Tables 11.10 and 11.11. Figure 11.4 shows the training and testing set performance of different numbers of *learning_rate* ranging from 0.1 to 0.9.

11.4.6 MLP: Deep learning

They are also known as feed-neural networks(vanilla) or simply as neural networks. This can be applied to both classification and regression problems. It consists of at least three layers, each containing one or more nodes, namely,

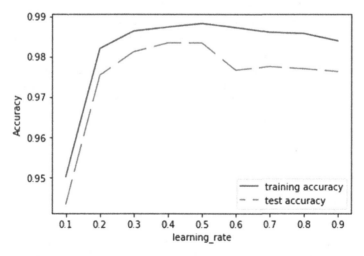

Figure 11.4 Gradient boosting: Ensemble of decision trees model results for multiple *learning_rate*.

Table 11.12 Computation results for the MLP: Deep learning

Data	Accuracy	RMSE
Training data	0.922	0.336
Testing data	0.922	0.345

Table 11.13 Computation results for tenfold cross-validation MLP

Data	Average accuracy	RMSE
Tenfold CV	0.792	0.456

Observations: The model achieved an accuracy of 89.2% when the model is trained without tuning the parameters. The model did not overfit. A hyperparameter tuning is also performed on the model by tuning the *number of hidden layers*, *hidden_units* in each layer, and the *alpha*. Now the model achieved an accuracy of 92.8%.

the input, hidden, and output layers. The number of hidden layers can be varied in each model. Each node except the ones in the input layer uses a non-linear activation function such as the rectified linear unit (ReLU) or the Tanh functions. The weights or the values of these nodes are updated at the end of each iteration using a method called backpropagation.

We have used two hidden layers, each with 100 nodes in the developed MLP. The ReLU activation function is used along with a constant learning rate of 0.001 and the Adam optimizer.

The results of MLP – deep learning are listed in Tables 11.12 and 11.13.

11.4.7 XGBoost regression

Recently, the XGBoost algorithm has become very popular among researchers. XGBoost stands for eXtreme gradient boosting. This algorithm comes from the gradient boosting of decision trees which is designed for speed and performance. This is an ensemble tree method that uses the gradient descent architecture by applying the principle of boosting weak learners.

The value of *n_estimators* is equal to 100 and the *learning_rate* = 0.2. The *max_depth* for each tree is set to 4. The results of the XGBoost Regression are listed in Tables 11.14 and 11.15. Figure 11.5 shows the training and testing set performance.

Table 11.16 shows the comparison between the various types of models that we have discussed above.

Table 11.14 Computation results for the XGBoost regression

Data	Accuracy	RMSE
Training data	0.993	0.100
Testing data	0.988	0.134

Table 11.15 Computation results for tenfold cross-validation XGBoost regression

Data	Average accuracy	RMSE
Tenfold CV	0.963	0.214

Observations: Upon tuning the hyperparameters, the model performance gradually increased and the model achieved an accuracy of 98.8%.

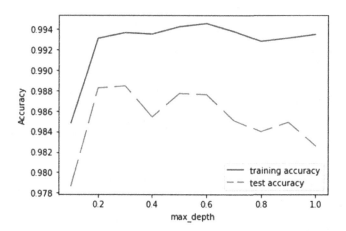

Figure 11.5 XGBoost regression model results for multiple *max_depth*.

Table 11.16 Model comparison among various types of machine learning models

Machine learning models	Train accuracy	Test accuracy	Train RMSE	Test RMSE	Tenfold CV accuracy	Tenfold CV RMSE
KNN	1.000	0.812	0.000	0.536	0.01	1.197
Linear regression	0.288	0.296	1.013	1.037	0.230	1.021
Decision tree	0.967	0.951	0.220	0.272	0.890	0.379
Random forest	0.987	0.980	0.139	0.176	0.929	0.300
Gradient boosting regression	0.988	0.983	0.130	0.159	0.956	0.231
Multilayer perceptron	0.922	0.922	0.336	0.345	0.792	0.456
XGBoost regression	0.993	0.988	0.100	0.134	0.963	0.214

11.5 STATISTICAL TEST

Statistical tests can be used for hypothesis testing. These tests are used for the following reasons:

1. To determine whether there exists a relationship between the predictor variable and the outcome variable
2. To determine the difference between two or more groups

They assume the null hypothesis of no relationships or no difference between the groups. After this, they observed the data that fall outside the range of values predicted by the null hypothesis. The following tests are done on the suicide dataset [11]:

1. *t-Test:* Male and female suicide rates
2. *Chi-squared Test:* Age and suicide rates

11.5.1 t-Test: Male and female suicide rates

We used the *t*-test to check the difference between the suicide rates of males and females. The two hypothesis statements are constructed:

- H_0: When there is no difference between the suicide rates of males and females (null)
- H_1: When there is a difference between the suicide rates of males and females (alternate)

If the obtained *p*-value is less than the significance level (0.05), then reject the null hypothesis, as shown in Figure 11.6.

Test Conclusion: On performing the *t*-test, the result obtained is to reject the null hypothesis. This means there is a difference between the suicide rates of males and females, as shown in Figure 11.7.

11.5.2 Chi-squared test: Age and suicide rates

We used the chi-squared test to check the difference between the suicide rates on age groups. The two hypothesis statements are constructed:

- H_0: Suicide rate and age groups are independent (null).
- H_1: Suicide rate and age groups are dependent (alternate).

The significance level is set to 0.05. Then the critical value is calculated which is 26,864; 70 is obtained. After this, the comparison is done between

```
[ ]   1 #calculating p value
      2 ttest,pval = stats.ttest_rel(male, female)
      3
      4 if pval<0.05:
      5     print("Reject null hypothesis")
      6 else:
      7     print("Accept null hypothesis")

   Reject null hypothesis
```

Figure 11.6 Code snippet of *t*-test.

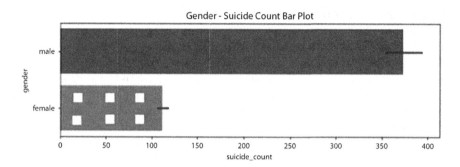

Figure 11.7 Suicide rate grouped by gender.

the *chi_square_statistic* with *critical_value* and *p*-value. The probability of getting *chi_square* is greater than 0.09 (*chi_square_statistic*). Figure 11.8 shows obtained results of the chi-squared test – age and suicide rates.

Test Conclusion: On performing the chi-squared test, the result obtained is to reject the null hypothesis. This means there is a dependency between age groups and suicide rate, as shown in Figure 11.9. The age group 35–54 years has a higher rate of suicide compared to other age groups.

```
[ ]   1  #compare chi_square_statistic with critical_value and p-value which is the
      2  #probability of getting chi-square>0.09 (chi_square_statistic)
      3  if chistat>=critical_value:
      4      print("Reject H0,There is a dependency between Age group & Suicide rate.")
      5  else:
      6      print("Retain H0,There is no relationship between Age group & Suicide rate.")
      7
      8  if p<=alpha:
      9      print("Reject H0,There is a dependency between Age group & Suicide rate.")
     10  else:
     11      print("Retain H0,There is no relationship between Age group & Suicide rate.")

Reject H0,There is a dependency between Age group & Suicide rate.
Reject H0,There is a dependency between Age group & Suicide rate.
```

Figure 11.8 Code snippet of chi-squared test: Age and suicide rates.

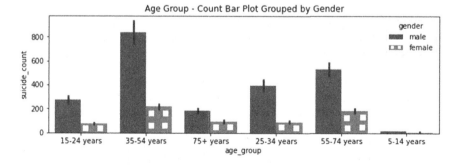

Figure 11.9 Suicide count grouped by age.

11.6 CONCLUSION

This chapter addresses the issue of suicidal risk in the healthcare industry. Traditional clinical prediction rules are better when the patients have less complex psychological and medical comorbidities. We have used various types of machine learning models on the suicide dataset to predict suicidal risk. These predictive models can help to improve the clinical predictions rule and help the mental healthcare provider in dealing the suicidal patients. These models can handle the highly complex dimensional data that can help in aiding the prognosis and diagnosis process. In addition, machine learning approaches are cost-effective and noninvasive. Therefore, machine learning approaches can be considered a potential complementary tool for researchers and mental healthcare providers. We have used various types of machine learning models, among them XGBoost outperforms the rest and attains a good result.

The medical and research community face several challenges when predicting the risk of suicidal tendencies, despite that machine learning holds the potential to improve detection and understanding of suicidal ideation and behavior. We believe that machine learning approaches will allow us to determine the important networks of molecular biomarkers that can be seen as a part of diagnosis, treatment, and monitoring of psychiatry patients, which enables a new era of precise and personalized medicine.

REFERENCES

1. S. J. Wolf, T. R. McCubbin, K. M. Feldhaus, J. P. Faragher, and D. M. Adcock, "Prospective validation of wells criteria in the evaluation of patients with suspected pulmonary embolism," *Annals of Emergency Medicine*, vol. 44, no. 5, pp. 503–510, 2004. doi: 10.1016/j.annemergmed.2004.04.002
2. C. Keogh, E. Wallace, C. Dillon, B. D. Dimitrov, and T. Fahey, "Validation of the CHADS2 clinical prediction rule to predict ischaemic stroke: A systematic review and meta-analysis," *Thrombosis and Haemostasis*, vol. 106, no. 3, pp. 528–538, 2011. doi: 10.1160/TH11-02-0061
3. S. T. Adams and S. H. Leveson, "Clinical prediction rules," *BMJ*, vol. 344, no. 7842, 2012. doi: 10.1136/bmj.d8312
4. M. Large, M. Kaneson, N. Myles, H. Myles, P. Gunaratne, and C. Ryan, "Meta-analysis of longitudinal cohort studies of suicide risk assessment among psychiatric patients: Heterogeneity in results and lack of improvement over time," *PLoS One*, vol. 11, no. 6, p. e0156322, 2016. doi: 10.1371/journal.pone.0156322
5. H. D. Nelson et al., "Systematic review of suicide prevention in veterans," *VA Evidence-based Synthesis Program Reports*, 2015. Available at https://pubmed.ncbi.nlm.nih.gov/27631045/ (accessed December 25, 2021).
6. M. K. Y. Chan et al., "Predicting suicide following self-harm: Systematic review of risk factors and risk scales," *British Journal of Psychiatry*, vol. 209, no. 4, pp. 277–283, 2016. doi: 10.1192/bjp.bp.115.170050
7. J. D. Ribeiro et al., "Self-injurious thoughts and behaviors as risk factors for future suicide ideation, attempts, and death: A meta-analysis of longitudinal studies," *Psychological Medicine*, vol. 46, no. 2, pp. 225–236, 2016. doi: 10.1017/S0033291715001804

8. K. Posner et al., "The Columbia-suicide severity rating scale: Initial validity and internal consistency findings from three multisite studies with adolescents and adults," *American Journal of Psychiatry*, vol. 168, no. 12, pp. 1266–1277, 2011. doi: 10.1176/appi.ajp.2011.10111704

9. J. D. Ribeiro et al., "Letter to the editor: Suicide as a complex classification problem: Machine learning and related techniques can advance suicide prediction – A reply to Roaldset (2016)," *Psychological Medicine*, vol. 46, no. 9, pp. 2009–2010, 2016. doi: 10.1017/S0033291716000611

10. R. C. Kessler, "Clinical epidemiological research on suicide-related behaviors: Where we are and where we need to go," *JAMA Psychiatry*, vol. 76, no. 8, pp. 777–778, 2019. doi: 10.1001/jamapsychiatry.2019.1238

11. Rusty, "Suicide Rates Overview 1985 to 2016," 2018. https://www.kaggle.com/russellyates88/suicide-rates-overview-1985-to-2016 (accessed December 25, 2021).

12. I. C. Passos et al., "Identifying a clinical signature of suicidality among patients with mood disorders: A pilot study using a machine learning approach," *Journal of Affective Disorders*, vol. 193, pp. 109–116, 2016. doi: 10.1016/j.jad.2015.12.066

13. R. C. Kessler et al., "Predicting suicides after psychiatric hospitalization in US army soldiers: The army study to assess risk and resilience in servicemembers (Army STARRS)," *JAMA Psychiatry*, vol. 72, no. 1, pp. 49–57, 2015. doi: 10.1001/jamapsychiatry.2014.1754

14. D. M. Ruderfer et al., "Significant shared heritability underlies suicide attempt and clinically predicted probability of attempting suicide," *Molecular Psychiatry*, vol. 25, no. 10, pp. 2422–2430, 2020. doi: 10.1101/266411

15. E. Baca-Garcia et al., "Nucleotide variation in central nervous system genes among male suicide attempters," *American Journal of Medical Genetics, Part B: Neuropsychiatric Genetics*, vol. 153, no. 1, pp. 208–213, 2010. doi: 10.1002/ajmg.b.30975

16. A. Kautzky et al., "The combined effect of genetic polymorphisms and clinical parameters on treatment outcome in treatment-resistant depression," *European Neuropsychopharmacology*, vol. 25, no. 4, pp. 441–453, 2015. doi: 10.1016/j.euroneuro.2015.01.001

17. D. Setoyama et al., "Plasma metabolites predict severity of depression and suicidal ideation in psychiatric patients: A multicenter pilot analysis," *PLoS ONE*, vol. 11, no. 12, p. e0165267, 2016. doi: 10.1371/journal.pone.0165267

18. A. A. Dargél et al., "Emotional hyper-reactivity and cardiometabolic risk in remitted bipolar patients: A machine learning approach," *Acta Psychiatrica Scandinavica*, vol. 138, no. 4, pp. 348–359, 2018. doi: 10.1111/acps.12901

19. Y. Bhak et al., "Depression and suicide risk prediction models using blood-derived multi-omics data," *Translational Psychiatry*, vol. 9, no. 1, pp. 1–8, 2019. doi: 10.1038/s41398-019-0595-2

20. M. A. Just et al., "Machine learning of neural representations of suicide and emotion concepts identifies suicidal youth," *Nature Human Behaviour*, vol. 1, no. 12, pp. 911–919, 2017. doi: 10.1038/s41562-017-0234-y

21. R. Cáceda, K. Bush, G. Andrew James, Z. N. Stowe, and C. D. Kilts, "Modes of resting functional brain organization differentiate suicidal thoughts and actions: A preliminary study," *Journal of Clinical Psychiatry*, vol. 79, no. 4, p. 2078, 2018. doi: 10.4088/JCP.17m11901

22. S. N. Gosnell, J. C. Fowler, and R. Salas, "Classifying suicidal behavior with resting-state functional connectivity and structural neuroimaging," *Acta Psychiatrica Scandinavica*, vol. 140, no. 1, pp. 20–29, 2019. doi: 10.1111/acps.13029

23. J. C. Weng, T. Y. Lin, Y. H. Tsai, M. T. Cheok, Y. P. E. Chang, and V. C. H. Chen, "An autoencoder and machine learning model to predict suicidal ideation with brain structural imaging," *Journal of Clinical Medicine*, vol. 9, no. 3, p. 658, 2020. doi: 10.3390/jcm9030658

24. P. Amini, H. Ahmadinia, J. Poorolajal, and M. Moqaddasi Amiri, "Evaluating the high risk groups for suicide: A comparison of logistic regression, support vector machine, decision tree and artificial neural network," *Iranian Journal of Public Health*, vol. 45, no. 9, pp. 1179–1187, 2016.

25. M. DelPozo-Banos et al., "Using neural networks with routine health records to identify suicide risk: Feasibility study," *JMIR Mental Health*, vol. 5, no. 2, p. e10144, 2018. doi: 10.2196/10144

26. S. B. Choi, W. Lee, J. H. Yoon, J. U. Won, and D. W. Kim, "Ten-year prediction of suicide death using Cox regression and machine learning in a nationwide retrospective cohort study in South Korea," *Journal of Affective Disorders*, vol. 231, pp. 8–14, 2018, doi: 10.1016/j.jad.2018.01.019

27. J. L. Gradus et al., "Prediction of sex-specific suicide risk using machine learning and single-payer health care registry data from Denmark," *JAMA Psychiatry*, vol. 77, no. 1, pp. 25–34, 2020. doi: 10.1001/jamapsychiatry.2019.2905

28. R. C. Kessler et al., "Predicting suicides after outpatient mental health visits in the army study to assess risk and resilience in servicemembers (Army STARRS)," *Molecular Psychiatry*, vol. 22, no. 4, pp. 544–551, 2017. doi: 10.1038/mp.2016.110

29. R. C. Kessler et al., "Developing a practical suicide risk prediction model for targeting high-risk patients in the Veterans health Administration," *International Journal of Methods in Psychiatric Research*, vol. 26, no. 3, p. e1575, 2017. doi: 10.1002/mpr.1575

Chapter 12

Information extraction and summarization of medical reports using Textract and GPT-2

Pratik Kanani, Tanay Gandhi, Yash Jhaveri, and Varun Mehta

12.1 INTRODUCTION

Healthcare is a significant subject to study across the world since it has a substantial impact on citizens' development and well-being. The healthcare system is critical in India, which is a massive country with a booming population. A country's healthcare system represents the amount of development and care offered to its population. There are, however, considerable variations in the quality and accessibility of healthcare services in India's urban and rural areas. Hospitals and clinics are easily accessible in India's metropolitan centers, and individuals have access to a variety of healthcare facilities. Urban medical infrastructure is better able to handle emergencies and provide specialized care. Yet, rural India, where a sizable proportion of the population resides, suffers from a serious lack of healthcare institutions and amenities. A lack of medical infrastructure in rural regions has resulted in a considerable portion of the population having insufficient access to healthcare services. Rural communities confront access issues to healthcare services due to a lack of basic medical infrastructure, a paucity of medical experts, a dearth of drugs and equipment, and poor transportation facilities. Furthermore, because of a lack of knowledge and education, individuals in rural regions are frequently uninformed of their rights and entitlements to healthcare services, exacerbating the issue. Further, while the majority of the Indian population live in rural areas, only 40% of the country's healthcare services are easily accessible to them [1]. This causes a load on these rural healthcare services and leads to people traveling over long distances. This creates a huge gap in the healthcare system of India, which needs to be looked into.

Medical tests and blood reports are critical in the diagnosis and treatment of a variety of disorders. Pathology laboratories do these tests to diagnose the ailment from which a patient is suffering. Blood tests are one of the most popular medical tests used to detect abnormalities in the levels of medical entities such as red blood cells, white blood cells, platelets, glucose, cholesterol, and other vital body components. The findings of these tests are essential indications of the patient's health and assist doctors in making appropriate treatment decisions. Despite their importance, medical reports can be difficult for the general public to grasp due to the complicated language and medical jargon utilized in these reports. Patients and their families may experience confusion, anxiety, and fear as a result of this lack of knowledge. According to the survey conducted by Max Super Specialty Hospital, Delhi, in 2020, it was discovered that approximately 70% of patients had trouble comprehending their diagnostic records [2]. To guarantee that people understand their medical status, the severity of the disease, and the treatment plan, healthcare professionals must explain the reports in simple words. Patients will be able to take an active role in their healthcare and make educated decisions about their treatment options as a result of this.

To tackle this problem, this chapter proposes a system which automatically parses and extracts important information from medical reports and highlights the deficiencies or excess of medical entities. The system extracts essential information from structured medical diagnosis reports and matches them with a custom-built lexicon of medical entities using OCR (optical character recognition) methods supplied by AWS Textract. Natural language processing (NLP) approaches are then used to generate a report summary based on the retrieved data, offering basic insights into the report. Users merely need to upload their medical reports to this system, and the system will offer them a summary of the report as well as natural cures based on the report's results. By making medical reports easier to read, this approach has the potential to enhance healthcare outcomes by empowering individuals to better understand their diseases and take necessary measures.

12.2 LITERATURE SURVEY

OCR can be used to transform physical copy reports into editable text information. Qader and Ameen [3] propose a diagnosis of the illness using the results of medical checks. They suggest the aforementioned technique, the Bag of Words (BOW) model for feature selection, and classification algorithms for disease prediction. SVM, naive Bayes, decision tree, and KNN algorithms were among the numerous classification algorithms utilized, and they obtained the best accuracy when combined with Adaboost and naive Bayes. The additional feature proposed by the chapter is presenting the predicted disease's actual image for patients not familiar with medical terms to help patients exactly understand the problem. The approach taken by the authors is to extract features like heart rate, hypertension, diabetes mellitus, etc. from the reports and based on these feature values, they predict the disease. They have mainly used three datasets related to heart, kidney, and thoracic data with an average of 450 data rows. The authors have received a maximum accuracy of about 97.9% after employing BOW and Adaboost. Though the work presented by the authors is accurate enough and commendable, there are a few drawbacks. The chapter only targets certain types of reports and only a few of the features or attributes of the report. Another drawback includes the dataset size to build the classifier is comparatively small which may not give the best accuracies in the long run. Finally, since the classifier is built specifically only on three diseases, it restricts the scope of use: undertaking an extensive analysis utilizing a bigger, more varied dataset. Additionally, evaluating the performance of the OCR technology and algorithms for precise disease detection is required by contrasting the proposed strategy with current approaches and using the right assessment criteria.

A document image processing method to extract information from medical reports is proposed by Xue et al. [4]. They use the segmentation approach where they use the top-down pipeline to segment the table areas and the text. Table lines are also picked up as a crucial localization cue. After segmentation, they look for text which may include Arabic numbers, mathematical symbols, and multilingual characters in these segments. The authors use various CNN-based and sequence model algorithms with the best accuracy of 92.3% provided by the RCNN model. The authors also provide a public dataset of 357 images of Chinese medical reports. The suggested system's main flaw is that it does not adequately depict the relationship between the texts within a single document table, which must be done in order to turn an image or PDF file into a source of data that can be edited. For medical laboratory report analysis and information extraction, the model lacks emphasis. Therefore, methods for table analysis and information extraction from medical laboratory data need to be developed. To precisely extract pertinent information from tabular data, investigate techniques like table recognition, structure extraction, and semantic comprehension.

Transformer models, for instance, Bidirectional Encoder Representations from Transformers (BERT), can be trained on report data to tackle the problem of text summarization. Vinod et al. [5] propose a strategy to be put forth for training the BERTSUMEXT, a model for summarizing based on BERT, on clinical report summarization datasets in an effort to boost the model's performance, particularly in the medical field. The approach is based on converting the medical report into a text file using OCR and then into a JSON file. After this, the authors modify the existing models of BERTSUM and apply cross-validation techniques to record the performance on the summarization task. The main issue the author of this paper encountered was the BERTSUMEXT model's insufficient exploration for clinical report summary. Therefore, extensive research is being done on optimizing the BERTSUMEXT model, specifically for the summarizing of clinical report. It is recommended that this research concentrate on strengthening the model's performance, addressing issues with clinical reports, and comparing its efficiency to currently used summarizing techniques.

A similar methodology was proposed by Karthikeyan et al. [6] who proposed to fill in the missing gaps and reduce the word error rate in the raw data obtained from medical reports. The reports when transformed into raw data using OCR may not be complete and may contain some missing words which the authors tackle with the use of deep neural networks and RoBERTa models, i.e., the authors propose a post-processing step after OCR which aids in making the text extracted to be more robust and accurately captured. They test their model on UK NHS medical reports dataset and MiBio dataset and provide good results in the reduction of the average WER and CER score. The drawback of the paper is that though the proposed system reduces the average WER and CER score, which are still considered to be high and hence need to be reduced since it is related to the medical domain where a high accuracy is required. OCR post-correction methods for medical records employing deep learning are likewise not given enough attention. Therefore, it is necessary to create reliable OCR post-correction methods that are especially suited for medical reports employing deep learning techniques. It is necessary to look at techniques that can efficiently fix OCR mistakes, enhance recognition accuracy, and guarantee the dependability of retrieved information for medical applications.

Hamad and Kaya [7] provide us with a review of OCR technology. They go on to explain the various phases involved in OCR, the challenges that might emerge during these phases, the developments and applications of OCR, and the history of OCR. The paper discusses the impact of OCR in healthcare and how it is useful for doctors and hospitals. Medical service experts need to continuously manage large amounts of patient documents but with the help of OCR, these documents can be transformed to be stored into an electronic database where they can be managed and easily accessed. The paper's shortcomings, which seems outmoded, is its limited consideration of OCR technology. The suggested approach calls for performing a thorough investigation of OCR technology, which should include a look at various OCR algorithms, performance assessment, accuracy rate comparison, and identification of potential issues. This study will provide a thorough understanding of OCR technology, especially as it relates to healthcare.

Alternatively, Uchimoto et al. [8] have suggested a way for creating sentences using keywords or headwords. They provide a strategy that is split into two components: the creation and assessment of candidate texts. In the creation phase, dependency trees are created by generating natural text sentences employing complementary information and other functional terms. When a keyword is provided, the evaluation component is employed to produce an acceptable text. The suggested model takes into account n-gram data and word dependence data. The model lacks studies on keyword-based text generation for medical reports. Investigate text generation techniques that can produce text from medical terms that is logical and contextually suitable in order to fill this gap. To produce meaningful and reliable content based on keyword input, methods like deep learning–based approaches and natural language generation should be investigated.

Long short-term memory (LSTM)–based architecture can also be used for creating phrases in order to correct the grammatical structure of medical reports. Das et al. [9] have created a similar technique for creating phrases that adhere to the correct grammatical structure. The paper describes the

LSTM architecture-based sentence creation system. After each repetition, the system generates a new set of words. When compared to other ways, this process ultimately produces meaningful words to create sentences or passages that are quite convincing. The insufficient investigation of sentence generation for medical reports using LSTM-based deep learning constitutes the research gap identified in this work. The suggested remedy is for LSTM-based deep learning approaches to be used in research on sentence generation specifically targeted for medical reports. Since medical reports have a specific vocabulary and structure, research should concentrate on creating models that can produce sentences that are grammatically correct and contextually appropriate.

A deep learning–based technique for text content extraction from photos of divided medical laboratory reports is provided by Xue et al. [10]. The first step is to use a patch-based training technique to create a set of bounding boxes containing text over an image of a medical test report. For text recognition, shallow and deep neural network layers are also employed. The proposed model obtains a precision of 98.6% and a recall of 99.5%. The detection and recognition of text in images of medical laboratory reports has received little focus. It is advised to create deep learning–based methods specifically for text identification and recognition in images of medical laboratory report to close this gap. To properly extract text from photos, methods like object detection, OCR, and sequence recognition should be researched.

Another workable method for extracting structured data from printed medical records that have been captured by smartphones has been proposed by Li et al. [11]. An OCR pipeline is used to recognize text in a document photo. This pipeline addresses the problems of low image quality and content complexity through image pre-processing and the establishment of several OCR engines. A collection of annotation techniques that offer customizable layouts are then used to establish the document type, entities of interest, and entity correlations, from which a structured PHR document is generated. Lack of research on creating organized personal health records from images of printed medical records is one issue. It is necessary to look for ways to automatically extract and organize pertinent data from images of printed medical records. Develop methods that can correctly categorize and arrange important medical data, allowing for the production of structured personal health records from such images.

Additionally, OpenAI GPT-2 Model can be trained to generate lengthy phrases and articles. This aforementioned work has been taken up by Qu et al. [12] using two fresh corpora before doing a comparative analysis. They used the BERT model to fulfill the task of context-based prediction of intermediate words concurrently. They employed different corpora to pretrain the model, then used it to perform the long-sentence production, and masked word generation prediction tasks. The former primarily create sentences by looping down from the start-word, whereas the latter bases its creation of intermediate words on the surrounding words. Therefore, research is being done on novel corpora specifically for medical applications using pretraining approaches like BERT and GPT-2. It is necessary to create text generation and prediction systems that are tailored to medical data in order to produce accurate and contextually appropriate text outputs.

A similar OCR methodology is proposed by Sirriani et al. [13] who examine the application of generative pretrained transformer models (GPT) to dental and clinical notes for the purpose of text prediction and recommendation. In order to prescribe the appropriate course of action based on the patient's medical history, the authors set out to develop a system that could synthesize dental medical records. The authors collected a large dataset of dental medical notes and fine-tuned different GPT models using a sequence-to-sequence approach. These models can be improved by adjusting them on a sizable dataset of dental medical notes, incorporating domain-specific knowledge, and comparing their performance to industry standards or feedback from experts.

On the other hand, Gifu [14] has explored the use of AI-backed OCR technology in healthcare to improve the digitization and management of patient data. The study outlines an approach for training OCR models using transfer learning to accurately extract and digitize data from medical records. The authors in the paper suggest that AI-backed OCR can improve healthcare data management efficiency and accuracy and can potentially lead to faster and more accurate diagnosis and better patient outcomes. However, the authors also acknowledge ethical and legal concerns related to patient data privacy and security. The analysis of healthcare AI-powered OCR is out dated. Updating the assessment to reflect more recent developments in AI-supported OCR in the medical field is required.

12.3 RESEARCH GAP

The need for extracting information and the use of various methods to do so are implemented in References [4–6, 8, 11, 12]. However, most of these papers are only limited to extracting information from medical reports by methods like OCR. Therefore, we have made an effort to close this gap by utilizing AWS Textract to solve OCR difficulties by making use of its sophisticated machine learning algorithms, table extraction capabilities, handwriting recognition, document understanding features, and interaction with other AWS services. This could improve the precision, effectiveness, and usefulness of OCR procedures, ultimately assisting with research projects in many different fields, such as healthcare and medical text analysis. Since English is the most widely spoken language in the world and papers like [4, 10–12] are primarily concerned with information extraction from Chinese reports, we have attempted to apply our approach specifically to the English language. The paper [7] uses the extracted data to make a dataset to predict specific types of diseases. These methodologies, along with the text generation and summarization techniques proposed by [8, 9], have motivated us to combine the two concepts and provide a system which not only extracts information from the medical reports but also summarizes the reports in simple terms for better understanding. Converting images of medical reports has been taken into focus using various OCR techniques and tools that can provide valuable information on complex medical terms and help the layman understand the gist of the report. The study [13] focused on dental medical notes, but the results may not generalize to other medical domains. The dataset used was limited to a single source, and the authors did not compare their approach with other existing NLP methods. This study [14] focuses on using OCR for digitizing and managing patient data from medical records, but further research is needed to explore the use of AI-backed OCR technology in other areas of healthcare. It does not address potential challenges and limitations of the technology, such as low recognition accuracy of handwritten text or errors caused by poor image quality. Additionally, the paper does not address the potential impact of OCR on the workflow and user experience of healthcare professionals. Future research can help progress medical report OCR technology by filling in these research gaps, which will enhance the systems' precision, interpretability, and usability in clinical settings.

12.4 METHODOLOGY

The three major stages required in the proposed system are as follows:

A. Text is extracted using *OCR* and data from the medical reports
B. *Medical Dictionary*, which consists of various probable medical terms used for mapping
C. *Report Summarizer*, which is used for generating a summary from the anomalies detected

These aforementioned stages work together to extract relevant information from medical documents and generate concise summaries. This streamlines the analysis of medical reports, enabling healthcare professionals to quickly grasp essential details and make informed decisions based on the summarized information. Figure 12.1 provides a synopsis for the stages required in the proposed system consisting of Text Extraction using OCR, Medical Dictionary, and Report Summarizer.

12.4.1 OCR

OCR is a technique that converts scanned pictures or handwritten text into machine-readable text that computers can process and analyze. In the medical field, OCR is often used to extract information from medical records, such as patient charts and prescriptions. OCR technology can quickly process large amounts of data, improve accuracy, and integrate data from different sources and formats to help analyze medical data and identify patterns and trends.

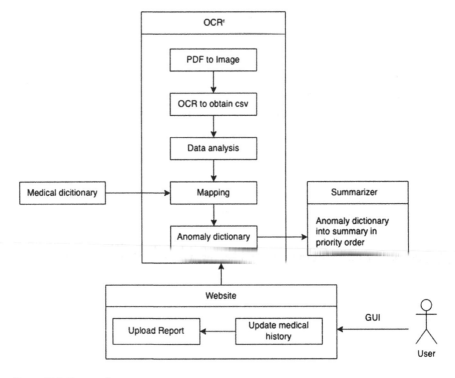

Figure 12.1 System flow.

The steps involved in OCR are as follows:

a. **Image pre-processing**

The image pre-processing stage involves several mathematical operations, such as image binarization, noise reduction, and image segmentation. One example of an equation used in image binarization is Otsu's
method, which automatically determines the threshold value to convert
a grayscale image to a binary image:

$$T = \operatorname{argmax}(t)\left\{\sigma^2 b(t)\sigma^2 w(t)\right\}$$

where T is the threshold value and $\sigma^2 b(t)$ and $\sigma^2 w(t)$ are the variances of
the pixel intensities in the foreground and background regions, respectively, at a threshold value of t.

b. **Text detection**

Text detection involves identifying the regions of the image that contain text. One approach to text detection is using a sliding window and
a classifier to determine whether each window contains text or not. The
classifier can be trained using a machine learning algorithm such as a

support vector machine (SVM), which can be represented by the following equation:

$$y = \text{sign}\left(w^x + b\right)$$

where y is the predicted class label, w is the weight vector, x is the feature vector of the sliding window, b is the bias term, and sign() is the sign function.

c. **Text recognition**

Text recognition involves recognizing the characters within the text regions detected in the previous stage. One popular approach to text recognition is using recurrent neural networks (RNNs), such as long short-term memory (LSTM) networks. The forward pass of an LSTM can be represented by the following equations:

$$f_t = \sigma\left(A_f\, x_t + M_f\, h_{\{t-1\}} + b_f\right)$$

$$i_t = \sigma\left(A_i\, x_t + M_i\, h_{\{t-1\}} + b_i\right)$$

$$o_t = \sigma\left(A_o\, x_t + M_o\, h_{\{t-1\}} + b_o\right)$$

$$g_t = \tan h\left(A_g\, x_t + M_g\, h_{\{t-1\}} + b_g\right)$$

$$c_t = f_t\, c_{\{t-1\}} + i_t\, g_t$$

$$h_t = o_t \tan h(c_t)$$

where x_t is the input vector at time t, $h_{\{t-1\}}$ is the hidden state vector at time $t-1$, and A, M, and b are the weight matrices and bias vectors of the LSTM, respectively. $\sigma()$ and $\tan h()$ are the sigmoid and hyperbolic tangent activation functions, respectively.

To extract the relevant data from the medical reports, the authors experimented with various popular Python libraries like Pytesseract [15], EasyOCR [16], and PDFplumber [17]. Most of these medical reports are generated electronically and have the target data represented in a structured table-like manner. However, these libraries failed to identify the structure of the data and instead provided all the text on the page in an unstructured manner. As a result, significant data cleaning and processing may be required to get the data in an appropriate format. This can be a cumbersome and time-consuming process, leading to suboptimal and less accurate results.

Therefore, the authors employ "AWS Textract" [18]. This tool uses advanced machine learning, OCR and text recognition algorithms to identify and extract structured and unstructured data such as text, tables and forms from scanned documents, PDFs, and images. The extracted data is transformed into a format that can easily be processed and analyzed, making it apt for extracting the necessary information from the clinical report. It also works well with a variety of file formats which include PDF, JPEG, PNG, and BMP, making it versatile and flexible.

When working with PDFs, AWS Textract first converts the PDF into images before performing OCR. Therefore, in the proposed system, the PDF file is first converted into temporary images using the "pypdfium2" [19] library before being passed through the AWS Textract algorithm. Since the system is only interested in extracting structured data, the algorithm first tries to identify table-like structures in the report and then extracts information from them.

This algorithm was then tested on approximately 50 medical reports from around 15 different pathological labs. During this testing, the authors noticed that different laboratories may use a different spelling or medical term for the same entity. Also, there might be slight differences in the arrangement of the columns and representation of the data. Hence, to ensure that the relevant text is extracted, the authors modify the AWS Textract algorithm to include certain conditions specific to clinical reports. This allows the algorithm to work well with various report formats. Once the data is extracted, the temporary images created are discarded, and the extracted data is stored in a dataframe format in the RAM. The system then processes the dataframe and analyzes the data to ascertain any abnormalities found in the report. To achieve this, the system uses an algorithm that parses through the dataframe and checks for parameters whose observed values do not fall within the reference intervals.

12.4.2 Medical dictionary

Designing a medical dictionary is a challenging endeavor that necessitates a thorough grasp of medical terminology, anatomy, physiology, and ailments (Figure 12.2). To ensure the medical dictionary's authenticity and relevance, cooperation from local doctors was sought, who offered their skills and knowledge in the field of medicine. The doctors have discussed the symptoms,

```
"haemoglobin": {
    "information": "Protein in your red blood cells that carries oxygen and carbon dioxide.",
    "high": [null, "physician"],
    "low": [null, null],
    "remedy_high": ["avoid alcohol"],
    "remedy_low": ["almonds", "walnuts", "dates"]
},
"rbc_count": {
    "information": "Red blood cells carry oxygen from your lungs to every cell in your body.",
    "high": [null, "physician"],
    "low": [null, "physician"],
    "remedy_high": ["exercise", "avoid meaty foods"],
    "remedy_low": ["leafy vegetables"]
},
```

Figure 12.2 Medical dictionary.

```
{
    "haemoglobin": {
        "priority": 3
    },
    "rbc_count": {
        "priority": 3
    },
    "total_leukocyte_count": {
        "priority": 2
    },
```

Figure 12.3 Priority dictionary.

causes, and treatments of several medical conditions while considering their experiences treating patients with various ailments. The authors have tried to incorporate this knowledge into a static medical dictionary focusing on blood parameters. They have tried to incorporate the basic understanding of the medical entity, the cases when the observed value is high or low, and some home remedies that could normalize the anomalies in the medical dictionary. This acts as one of the key reference points when generating the report summary.

Collaboration with local doctors aided not only in the creation of a complete medical dictionary but also in their understanding of the significance of each component. The physicians most likely gave insight into how different factors interact with one another and how treating one element might impact treating another. For example, if a patient has low sodium levels but high blood sugar glucose levels, the doctor must consider both when making therapy suggestions. If the doctor merely addresses the high blood sugar glucose levels and ignores the low salt levels, it may lead to further issues. Therefore, a priority dictionary comprising all components and their priority order has been developed. This empowers the algorithm to think and function like a human doctor since human physicians similarly prioritize the treatment of medical disorders depending on their severity and possible influence on the patient's health. By including the priority dictionary in the algorithm, a more complex tool that can deliver medical opinions based on the priority of medical issues has been developed. The snippet of the priority dictionary is shown in Figure 12.3.

12.4.3 Report summarization

After obtaining a list of aberrant parameters and their values, several strategies may be used to provide a thorough report summary. Depending on the circumstances, multiple ways may be adopted to provide the data in an intelligible and practical manner. The goal of creating a summary report is to offer a clear and concise depiction of the aberrant parameters and their related values, as well as any pertinent insights or recommendations for further inquiry or action. The initial stage in our approach was to experiment with GPT-2, a cutting-edge language model. OpenAI created this model, which is based on transformer architecture, to enable autonomous human-like text generation. Although being the forerunner of the more complex GPT-3 model, GPT-2 has already been trained on a large dataset, including information on a variety of topics.

The proposed system intends to employ the GPT-2 model for automatic text summary of medical reports based on the extracted information. The system will feed the model aberrant parameters and their observed high/low flags, which will then create numerous replies. However, the authors noticed that the output generated by this model was not always accurate and up to the mark. This is because it is not explicitly trained on medical report data. Also, the model was trained on data available on the Internet which may sometimes lead to learning from incorrect data and since there is no way the model can verify the accuracy of the data, it can lead to potential problems, especially when dealing with sensitive topics like medicine which directly can impact the lives of people. Hence, to ensure the correctness of the generated output, several GPT-2 outputs were generated, and the best ones were picked based on its overlap with the dictionary-based values. Once the best output was selected, it is combined further with the values from the medical dictionary, thereby generating an accurate report summary.

In case when the medical entity is missing from the medical vocabulary, the GPT-2-produced answer is delivered in such instances, but with a caution concerning its correctness. This method guarantees that the user is aware of the output's limits and may take necessary steps to confirm the information.

12.5 IMPLEMENTATION AND RESULTS

To generate the summary from an uploaded medical report, the proposed algorithm proceeds with the following steps (Figures 12.4–12.6):

i. The first stage includes extracting information from medical report using OCR. The steps involved in OCR is as follows:
- Converting report from PDF to images using pypdfium2 library.
- Passing the converted images through the normal AWS Textract algorithm to obtain the target data extracted. *Note:* Only that data is extracted which is in a structured format.
- Identifying the columns based on the first row and processing the text into a standard form.
- Creating the dataframe by filling up the columns with the corresponding data.
- Looping through each row and identifying the medical entities not lying in the specified range.

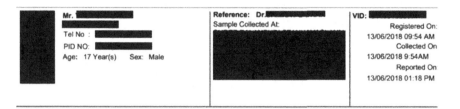

Investigation	Observed Value	Unit	Biological Reference Interv
CBC Haemogram			
Erythrocytes			
Haemoglobin (Hb)	13.6	gm/dL	12.5-16.5
Erythrocyte (RBC) Count	5.15	mill/cu.mm	4.2-5.6
PCV (Packed Cell Volume)	40.9	%	36-47
MCV (Mean Corpuscular Volume)	79.4	fL	78-95
MCH (Mean Corpuscular Hb)	26.4	pg	26-32
MCHC (Mean Corpuscular Hb Concn.)	33.3	g/dL	32-36
RDW (Red Cell Distribution Width)	12.8	%	11.5-14.0
Leucocytes			
Total Leucocytes (WBC) count	5,700	cells/cu.mm	4000-10500
Absolute Neutrophils Count	2622	/c.mm	2000-7000
Absolute Lymphocyte Count	2280	/c.mm	1000-3000
Absolute Monocyte Count	285	/c.mm	200-1000
Absolute Eosinophil Count	456	/c.mm	20-500
Absolute Basophil Count	57	/c.mm	20-100
Neutrophils	46	%	44-76
Lymphocytes	40	%	15-43
Monocytes	5	%	4.0-9.0
Eosinophils	8	%	0-6
Basophils	1	%	0-2
Platelets			
Platelet count	245	10^3 / µl	150-450
MPV (Mean Platelet Volume)	9.9	fL	6-9.5
PCT (Platelet Haematocrit)	0.24	%	0.2-0.5
PDW (Platelet Distribution Width)	11.5	%	9-17

EDTA Whole Blood - Tests done on Automated Five Part Cell Counter. (WBC, RBC Platelet count by impedance method, WBC differential by VCS technology other parameters calculated) All Abnormal Haemograms are reviewed confirmed microscopically. Differential count is based on approximately 10,000 cells.

Figure 12.4 Example of a medical report.

ii. The next step in the system is report summarization. The steps involved in report summarization are as follows:
- Map anomalies with priority dictionary to get the order.
- If not exact match, use string matching algorithm based on common subsequence.
- Give anomaly as input along with its high/low flag to generate multiple GPT-2 responses.
- Map anomalies with medical dictionary to get the most accurate output.
- Combine the data to get the summary for that parameter which would include the definition of the entity in simple terms, the effects, and issues if the anomaly is low or high and the potential household remedies to get the anomalies under control.

	Investigation	Observed Value	Unit	Biological Reference Interval	Our Analysis	Doctor Opinion
0	Erythrocytes	-1		-1		
1	Haemoglobin (Hb)	13.6	gm/dL	12.5-16.5	Moderate	Moderate
2	Erythrocyte (RBC) Count	5.15	mill/cu.mm	4.2-5.6	Moderate	Moderate
3	PCV (Packed Cell Volume)	40.9	%	36-47	Moderate	Moderate
4	MCV (Mean Corpuscular Volume)	79.4	fL	78-95	Moderate	Low
5	MCH (Mean Corpuscular Hb)	26.4	pg	26-32	Moderate	Low
6	MCHC (Mean Corpuscular Hb Concn.)	33.3	g/dL	32-36	Moderate	Moderate
7	RDW (Red Cell Distribution Width)	12.8	%	11.5-14.0	Moderate	Moderate
8	Leucocytes	-1		-1		
9	Total Leucocytes (WBC) count	5700	cells/cu.mm	4000-10500	Moderate	Low
10	Absolute Neutrophils Count	2622	/c.mm	2000-7000	Moderate	Low
11	Absolute Lymphocyte Count	2280	/c.mm	1000-3000	Moderate	Moderate
12	Absolute Monocyte Count	285	/c.mm	200-1000	Moderate	Low
13	Absolute Eosinophil Count	456	/c.mm	20-500	Moderate	High
14	Absolute Basophil Count	57	/c.mm	20-100	Moderate	Moderate
15	Neutrophils	46	%	44-76	Moderate	Low
16	Lymphocytes	40	%	15-43	Moderate	High
17	Monocytes	5	%	4.0-9.0	Moderate	Moderate
18	Eosinophils	8	%	0-6	High	High
19	Basophils	1	%	0-2	Moderate	Moderate
20	Platelets	-1		-1		
21	Platelet count	245	10^3 pl	150-450	Moderate	Moderate
22	MPV (Mean Platelet Volume)	8.8	fl	6-9.5	High	High
23	PCT (Platelet Haematocrit)	0.34	%	0.2-0.5	Moderate	Low
24	PDW (Platelet Distribution Width)	11.5	%	Sep-17		

Figure 12.5 Dataframe generated after OCR.

{'Eosinophils': ['high', 1], 'MPV (Mean Platelet Volume)': ['high', 0]}

Figure 12.6 Abnormal parameters obtained after OCR and its analysis.

Fasting glucose is a measurement of the amount of glucose (sugar) in a person's blood after they have gone without food for at least 8 hours. It is used to diagnose and monitor diabetes, as well as to assess a person's overall glucose metabolism. Since the observed glucose fasting level is high, there are chances of diabetes and it is preferable to show a physician. It is recommended to consume non-starchy vegetables, high-fibre carbohydrates, lean proteins and low-fat dairy products.

Figure 12.7 Summary generated by the system.

If the high blood sugar level is detected, then the summary generated is as shown in Figure 12.7.

After testing on multiple reports and for multiple instances, the authors found that the entire process from uploading a medical report to the generation of the output takes an average of 7 seconds. This is so because the OCR process and the summary generation process are computationally heavy and slow.

12.6 CONCLUSION

Medical reports are a crucial tool for the diagnosis and treatment of medical conditions. They provide essential information about a patient's health and can help healthcare providers identify any abnormalities or issues that need to be addressed. It is important for patients to understand their medical reports and seek the support they need to do so, whether from their healthcare provider or other reliable sources. However, there might be cases where healthcare professionals might not be immediately available. Therefore, it becomes imperative for patients to understand their medical reports in order to take an active role in their own healthcare and make informed decisions about their treatment. The proposed system aids patients to generate a simplified summary and version of their medical reports from the comfort of their phones. All they require is the medical report and a secure Internet connection. This system allows different formats of the medical reports, i.e., image format or pdf format to be uploaded by the patients which can be analyzed. Upon uploading the report, the system analyzes the report and extracts the major anomalies in the report. Based on this extraction of information, the system explains the details of the anomalies and provides a summary of the report. It recommends household remedies and foods which need to be avoided so that the abnormal medical parameters are normalized.

REFERENCES

1. "India's Villages Don't Have Enough Health Workers. But Here Is How Modicare's Wellness Drive Can Still Succeed." https://www.indiaspend.com/indias-villages-dont-have-enough-health-workers-but-here-is-how-modicares-wellness-drive-can-still-succeed/
2. "Max Healthcare Institute Limited Annual Report 2020–21." https://max-website20-images.s3.ap-south-1.amazonaws.com/Annual_Report_FY_2020_21_1bab38c3ff.pdf
3. W. Qader and M. M. Ameen, "Diagnosis of Diseases from Medical Check-up Test Reports Using OCR Technology with BoW and AdaBoost Algorithms," 2019 International Engineering Conference (IEC), pp. 205–210, 2019. doi: 10.1109/IEC47844.2019.8950605
4. W. Xue, Q. Li, Z. Zhang, Y. Zhao and H. Wang, "Table Analysis and Information Extraction for Medical Laboratory Reports," 2018 IEEE 16th International Conference on Dependable, Autonomic and Secure Computing, 16th International Conference on Pervasive Intelligence and Computing, 4th International Conference on Big Data Intelligence and Computing and Cyber Science and Technology Congress, pp. 193–199, 2018. doi: 10.1109/DASC/PiCom/DataCom/CyberSciTec.2018.00043
5. P. Vinod, S. Safar, D. Mathew, P. Venugopal, L. M. Joly and J. George, "Fine-tuning the BERTSUMEXT Model for Clinical Report Summarization," 2020 International Conference for Emerging Technology (INCET), 2020, pp. 1–7. doi: 10.1109/INCET49848.2020.9154087
6. S. Karthikeyan, A. G. S. de Herrera, F. Doctor and A. Mirza, "An OCR Post-Correction Approach Using Deep Learning for Processing Medical Reports," IEEE Transactions on Circuits and Systems for Video Technology, vol. 32, no. 5, pp. 2574–2581, 2022. doi: 10.1109/TCSVT.2021.3087641

7. K. Hamad and M. Kaya, "A Detailed Analysis of Optical Character Recognition Technology," International Journal of Applied Mathematics, Electronics and Computers, vol. 4. pp. 244–244, 2016. doi: 10.18100/ijamec.270374

8. K. Uchimoto, S. Sekine and H. Isahara, "Text Generation from Keywords," Proceedings of the 19th International Conference on Computational linguistics, Association for Computational Linguistics, 2002. doi: 10.3115/1072228.1072292

9. S. Das, S. B. Partha and K. N. Imtiaz Hasan, "Sentence Generation Using LSTM Based Deep Learning," 2020 IEEE Region 10 Symposium (TENSYMP), IEEE, pp. 1070–1073, 2020. doi: 10.1109/TENSYMP50017.2020.9230979

10. W. Xue, Q. Li and Q. Xue, "Text Detection and Recognition for Images of Medical Laboratory Reports with a Deep Learning Approach," IEEE Access, vol. 8, pp. 407–416, 2020. doi: 10.1109/ACCESS.2019.2961964

11. X. Li, G. Hu, X. Teng and G. Xie, "Building Structured Personal Health Records from Photographs of Printed Medical Records," AMIA Annual Symposium Proceedings, vol. 2015, pp. 833–842, 2015.

12. Y. Qu, P. Liu, W. Song, L. Liu and M. Cheng, "A Text Generation and Prediction System: Pre-training on New Corpora Using BERT and GPT-2," 2020 IEEE 10th International Conference on Electronics Information and Emergency Communication (ICEIEC), IEEE, pp. 323–326, 2020. doi: 10.1109/ICEIEC49280.2020.9152352

13. J. Sirriani, E. Sezgin, D. Claman and S. L. Linwood, "Medical Text Prediction and Suggestion Using Generative Pre-trained Transformer Models with Dental Medical Notes", medRxiv 2022.04.29.22274513. doi: 10.1101/2022.04.29.22274513

14. D. Gifu, "AI-backed OCR in Healthcare," Procedia Computer Science, vol. 207, pp. 1134–1143, 2022. doi: 10.1016/j.procs.2022.09.169

15. https://pypi.org/project/pytesseract/

16. https://huggingface.co/spaces/tomofi/EasyOCR

17. https://pypi.org/project/pdfplumber/0.1.2/

18. https://aws.amazon.com/textract/

19. https://pypi.org/project/pypdfium2/

Chapter 13

A comparative study on prediction of soil health and crop recommendation using machine learning models

Mithun Shivakoti and Srinivasa Reddy K.

13.1 INTRODUCTION

Agriculture is a vital part of many countries' economies. India is one of the largest countries that depends solely on agriculture and related products. Agriculture employs more than 50% of the working population across the world and is one of the key drivers of the industrial revolution and a specific region's economy. Soil management plays a critical role to ensuring agricultural sustainability, and it is critical to understand the long-term repercussions of the various ways of managing soil and to pay close attention to soil quality. Like air and water, soil is considered a vital natural resource that offers a diverse range of paybacks to human beings in the form of commodities and services provided by various ecosystems. In agriculture, the soil is the most important and fundamental thing [1].

The quality of soil is the single most significant factor in crop production in any form. The term "soil" can be understood in a variety of ways depending on who you ask. To a geologist, the term "soil" refers to the products of past surface products. It is significant to a penologist because it depicts the ongoing physical and chemical processes that are taking place. According to the civil engineering perspective, soil is considered as the solid material that serves as a base for constructing the foundations of various structures such as buildings, roads, and other infrastructure. When referring to the rocks or minerals that are being extracted or mined, a mining engineer will refer to the soil as the dispersed particles of debris or residues that surround the target material. When it comes to highway engineering, the soil is the material that will be used as the base for the track bed.

It is possible for different people, like geologists, penologists, civil engineers, mining engineers, and highway engineers, for their own unique reasons, to define soils in a variety of distinct ways. The term "environmental medium" refers to the role that soil plays in agriculture from the perspective of an agriculturist. The study of soil involves the identification of externally observable patterns present in the soil. The study of soil characteristics is essential for understanding and managing the natural resources of a region. There are many different kinds of soil, and not all of them are ideal for growing every kind of crop because each type of soil contains its own unique set of qualities that make them ideal for growing specific types of crops. Take sandy soil as an example; it requires a significant amount of water. Clay soil, on the other hand, has a greater capacity to store water; hence, it has a lower overall water requirement. The study of soil entails becoming familiar with the distinct patterns that can be observed on soil. The soil classification system is utilized to categorize soil types into groups according to their respective soil properties [2]. The process of soil classification encompasses various stages, including analyzing the composition and structure of the soil, determining its classification levels, and ultimately applying this knowledge in practical settings.

In recent years, there has been a rise in interest in the study of soil texture and color classification by utilizing digital methods on photographs of soil. The classification of soils is an especially fundamental component of any viable agricultural enterprise. Studies classify the soil based on the color of the soil and the texture of the soil.

The classification of soil can be carried out using a variety of standard approaches, both in the lab and in the field. Chemical analysis and image analysis are the two methods that can be utilized to determine the type of soil. Chemical analysis is often carried out in a laboratory using a variety of chemicals, a process that is not only expensive but also time-consuming, making it difficult for average farmers to access. [3–5] Through image analysis, in most cases, soils are categorized based on the engineering properties of the soil. The latest categorizations enable a seamless progression from the on-site examination to the initial projections of the characteristics and performance of soil mechanics. Soil sections captured with conventional cameras, microscopes, or scanners and observed under polarized light can be digitized to generate three-dimensional models that exhibit diverse geometric properties. The perspective that soil is a resource and that soil itself is a material are useful places to start when attempting to classify soil.

The pH value of the soil is the most important element to be examined before beginning the cultivation of any crop [6]. The pH level of soil is a crucial determinant of crop health and productivity, as well as the general well-being of an ecosystem. The determination of soil pH is crucial in identifying its inherent acidity or alkalinity, and optimal plant growth is contingent upon achieving the appropriate pH equilibrium, which can be ascertained via testing. The pH value of soil indicates its acidity or basicity [7]. Table 13.1 shows the pH value and its meaning. Effective crop management and sustainable agriculture necessitate accurate and efficient soil pH measurement and prediction systems.

Table 13.1 The pH value of the soil and meaning

pH value	7	<7	>7	≥5.5 and <7.0
Meaning	Neutral	Acidity	Basicity	Ideal for cultivation

Farmers usually provide soil samples to specialized laboratories for the purpose of evaluating soil pH or referring to soil pH color charts. An expert periodically aids agricultural producers in ascertaining the soil's pH level. Nevertheless, obtaining proficient perspectives may not always be feasible in every circumstance. Each of the aforementioned alternatives necessitates a certain amount of time, exertion, and specialized expertise. The utilization of a soil pH chart as a sole means of assessing soil pH is deemed inadequate due to its reliance on human perception and the expertise of a trained specialist. To determine the pH level of soil in a laboratory setting, it is necessary to employ a soil pH meter and a soil color pH card. The procedure of utilizing a pH meter on soil for a comparatively uncomplicated soil sample necessitated over an hour. The proliferation of technological advancements and greater computer usage has led to an increased prevalence of automation in daily life. Consequently, the acceleration of the process is accompanied by a reduction in the susceptibility of the final product to inaccuracies. Two techniques, namely, image processing and regression, will be utilized to attain the objective of estimating the soil's pH [7].

In recent years, the use of machine learning and deep learning techniques has become increasingly popular in the field of soil science, as they offer a powerful tool for characterizing and predicting soil properties. On soil images, by applying image processing and machine learning approaches, the soil pH can be forecasted. Regression analysis is a statistical method employed to establish the correlation between a dependent variable (soil pH) and one or more independent variables (image features). The objective of this chapter is to investigate the application of machine learning and deep learning methodologies in the categorization of soil varieties and the estimation of soil pH. This research aims to present an analysis of the current state of the art in soil characterization through the utilization of machine learning and deep learning. Additionally, the study will showcase the outcomes of a case study that highlights the efficacy of these techniques in soil type classification and pH prediction.

13.2 LITERATURE SURVEY

The hue of the soil plays a crucial role in distinguishing diagnostic strata and features, which are utilized for the taxonomic categorization of the soil, such as mollic and umbric epipedons [8]. The absence of well-defined standards makes the task of ascertaining the hue of the soil a challenging endeavor. As per the American Standards Association [9, 10], the Munsell Soil Color Chart (MSCC) [11] is solely employed for visual characterization purposes. According to Kirillova et al., the measurement of color is typically conducted through the use of a spectrophotometer. The MSCC has been the preferred technique for soil color determination in the past due to its comparative simplicity.

The color chips of MSCC are generally expected to correspond with the color of the soil. However, the degree of similarity between the two may be contingent upon the nature of the illumination and the dispersion of the lamp spectrum. Furthermore, the MSCC exhibits a high degree of subjectivity to human perception, thereby rendering the presentation of soil organic matter (SOM) prediction utilizing MSCC notation a challenging undertaking.

Diffuse reflectance spectroscopy (DRS) has been identified as a promising alternative approach for measuring soil organic carbon (SOC) and SOM due to the strong correlations observed between SOM and reflectance values in the visible and near-infrared or mid-infrared range. This has been demonstrated in previous studies [12–14].

Morais and colleagues proposed a method of multivariate image analysis that utilizes picture segmentation to differentiate between clay and sandy soil types. This approach has been documented in several studies [3, 4, 5, 15]. Soil micromorphology-based image analysis was utilized for soil classification [16]. Liu et al. [17] proposed a categorization system for urban soil utilizing a support vector machine (SVM) approach.

Bhattacharya and Solomatine [18] employ segmentation, feature extraction, and classification techniques in their study. Segmentation algorithms are utilized to segregate measured signals. By means of the boundary energy method, characteristics are derived from the input data. Based on these identified characteristics, classifiers such as artificial neural networks (ANN), SVM, and decision trees (DTs) are employed to generate desirable outcomes.

Chung et al. [19] investigated the soil texture classification system based on RGB form images. Each segmented soil sample was subjected to image acquisition using a CCD camera that had been reduced in size, resulting in the acquisition of four surface pictures. The utilization of the pipette method was also employed in the analysis of texture fractions. The results indicate that 48% of the soil samples yielded identical findings when comparing the in situ image processing method and the laboratory method. The previously mentioned standards were employed to categorize the soil.

Shenbagavalli and Ramar [20] devised an algorithm for classifying soil based on its texture that makes use of mask convolution. In order to investigate the soil photos, feature extraction 3×3 Law's mask convolution was utilized. In order to construct the feature vector that will be used in the subsequent operations, the absolute mean, mean, skewness, kurtosis, and standard deviation of the soil picture were computed.

Bose Chaudhuri Hocquenghem codes (BCH) used multiclass SVMs. The decoding process of a standard method remains constant irrespective of the signal-to-noise ratio (SNR) conditions. The absence of local minima in Thaw, coupled with the high decoding capability of outlier resilient SVM for BCH codes [21], is noteworthy. ABDF is a software tool that offers a wide range of features and practical applications. Additionally, it presents a graphical user interface that facilitates the exploration of extensive data sets [22].

Zhang et al. have reported that a degree of uncertainty may exist between the correlation of soil composition and the mechanical behavior of soil when obtained through the use of CPT. The lack of clarity leads to the convergence of numerous categories of soil. The present methodology involves the utilization of point and region estimation. In this context, the writer presents a novel fuzzy approach that is independent of CPT, as documented in Reference [23].

Young and Calvert [24] present a notion for bending energy-based analysis of biological shape techniques. It also explains sampling theorem for connected and closed contours and provides a quick approach for determining bending energy. The utilization of RGB image processing in order to detect iron and carbon from soil images has been documented in References [25, 26]. Vibhute et al. [27] have devised a methodology for categorizing soil utilizing hyperspectral image data. Furthermore, the hyperspectral image was utilized in References [28, 29]. Nevertheless, the cost of a hyperspectral imaging camera exceeds that of a smartphone camera. Stiglitz and colleagues utilized the cyan, magenta, yellow, and black color conversion method derived from Munsell color [25] to develop a software for instantaneous identification of soil types [30].

The CIEL*a*b* mode was utilized to determine the soil moisture content [31], while the L*a*b* mode was employed to evaluate the soil depth. In Reference [32], a mobile application utilizing RGB image processing techniques has been developed for the purpose of identifying soil color classification. The images were converted from the RGB color space to the CIExyz and Munsell HVC color models.

The classification of dry and moist sample photos obtained by GPS-enabled devices was the subject of a second investigation [33]. They also processed images in RGB, CMYK, CIElab, and XYZ modes.

An image was subjected to a computer vision-based texture analysis, as suggested by Sofou et al. [26]. The morphological partial differential equation–based method, which depended on the contrast of the picture, was utilized for the segmentation process. It was proposed to use variations in surface texture images as a local modulation component for the purpose of texture analysis. The in-field method that Breul and Gourves [34] presented for characterizing soil on the basis of its textural properties using third-order moment is described below. Textural investigation in the field using spectral methods applied to subsurface soil pictures is one of the proposed investigations. This method seeks to rapidly distinguish fine material from coarse material and characterize a large percentage of materials with a grain size of 80 μm or finer. A proposal for a soil image retrieval system was made by Shenbagavalli and Ramar [20]. As a result of the findings, we concluded that the proposed retrieval method is effective.

The pH of the soil was predicted using the RGB color space of soil images [7, 35–40]. The soil is photographed using a digital camera, and the following characteristics shown in Equation (13.1) were utilized to forecast the pH of the soil.

Soil feature = Red/Green/Blue $\qquad\qquad$ (13.1)

Abu et al. [41] devised an expert system utilizing fuzzy logic to control soil pH. The method involved the correction of soil pH levels to facilitate the replacement of fertilizer by farmers and to ensure optimal plant quality. The physical properties of soil were demonstrated by Babu and Pandian [37] with a presented methodology. LabView was employed to construct the technology for fractal dimension measurement. The fractal dimension is depicted in Equation (13.2).

$$\text{Fractal dimension} = \frac{\log\big(Y(f)\big)}{\log\,(1\,/\,f)} \qquad (13.2)$$

Color photographs of 24-bit are employed as input to assess the model's performance subsequently transformed into 8-bit, and the features are extracted utilizing an equation suggested by Kumar et al. [39]. In their study, Aziz et al. [35] employed the RGB values of images as provided by Kumar et al. [39] to train and test a neural network. The authors achieved an accuracy rate of 80% by utilizing a hidden layer comprising 10 neurons. The pH value of the soil was determined through the computation of the mean RGB values of soil images by Gurubasava and Mahantesh [38]. The mean RGB values were contrasted against both the factual soil pH and their projected pH. Barman et al. [7] have proposed a technique for soil pH estimation that involves the utilization of HSV color image processing and regression methodologies, including linear, logarithmic, exponential, and quadratic models. The approach also involves the computation of hue, saturation, and value of soil images.

13.3 PROPOSED SYSTEM

13.3.1 Dataset description

In this work, two different datasets are being used, the first being an image dataset for classifying the type of soil, consisting of 235 images (approximately 30 per class) which has been manually created by the authors. Soil is classified into eight types: "alluvial soil", "arid and desert soil", "black soil", "cinder soil", "laterite soil", "peat soil", "red soil", and "yellow soil". Figure 13.1 shows the sample images of the dataset from each class. The second dataset utilized in this study is pH-recognition, a Comma Separated Value file, collected from Kaggle [42], which contains pH values for a range of R, G, and B combinations within an image, i.e., between 0 and 255. The dataset consists of four attributes, specifically blue, green, red, and label (pH). Table 13.2 shows the sample RGB values of the dataset. Figures 13.2–13.4 display scatter plots that illustrate the relationship between red, green, and blue values, ranging from 0 to 255, and their corresponding pH values, ranging from 0 to 14, within the dataset. It is evident from the plots that the data points are not linearly distributed, but rather exhibit a wide dispersion across the plot's dimensions.

| Alluvial Soil | Arid and Desert Soil | Black Soil | Cinder Soil |
| Laterite Soil | Peat Soil | Red Soil | Yellow Soil |

Figure 13.1 Sample images of the dataset from each class of soils.

Table 13.2 Sample RGB values of the dataset

Red (R)	25	55	67	67	104	183	207	166
Green (G)	212	197	185	170	181	185	143	82
Blue (B)	180	130	72	143	16	2	65	54

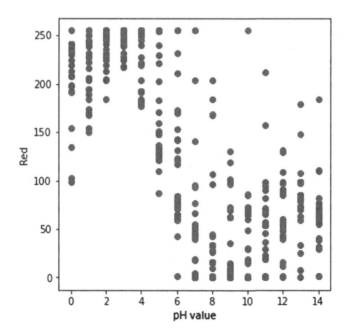

Figure 13.2 Plot of all the values of red w.r.t. pH.

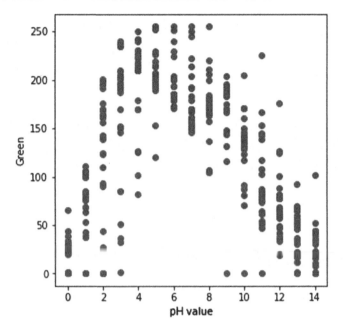

Figure 13.3 Plot of all the values of green w.r.t. pH.

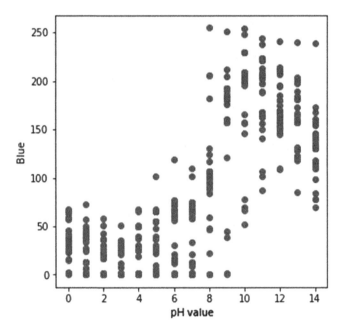

Figure 13.4 Plot of all the values of blue w.r.t. pH.

13.3.2 Methodology

13.3.2.1 Linear regression

Linear regression is a statistical methodology employed to establish a linear correlation between a reliant variable and one or more autonomous variables. The objective is to formulate a mathematical equation that can forecast the dependent variable's value by considering the independent variables' values. Linear regression is a statistical technique utilized to construct a model that describes the association between two variables by employing a linear equation to the gathered data.

The fundamental formula for simple linear regression with a single predictor variable (X) is given in Equation (13.3).

$$Y = \beta 0 + \beta 1 X + \varepsilon \qquad (13.3)$$

Here:

Y is the dependent variable or outcome we want to predict.
$\beta 0$ represents an intercept or constant term.
$\beta 1$ is the slope coefficient.
X is the variable of interest or predictor.
ε is the random noise or error component t.

The primary aim of linear regression is to ascertain the optimal values for $\beta 0$ and $\beta 1$ that minimize the sum of squared errors between the predicted and actual Y values. The conventional approach for this task involves the utilization of either the least squares technique or the gradient descent optimization algorithm.

13.4 RANDOM FOREST REGRESSION

The random forest regressor is a form of ensemble learning technique that integrates numerous DTs to generate forecasts. The concept underlying random forest regression involves the construction of numerous DTs utilizing distinct subsets of both the data and features. Subsequently, the predictions of these trees are averaged to yield a more precise and resilient outcome.

The construction of each DT within a random forest involves the utilization of a random subset of the available features and training data. The implementation of this technique aids in mitigating overfitting while simultaneously augmenting the heterogeneity of the trees within the forest. In the course of the training procedure, every DT within the random forest is constructed via a recursive partitioning of the data into increasingly smaller subsets, utilizing the features that yield the highest information gain. After constructing the trees, they can be employed to generate forecasts on novel data by transmitting it through every tree and computing the mean outcomes.

The algorithm can be mathematically represented as follows:

1. Let X represent the matrix of input data, where each row represents an observation and each column represents a feature.
2. Consider y to be the variable-vector target.
3. Let T represent the total number of DTs within the forest.
4. For every tree from t = 1 to T:
   4.1 A bootstrap sample is a subset of the data selected at random with replacement. Let X_t and y_t represents the vectors of data input and variable target for this sample.
   4.2 Select at random a feature subset, often known as a feature subset. Let F_t represent the set of chosen features.
   4.3 Train a DT using only the features in F_t and the data X_t and y_t.
   4.4 The forest is where the DT is stored.
5. To make a prediction for a new observation x, compute and average the prediction for each DT in the forest, as shown in Equation (13.4).

$$y\_hat(x) = 1/T * sum(y\_t(x)) \tag{13.4}$$

Here, y_t(x) is the output of the DT t for the input x.

13.5 LEAST ABSOLUTE SHRINKAGE AND SELECTION OPERATOR (LASSO) REGRESSION

The LASSO regression is a linear regression approach that is employed to identify a subset of features for utilization in the model. This is accomplished by reducing the coefficients of irrelevant features to zero. The LASSO regression technique operates by incorporating a penalty term into the cost function of least squares, thereby imposing a restriction on the magnitude of the coefficients. The penalty term in question exhibits proportionality to the absolute value of the coefficients. This property results in the tendency of small coefficients to approach zero, leading to the exclusion of the corresponding features from the model.

The following is the mathematical formulation of LASSO regression:

1. The matrix of input data can be represented by X, where each row denotes an observation and each column denotes an independent variable.
2. Consider y to be the variable-vector target.
3. Let $\beta = (\beta 0, \beta 1, ..., \beta p)$ be the estimated vector of coefficients, where $\beta 0$ is the intercept term.
4. The LASSO regression problem may be expressed as shown is Equation (13.5):

$$\text{minimize} \|y - X\beta\|^2 + \lambda * \|\beta\|\_1 \tag{13.5}$$

where $\|.\|\_1$ is the L1 norm and λ is a hyperparameter that controls the strength of the penalty term. The larger the value of λ, the more the coefficients pushed toward zero, resulting in sparser solutions.

5. The norm of in L1 is defined as follows:

$$\|\beta\|\_1 = |\beta 1| + |\beta 2| + \cdots + |\beta p|$$

6. Optimization techniques such as coordinate descent and gradient descent can be used to deal with the optimization problem.

Coordinate descent updates is given by Equation (13.6).

$$\beta\_j = S(z\_j, \lambda/2) / \left(X\_j^T X\_j \right) \qquad (13.6)$$

where $S(z, \lambda/2)$ is the soft-thresholding operator defined as given in Equation (13.7):

$$S(z, \lambda/2) = \text{sign}(z) * \max(0, |z| - \lambda/2) \qquad (13.7)$$

and $z\_j = X\_j^T (y - X\_{-j} \beta\_{-j})$ is the residual, where X_{-j} and β_{-j} are the matrices and vectors without the jth column.

Gradient descent updates are shown in Equation (13.8).

$$\beta = \beta - \eta * \nabla \left(\|y - X\beta\|^2 + \lambda * \|\beta\| \right)\_1 \qquad (13.8)$$

where η is the rate of learning and (.) is the gradient operator.

13.6 XGB REGRESSION

Extreme Gradient Boosting (XGBoost) regression algorithm is a widely used machine learning technique for performing regression tasks. The XGBoost algorithm is a boosting technique that leverages an ensemble of weak prediction models, specifically DTs, to construct a robust model for predictive tasks. The XGBoost algorithm operates through a process of iteratively augmenting the ensemble model with DTs, wherein each subsequent tree is designed to minimize the residual errors of its predecessor. The aforementioned procedure is iterated until either a predetermined limit of trees is attained or until no additional enhancements can be achieved.

In order to mitigate the issue of overfitting, XGBoost employs regularization methods, such as L1 and L2 regularization, as well as early stopping, which enables the algorithm to halt the addition of new trees when the validation loss fails to demonstrate improvement beyond a specified number of iterations.

The XGBoost regression algorithm is mathematically described as follows:

1. The matrix of input data can be represented by X, where each row denotes an observation and each column denotes an independent variable.
2. Consider y to be the variable-vector target.
3. Let h_i(x) represent the ith DT's forecast.
4. The objective function of XGBoost is specified as shown in Equation (13.9).

$$\text{Obj} = 1/2 * \text{sum}\_i^n [y\_i - \text{sum}\_k^M f\_k(x\_i)]^2$$
$$+ \text{gamma} * \text{sum}\_k^M \text{Omega}(f\_k) \tag{13.9}$$

where n represents the number of observations, M represents the number of DTs, f_k represents the prediction of the kth tree, gamma controls the complexity of the trees, and Omega(f_k) penalizes the complexity of the kth tree.
5. Optimize the objective function using gradient descent.
   Gradient updates are given in Equation (13.10).

$$g\_i = \partial(y\_i - \text{sum}\_k^M f\_k(x\_i))/\partial f\_M(x\_i)$$
$$h\_i = \partial^2(y\_i - \text{sum}\_k^M f\_k(x\_i))/\partial f\_M(x\_i)^2 \tag{13.10}$$
$$f\_k = f\_k - \eta * [\text{sum}\_i \, g\_i/(\text{sum}\_i \, h\_i + \text{lambda})]$$

where g_i is the first derivative and h_i is the second derivative of the loss function with respect to the prediction, respectively, η is the learning rate, and lambda is the L2 regularization parameter.
6. When a maximum number of trees is achieved or when the improvement in the goal function falls below a specific level, the algorithm terminates.

13.7 RIDGE REGRESSION

Ridge regression is a linear regression methodology that is used to examine data that exhibits multicollinearity, a phenomenon characterized by the existence of independent variables that are highly correlated. The conventional approach to linear regression involves minimizing the sum of squared residuals. However, ridge regression introduces an extra penalty term to the cost function. The penalty term is a mathematical function that is dependent on the squared magnitude of the coefficients and is subsequently multiplied by a parameter referred to as lambda, which is also recognized as the regularization parameter. The inclusion of a penalty term aids in the contraction of coefficients toward zero, thereby diminishing their variance and subsequently mitigating the impact of multicollinearity. Consequently, ridge regression is more appropriate for datasets exhibiting a high degree of correlation among independent variables. The determination of the optimal lambda value can be achieved through various methods, including cross-validation. It is worth noting that an increase in lambda values leads to a greater degree of shrinkage of the coefficients.

The following is the mathematical formulation of ridge regression:

1. The matrix of input data can be represented by U, where each row denotes an observation and each column denotes an independent variable.
2. Consider y to be the variable-vector target.
3. Let $\beta = (\beta 0, \beta 1, ..., \beta p)$ be the estimated vector of coefficients, where $\beta 0$ is the intercept term.
4. The ridge regression problem is stated in Equation (13.11):

$$\text{minimize } \left\| y - U\beta \right\|^2 + \lambda * \left\| \beta \right\|^2 \tag{13.11}$$

   where ||.|| is the L2 norm and λ is a hyperparameter that controls the strength of the penalty term. The larger the value of λ, the smaller the coefficients, resulting in a more stable and less flexible model.
5. The L2 norm is defined as follows:

$$\left\| \beta \right\|^2 = \beta 1^2 + \beta 2^2 + \cdots + \beta p^2$$

6. Using linear algebra techniques such as matrix inversion or singular value decomposition, the optimization problem can be solved.

The answer to the problem of ridge regression is given by Equation (13.12).

$$\beta = (U^T U + \lambda I)^{(-1)} U^T y \tag{13.12}$$

where I represents the p × p identity matrix.

13.8 ELASTIC NET

Elastic net linear regression utilizes regularization techniques from both the LASSO and ridge methodologies to impose penalties on regression models. The proposed approach integrates the LASSO and ridge regression techniques, leveraging their respective limitations to enhance the efficacy of statistical model regularization.

The elastic net approach addresses the limitations of the LASSO method, which is restricted to a small number of samples in the context of high-dimensional data. The elastic net methodology permits the inclusion of "n" predictors until reaching saturation. In cases where the variables exhibit high interconnectivity, the LASSO method tends to favor the selection of a single variable from each group while disregarding the remaining variables.

The elastic net is a regularization technique that addresses the limitations of LASSO by incorporating a quadratic term ($\|\beta\|2$) in the penalty function. When utilized independently, this term corresponds to ridge regression. The quadratic expression of the penalty term induces convexity in the loss function. The elastic net model integrates the favorable attributes of both LASSO and ridge regression techniques.

The elastic net method's estimate is determined through a two-stage procedure that involves the utilization of the LASSO and regression approaches. The initial step involves the identification of the coefficients for ridge regression, followed by a subsequent stage wherein the coefficients are subjected to shrinkage via LASSO.

Consequently, the coefficients undergo dual forms of shrinkage through the utilization of this approach. The utilization of the naive form of the elastic net leads to a dual shrinkage phenomenon that yields diminished predictability and notable bias. The rescaling of coefficients is performed by multiplying them with $(1 + \lambda2)$ in order to accommodate the aforementioned impacts.

The mathematical formulation of elastic net is as follows:

1. The matrix of input data can be represented by X, where each row denotes an observation and each column denotes an independent variable.
2. Consider y to be the variable-vector target.
3. Let $\beta = (\beta0, \beta1, ..., \beta p)$ be the estimated vector of coefficients, where $\beta0$ is the intercept term.
4. The elastic net problem can be expressed as shown in Equation (13.13).

$$\text{minimize} \|y - X\beta\|^2 + \lambda1 * \|\beta\|\_1 + \lambda2 * \|\beta\|^2 \tag{13.13}$$

   Here $\|.\|\_1$ is the L1 norm and $\|.\|2$ is the L2 norm, $\lambda1$ and $\lambda2$ are hyperparameters that determine the penalty term strengths. The greater the values of $\lambda1$ and $\lambda2$, the lower the coefficients, resulting in a model that is more stable and less flexible.
5. The norm of β in L1 is defined as follows: $\|\beta\|\_1 = |\beta1| + |\beta2| + \cdots + |\beta p|$
6. It is possible to tackle the optimization problem using iterative techniques such as coordinate descent or gradient descent.

The following updating rules shown in Equation (13.14) apply to the elastic net algorithm.

$$\beta j = S\left(\sum\_i = 1 ^ n(xij)\left(yi - \sum\_k \neq j xik * \beta k\right), \lambda1\right) / \left(\sum\_i = 1 ^ n(xij) ^ 2 + \lambda2\right) \tag{13.14}$$

where S represents the soft-thresholding operator and is defined as shown in Equation (13.15).

$$S(z, \gamma) = \text{sign}(z) * \max(0, |z| - \gamma) \tag{13.15}$$

13.9 POLYNOMIAL REGRESSION

The polynomial regression technique is utilized to model the association between a dependent variable y and an independent variable c as a polynomial of nth degree. Polynomial regression is a type of linear regression that involves modeling a nonlinear relationship between the independent and dependent variables using a polynomial equation. This approach is used when there is a curvilinear pattern in the data points.

Polynomial regression can model relationships between variables of any degree, as contrast to linear regression, which only models a linear relationship between the input variables and the output. Finding the optimal coefficients to minimize the discrepancy between the expected and actual values entails fitting a polynomial equation to the data.

The following is the mathematical formulation of polynomial regression:

1. The matrix of input data can be represented by C, where each row denotes an observation and each column denotes an independent variable.
2. Consider y to be the target variable-vector.
3. Let n indicate the degree of the polynomial function.
4. The following expression describes the polynomial regression model:

$$y = \beta 0 + \beta 1 c + \beta 2 c^2 + \cdots + \beta n * c^n + \varepsilon$$

   where 0, 1,..., c are the estimated coefficients, c^n is c raised to the power of n, and ε is the error term.
5. The objective of OLS regression is to minimize the sum of squared errors, as in Equation (13.16).

$$SSE = \Sigma(yi - f(ci))^2 \tag{13.16}$$

   where (ci) is the expected value of y from the ith observation.
6. Minimizing the SSE yields the coefficient OLS estimator as given in Equation (13.17).

$$\beta = (C^T C)^{(-1)} C^T y \tag{13.17}$$

   where C^T represents the transposition of C and $(C^T C)^{(-1)}$ represents the inverse of the matrix product $C^T C$.

13.10 ADABOOST REGRESSOR

The AdaBoost regressor is a meta-estimator that initiates the modeling process by fitting a regressor on the initial dataset. Subsequently, the dataset is subjected to fitting of additional regressor copies, wherein the weights of instances are modified based on the error of the present prediction. Subsequently, the AdaBoost regressor is trained on the initial dataset once more. Consequently, as a result of this phenomenon, subsequent regressors tend to prioritize cases that present greater difficulties. The current study utilized multiple models as base estimators, with the specific choice of base estimator being the random forest regressor and DT regressor for prediction purposes.

The following is the mathematical formulation of the AdaBoost regressor:

1. The matrix of input data can be represented by R, where each row denotes an observation and each column denotes an independent variable.
2. Consider y to be the variable-vector target.
3. Let h(r) be a model of weak regression with a maximum depth of 1.
4. Let E be the number of weak learners, also known as the number of iterations.
5. Initialize the weights a_h associated with each observation as follows:

$$a\_h = 1/o$$

   where n represents the number of observations.
6. For every iteration m between 1 and E:
   a. Fit a weak regression model z_e(r) using the current weights a to the training data.
   b. Determine the weak learner's weighted mean absolute error (MAE) as per Equation (13.18).

$$\varepsilon\_e = \sum\_i = 1 ^ o a\_h \,|\, y\_h - m\_e(r\_h)\,|/\sum\_h = 1 ^ o a\_h \quad (13.18)$$

   c. Calculate the weak learner's weight as given in Equation (13.19).

$$\alpha\_e = \log((1 - \varepsilon\_e)/\varepsilon\_e) \quad\quad\quad (13.19)$$

   d. Update each observation's weights w_i as shown in Equation (13.20).

$$a\_h = a\_h * \exp(\alpha\_e * |\, y\_h - z\_e(r\_h)\,|) \quad\quad (13.20)$$

   e. Normalize the weights so their sum equals 1 as in Equation (13.21).

$$a = a/\sum\_h = 1 ^ o a\_h \quad\quad\quad (13.21)$$

7. The conclusive prediction as the weighted total of the weak learners is given by Equation (13.22).

$$f(r) = \sum\_e = 1 ^ E \alpha\_e\, z\_e(r) \quad\quad\quad (13.22)$$

13.11 DT REGRESSOR

A DT regressor creates a tree-like structure to depict the relationship between a dependent variable and one or more independent variables. Each node in the tree represents a decision or branch depending on the value of a certain independent variable, and each branch reflects the possible outcomes of that decision.

The final predictions are made by tracing the tree's branches to the correct leaf node. Finding the splits that minimize the variance of the dependent variable is how the algorithm operates. The ultimate result of the tree is the mean target value of the training instances located in the corresponding terminal node. The DT regressor model is characterized by its ease of comprehension and interpretability, as well as its capacity to handle both linear and nonlinear associations between features and target variables.

The following is the mathematical description of DT regression:

1. The matrix of input data can be represented by M, where each row denotes an observation and each column denotes an independent variable.
2. Consider y to be the variable-vector target.
3. Let T represent a DT with internal nodes. Each internal node represents a feature-based split, whereas each leaf node represents a prediction.
4. For each internal node j, let f_j represent the feature upon which the split is based, and let s_j represent the split threshold value. The division can then be stated as follows:

    If x_fj s_j, then proceed to the left child; otherwise, proceed to the right child.
5. Let c_k represent the anticipated value for the observations that fall under each leaf node k.
6. The objective is to identify the tree T that minimizes the variance of the dependent variable across all leaf nodes. The definition of the variance of the dependent variable at a leaf node k is given by Equation (13.23).

$$\text{Var}(y\_q) = 1/g\_q \sum\_i = 1^\wedge g\_k \, (y\_i - v\_q)^2 \qquad (13.23)$$

    where g_q is the number of observations that fall under node q and v_q represents the expected value for those data.
7. The criterion for dividing each internal node is the variance reduction that results from the split. The variance reduction for split j is defined as shown in Equation (13.24).

$$\Delta \text{Var}(p) = \text{Var}(y) - (\text{Var}(y\_\text{left}) + \text{Var}(y\_\text{right}))/2 \qquad (13.24)$$

    where Var(y) is the variance of the dependent variable in the parent node, Var(y_left) is the variance of the dependent variable in the child node that is toward the left, and Var(y_right) is the variance of the dependent variable in child node that is toward the right.

8. The tree grows recursively by selecting the feature and threshold that yields the largest variance reduction and continuing the process on the subsequent subsets until a stopping requirement is reached.

9. The final prediction for a new observation x is obtained by traversing the DT and obtaining the expected value of the leaf node into which x falls.

13.12 MLP REGRESSOR

The MLP regressor, also referred to as the multi-layer perceptron regressor, is a neural network utilized for the purpose of addressing regression-related problems. The system is composed of multiple layers of synthetic neurons that analyze and alter the input information in order to anticipate the desired outcome. Neurons receive inputs, undergo a nonlinear activation process, and subsequently transmit the modified outputs to the succeeding layer. The intermediate layers are utilized to obtain complex representations of the input data. The algorithm is trained through the utilization of the gradient descent method, with the objective of minimizing the difference between the predicted and actual target values. The MLP regressor exhibits the ability to effectively manage intricate and nonlinear connections between the input and output variables.

The MLP regressor can be mathematically represented as follows:

1. The matrix of input data can be represented by S, where each row denotes an observation and each column denotes an independent variable.
2. Consider y to be the variable-vector target.
3. Let D and h represent, respectively, the weight matrix and bias vector for each neuron in the MLP regressor.
4. Let f represent the activation function applied to the weighted sum of each neuron's inputs.
5. The MLP regressor output for a given input s is given by Equation (13.25).

$$y\_pred(s) = f(D\_2 * f(D\_1 * x + h\_1) + h\_2) \qquad (13.25)$$

where D_1 and h_1 represent the weight matrix and bias vector for the first layer of neurons, D_2 and h_2 represent the weight matrix and bias vector for the second (output) layer of neurons, and f represents the activation function.

6. Determining the weight matrices D_1 and D_2 and bias vectors h_1 and h_2 that minimize the mean squared error (MSE) between the predicted values y_pred(s) and the actual target values y in the training set is the goal as in Equation (13.26).

$$MSE = 1/m * \sum\_i = 1 \wedge m (y\_i - y\_pred(s\_i))^2 \qquad (13.26)$$

where m is the number of training set observations.

7. Using gradient descent, the optimization problem can be handled by updating the weights and biases in the direction of the negative gradient of the MSE with respect to the weights and biases as in Equation (13.27).

$$
\begin{aligned}
D\_1 &= D\_1 - \alpha * \partial MSE/\partial D\_1 \\
h\_1 &= h\_1 - \alpha * \partial MSE/\partial h\_1 \\
D\_2 &= D\_2 - \alpha * \partial MSE/\partial D\_2 \\
h\_2 &= h\_2 - \alpha * \partial MSE/\partial h\_2
\end{aligned}
\tag{13.27}
$$

where α is the learning rate, which controls the size of the weight updates, and $\partial MSE/\partial D$ and $\partial MSE/\partial h$ are the partial derivatives of the MSE with respect to the weights and biases, respectively.

8. The partial derivatives can be calculated using the backpropagation technique, which propagates the error from the output layer back through the network and uses the chain rule to calculate the derivatives.

The MSE is a statistical metric utilized for assessing the accuracy of a predictive or estimation model, as shown in Equation (13.28). The MSE value of zero signifies an exact correspondence between the anticipated and factual values. Conversely, higher MSE values indicate more substantial deviations between the predicted and actual values.

$$
MSE = 1/h^* \sum_{i=1}^{h} \left(a(i) - \hat{a}(i) \right)^2
\tag{13.28}
$$

Here,

h is the count of number of data points.
$a(i)$ is the actual value of the datapoint.
$\hat{a}(i)$ is the corresponding predicted value of the datapoint.

13.12.1 Root mean squared error (RMSE)

The RMSE is a widely employed statistical metric as shown in Equation (13.29), utilized for assessing the accuracy of a prediction or forecasting model. RMSE serves as an indicator of the degree of deviation between the predictions and actual values. A reduced RMSE value is indicative of a superior model fit to the data, as it implies a decreased discrepancy between the projected and observed values.

$$
RMSE = \sqrt{\sum_{i=1}^{F} \left\| a(i) - \hat{a}(i) \right\|^2 \div F}
\tag{13.29}
$$

Here

F is the count of number of data points.
$a(i)$ is the actual value of the datapoint.
$\hat{a}(i)$ is the corresponding predicted value of the datapoint.

13.12.2 Mean absolute error

MAE is a performance metric for regression models. The MAE is computed by accumulating the absolute value of the difference between the predicted and actual values and dividing by the total number of observations, as shown in Equation (13.30). The resultant value represents the average deviation between the predicted and actual values, with smaller values indicating superior model performance.

$$\text{MAE} = \left| \left(s_i - s_j \right) \right| / j \tag{13.30}$$

Here:

j is the number of datapoints.
s_i is the actual value.
s_j is the predicted value.

13.12.3 Coefficient of determination(R^2)

R^2 score as per Equation (13.31) is a statistical indicator of the proportion of variance in the dependent variable (target variable) that can be explained by the independent variables (features) in a regression model. The correlation is expressed as a numeric value between 0.0 and 1.0, where 1.0 represents a perfect fit, which is highly reliable for making future predictions. A value of 0.0, on the other hand, indicates that the model is erroneous and fails to model the data effectively.

$$R = \frac{m(\Sigma cd) - (\Sigma c)(\Sigma d)}{\sqrt{\left[m\Sigma c^2 - (\Sigma c)^2 \right]\left[m\Sigma d^2 - (\Sigma d)^2 \right]}} \tag{13.31}$$

Here,

m is the total number of observations.
Σc is the sum of values of variable c.
Σd is the sum of values of variable d.
Σcd is the sum of the product of variables c and d.
Σc^2 is the sum of squares of the variable c
Σd^2 is the sum of squares of the variable d
Coefficient of determination = Square of correlation coefficient = R^2

13.12.3.1 Process flow and architecture of the proposed work

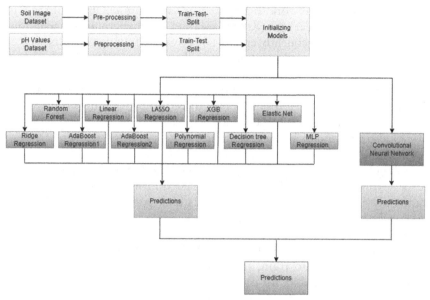

Figure 13.5 Process flow of the proposed work.

13.12.3.2 Convolutional neural network (CNN)

CNN is a class of deep learning models that are commonly employed in tasks related to the recognition of images and videos. The convolutional layer is a fundamental element of a CNN and executes a mathematical function known as convolution.

The convolution operation takes in an input (image), a set of filters (also known as kernels or weights), and applies the dot product of each filter to the overlapping regions of the input. The result is a new feature map that summarizes the local features in the input. By repeating this operation multiple times, CNN is able to extract high-level features from the input image.

The key mathematics behind convolutions include linear algebra and calculus. Specifically, the dot product and matrix multiplication are used to compute the convolution, while gradient descent and backpropagation are used to update the network weights during training.

Convolution: It is a mathematical operation that computes the sum of element-wise multiplications between the input and a small, fixed filter.

Pooling: Pooling is a technique used in deep learning that involves downsampling the input data to reduce its spatial dimensions. This process is designed to retain critical features while discarding nonessential information. Max pooling is the most frequently used pooling operation.

Activation functions: These functions are mathematical functions that are utilized to introduce nonlinearity into a neural network. This nonlinearity enables the network to acquire intricate representations of the data. The rectified linear unit (ReLU), sigmoid, and hyperbolic tangent (tan*h*) are among the frequently employed activation functions in CNNs.

Matrix multiplication: It is a fundamental operation in linear algebra that is used in the fully connected layers of a CNN to make the final predictions.

Backpropagation: It is an algorithm that is commonly utilized to calculate the gradients of the loss function in relation to the network weights. These gradients are subsequently used to modify the weights through the application of gradient descent.

Pooling layers are frequently employed in CNNs to perform downsampling of the feature maps, thereby decreasing their dimensionality. The process is commonly executed via operations such as max pooling, wherein the maximum value within each region of the feature map is selected.

Firstly, Figure 13.5 shows the process flow of the proposed work. Secondly, the 235-image dataset was imported, minimal preprocessing has been done, and then it is split into train, test, and validation datasets in the ratio of 0.8:0.1:0.1 (i.e., 80% data for train set and 10% each for test and validation sets) and has been run for 100 epochs. As the dataset consists of images, CNN has been chosen for the current work. An image size of 256*256 has been set and passed to a CNN consisting of six convolutional layers and six max pooling layers alternatively placed followed by a flatten and couple of dense layers. Sparse categorical cross-entropy has been used as the loss function as the current work is a multiclass classification and optimizer is set to Adam which has been clearly depicted in Figure 13.6. Results with graphical

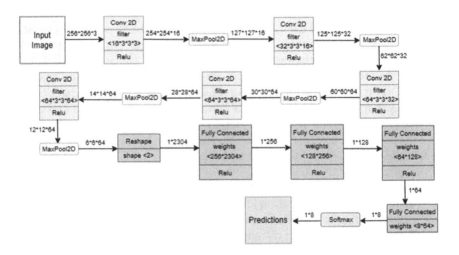

Figure 13.6 CNN architecture.

interpretation have been discussed in the following section. The current dataset would predict the type of soil. The pH-recognition dataset [42] contains 653 rows and four attributes, namely, blue, green, red, and label (pH), in which 80% of the dataset is used for training and 20% is used for testing. As the dataset appeared to be flawless and did not contain any null values or superfluous attributes, a significant amount of the pre-processing of the data was skipped. Both the quality and quantity of the data that were acquired are considered in the analysis. The values that were determined are also presented in a graphical form.

The predictions were done using multiple regression models: DT regressor, XGB regressor, LASSO regressor, elastic net, linear regressor, ridge regressor AdaBoost regressor (base_estimator = Random Forest Regressor), random forest regressor, AdaBoost regressor (base_estimator = Decision Tree Regressor), polynomial regressor, and MLP regressor.

Various parameters have been customized during the training of the model which includes setting degree to 4 for polynomial regression, maximum depth of 2 for the random forest regressor, regularization hyperparameter 0.0001 for elastic net, LASSO, and ridge regressors, learning rate of 0.5 and 220 estimators for XGB regressor, maximum iterations set to 50, early stopping being true, and solver being 'Limited-memory BFGS'(Broyden–Fletcher–Goldfarb–Shanno) for MLP regressor. AdaBoost regressor with base estimator being DT regressor and DT regressor with default parameters have been used and no customizations have been done.

13.12.3.3 Results and discussions

Figures 13.7 and 13.8 depict the performance of CNN model where our test and train accuracies have been 90.62% and 91.66%, respectively, followed by loss and validation loss 0.27 and 0.17, respectively.

MAE, MSE, RMSE, and R^2 score values of various models are shown in Table 13.3. From Table 13.3, XGBoost regressor has been the best among all the regressors with the highest R^2 score of 98% followed by AdaBoost regression (be = Decision Tree Regressor) and polynomial regression (d = 4) with R^2 scores of 97% and 95%, respectively.

Based on the outcomes of models such as DT regression and random forest regression outperformed linear regression due to the nonlinear nature of the data, which can be readily deduced from Figure 13.9. Since the data were widely dispersed, these algorithms outperformed linear regression.

Figures 13.10–13.13 show the comparison in terms of performance between all 11 regression models in terms of MAE, MSE, RMSE, and R² score, respectively.

The input image has been separated into three layers (i.e., R, G, B) and the average of red, green, and blue values have been calculated after parsing through each and every pixel of the image. Then these RGB values are sent to our model for pH predictions, which would also predict the chemical

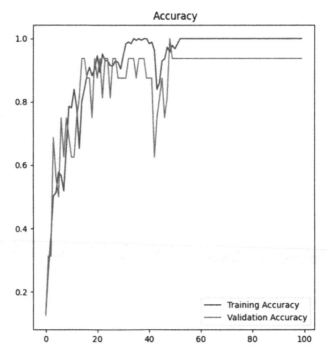

Figure 13.7 Test and train accuracies of proposed CNN model.

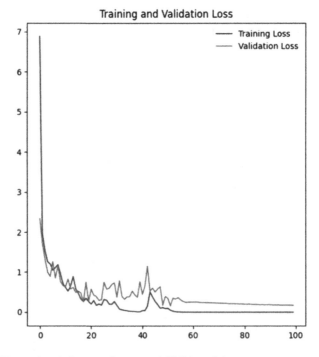

Figure 13.8 Test and train losses of proposed CNN model.

Table 13.3 MAE, MSE, RMSE, and R^2 score values of machine learning models

S. No.	Model	MAE	MSE	RMSE	R^2
1	XGB regression	0.38	0.38	0.61	0.98
2	AdaBoost regression (be = Decision Tree Regressor)	0.36	0.56	0.75	0.97
3	Polynomial regression (d = 4)	0.65	0.87	0.93	0.95
4	Decision tree regression	0.46	1.02	1.01	0.94
5	AdaBoost regression (be = Random Forest Regressor)	0.90	1.25	1.11	0.93
6	Random forest regression	0.94	1.43	1.19	0.92
7	MLP regressor	0.86	2.13	1.46	0.89
8	Elastic net	1.79	4.90	2.21	0.75
9	LASSO regression	1.79	4.90	2.21	0.75
10	Linear regression	1.79	4.90	2.21	0.75
11	Ridge regression	1.79	4.90	2.21	0.75

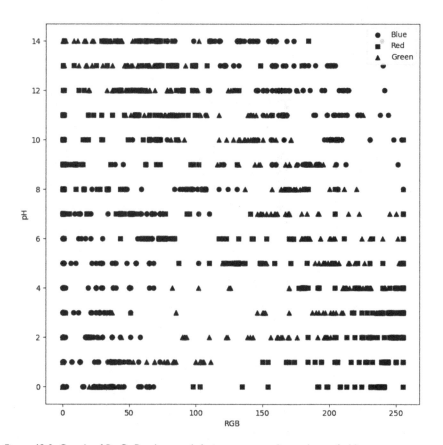

Figure 13.9 Graph of R, G, B values and their corresponding values of pH.

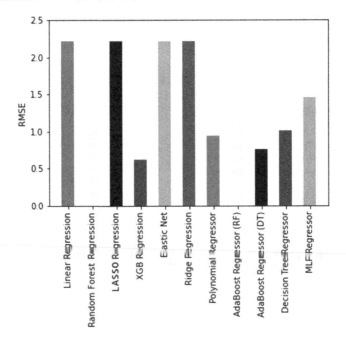

Figure 13.10 RMSE of proposed models.

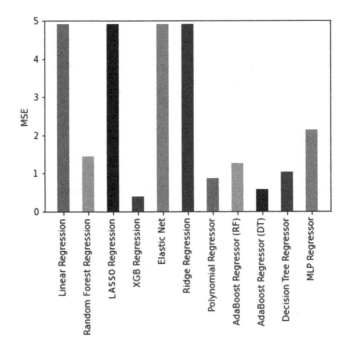

Figure 13.11 MSE of proposed models.

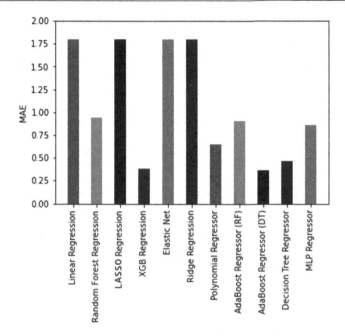

Figure 13.12 MAE of proposed models.

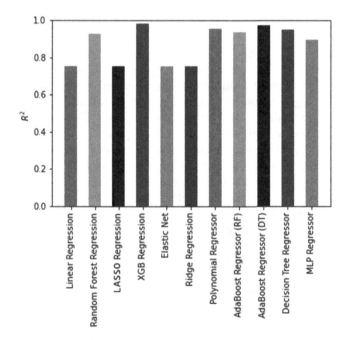

Figure 13.13 R^2 of proposed models.

Table 13.4 Predictions of the model with respect to corresponding pH range

S. No.	pH range	Chemical characteristics	Deficient nutrients	Suitable crops
I	Below 4.0	Strongly acidic	All nutrients	Not suitable for any crop
2	4.0–6.0	Moderately acidic	B, Ca, K, Mg, Mo, N, P	Wheat, soyabean, rice, potato, pea, peanut
3	6.0–6.5	Slightly acidic	Ca, Mg, N, P, S	Wheat, soyabean, rice, sweet potato, corn, beetroot
4	6.5–7.5	Neutral	No deficient nutrients	Wheat, soyabean, barley, vegetables, oilseeds, mushrooms, oats, cotton
5	7.5–8.5	Slightly alkaline	Fe, Mn, N, P	Vegetables, oilseeds, mushrooms, oats, cotton, cucumber, garlic
6	Above 8.5	Strongly alkaline	All nutrients	Not suitable for any crops

B: boron; Ca: calcium; Fe: iron; K: potassium; Mg: magnesium; Mn: manganese; Mo: molybdenum; N: nitrogen; P: phosphorus; S: sulfur.

characteristics, deficient nutrients, and suitable crops based on pH, as depicted in Table 13.4.

13.13 CONCLUSION

The objective of the proposed work is to classify different soil types and forecast their pH levels using a combination of machine learning algorithms and image processing techniques to create a soil health intelligence system that can suggest suitable crops. The system is trained on two datasets consisting of soil images, and red, green, and blue (RGB) values. From the results, the XGBoost regressor has effectively predicted soil pH and its characteristics with a very good R^2 score of 98%, and CNN has also performed well, with test and training accuracy of 90.62% and 91.66%, respectively, followed by train loss and validation loss of 0.27 and 0.17, respectively. The proposed approach examines and categorizes the data, resulting in a stable and effective method for soil classification and pH prediction. This research work has major implications for agriculture and soil sciences since it provides a rapid, inexpensive, and noninvasive technique for soil assessment. In addition, the proposed method can be extended in future work to predict other soil parameters, such as nutrient levels, organic matter content, and water retention capacity, by applying machine learning and deep learning techniques to enhance our understanding of soil parameters and recommended farming.

REFERENCES

1. Rahman, Sk, Mitra, Kaushik & Islam, S. M. (2018). Soil classification using machine learning methods and crop suggestion based on soil series. 2018 21st International Conference of Computer and Information Technology (ICCIT). 1–4. doi: 10.1109/ICCITECHN.2018.8631943

2. Park, J. & Santamarina, J. (2017). Revised soil classification system for coarse-fine mixtures. Journal of Geotechnical and Geoenvironmental Engineering. 143, 1–13. doi: 04017039. 10.1061/(ASCE)GT.1943-5606.0001705.

3. Morais, P. A. O., de Souza, D. M., Madari, B. E., Soares, A. S. & deOliveira, A. E. (2019). Using image analysis to estimate the soil organic carbon content. Microchemical Journal. 147. 775–781.

4. Morais, Pedro Augusto, Souza, Diego, Carvalho, Márcia Thaís, Madari, Beáta & Oliveira, Anselmo. (2019). Predicting soil texture using image analysis. Microchemical Journal. 146. 455–463. doi: 10.1016/j.microc.2019.01.009

5. Kovačević, Miloš, Bajat, Branislav & Gajic, Bosko. (2010). Soil type classification and estimation of soil properties using support vector machines. Geoderma. 154. 340–347. doi: 10.1016/j.geoderma.2009.11.005

6. Barman, Utpal. (2019). Prediction of soil pH using smartphone based digital image processing and prediction algorithm. Journal of Mechanics of Continua and Mathematical Sciences. 14. doi: 10.26782/jmcms.2019.04.00019

7. Barman, Utpal, Choudhury, Ridip, Talukdar, Niyar, Deka, Prashant, Kalita, Indrajit & Rahman, Naseem. (2018). Predication of soil pH using HSI color image processing and regression over Guwahati, Assam, India. Journal of Applied and Natural Science. 10. 805–809. doi: 10.31018/jans.v10i2.1701

8. Soil Survey Staff. (2014). Keys to soil taxonomy (12th ed.). Washington, DC: USDA-Natural Resources Conservation Service, US Government Print Office.

9. Kirillova, Nataliya, Grauer-Gray, Jenna, Sileva, T., Artemyeva, Zinaida & Burova, E. (2018). New perspectives to use Munsell color charts with electronic devices. Computers and Electronics in Agriculture. 155. 373–385. doi: 10.1016/j.compag.2018.10.028

10. Marqués-Mateu, Angel, Moreno-Ramón, Héctor, Balasch, Sebastià & Ibáñez-Asensio, Sara. (2018). Quantifying the uncertainty of soil colour measurements with Munsell charts using a modified attribute agreement analysis. Catena. 171. doi: 10.1016/j.catena.2018.06.027

11. Munsell Color. (2000). Munsell soil color charts: Year 2000 revised washable edition. New York: Greta Macbeth.

12. Chang, Cheng-Wen, Laird, David, Mausbach, Maurice & Hurburgh, Charles. (2001). Near-infrared reflectance spectroscopy: Principal components regression analyses of soil properties. Soil Science Society of America Journal. 65. 480–490. doi: 10.2136/sssaj2001.652480x

13. Viscarra Rossel, Raphael, Walvoort, D. J. J., Mcbratney, Alex, Janik, L. & Skjemstad, J. O. (2006). Visible, near infrared, mid infrared or combined diffuse reflectance spectroscopy for simultaneous assessment of various soil properties. Geoderma. 131. 59–75. doi: 10.1016/j.geoderma.2005.03.007

14. Nocita, Marco, Stevens, Antoine, Tóth, Gergely, Panagos, Panos, Wesemael, Bas & Montanarella, Luca. (2013). Prediction of soil organic carbon content by diffuse reflectance spectroscopy using a local partial least square regression approach. Soil Biology and Biochemistry. 68. 337–347. doi: 10.1016/j.soilbio.2013.10.022

15. Heung, Brandon, Ho, Hung Chak, Zhang, Jin, Knudby, Anders, Bulmer, Chuck & Schmidt, Margaret. (2016). An overview and comparison of machine-learning techniques for classification purposes in digital soil mapping. Geoderma. 265. 62–77. doi: 10.1016/j.geoderma.2015.11.014

16. Sofou, Anastasia, Evangelopoulos, Georgios & Maragos, Petros. (2005). Soil image segmentation and texture analysis: A computer vision approach. Geoscience and Remote Sensing Letters. 2. 394–398. doi: 10.1109/LGRS.2005.851752

17. Liu, Yong, Wang, Huifeng, Zhang, Hong & Liber, Karsten. (2016). A comprehensive support vector machine-based classification model for soil quality assessment. Soil and Tillage Research. 155. 19–26. doi: 10.1016/j.still.2015.07.006

18. Bhattacharya, B. & Solomatine, D. P. (2003). An algorithm for clustering and classification of series data with constraint of contiguity. Third International Conference on Hybrid and Intelligent Systems, Melbourne, Australia, pp. 489–498.

19. Chung, Sun-Ok, Cho, Ki-Hyun, Cho, Jin-Woong, Jung, Ki-Youl & Yamakawa, Takeo. (2012). Soil texture classification algorithm using RGB characteristics of soil images. Journal of the Faculty of Agriculture Kyushu University. 57. 393–397. doi: 10.5109/25196

20. Shenbagavalli R, Ramar K. (2011). Classification of soil textures based on laws features extracted from preprocessing images on sequential and random windows. Bonfring International Journal of Advances in Image Processing. 1. 15–18. doi: 10.9756/BIJAIP.1004

21. Sudharsan, V. & Yamuna, B. (2016). Support vector machine based decoding algorithm for BCH codes. Journal of Telecommunications and Information Technology, 2, 108–112.

22. Unmesha Sreeveni, U. B., Shiju Sathyadevan. (2015). ADBF Integratable Machine Learning Algorithms: Map reduce Implementation. Second International Symposium on computer vision and the Internet (VisionNet'15).

23. Zhang, Z. & Tumay, M. T. (2000). Statistical to fuzzy approach toward CPT soil classification. Journal of Geotechnical and Geoenvironmental Engineering. 125. 179–186.

24. Young, I. T. & Calvert, T. W. (1974). An analysis technique for biological shape. Information and Control. 25. 357–370.

25. Fan, Z., Herrick, J. E., Saltzman, R., Matteis, C., Yudina, A., Nocella, N., Crawford, E., Parker, R. & Van Zee, J.. (2017). Measurement of soil color: A comparison between smartphone camera and the Munsell color charts. Soil Science Society of America Journal. 81, 5. 1139–1146.

26. Viscarra Rossel, Raphael, Fouad, Youssef & Walter, Christian. (2008). Using a digital camera to measure soil organic carbon and iron contents. Biosystems Engineering. 100. 149–159.

27. Vibhute, Amol, Kale, Karbhari, Dhumal, Rajesh & Mehrotra, Suresh. (2015). Soil type classification and mapping using hyperspectral remote sensing data. MAMI 2015. pp. 1–4.

28. Qiu, Z., Chen, J., Zhao, Y., Zhu, S., He, Y. & Zhang, C. (2018). Variety identification of single rice seed using hyperspectral imaging combined with convolutional neural network. Applied Sciences. 8, 2. 212.

29. Chatnuntawech, I., Tantisantisom, K., Khanchaitit, P., Boonkoom, T., Bilgic, B. & Chuangsuwanich, E. (2018). Rice classification using hyperspectral imaging and deep convolutional neural network. arXiv:1805.11491

30. Stiglitz, R., Mikhailova, E., Post, C., Schlautman, M. & Sharp, J. (2016). Evaluation of an inexpensive sensor to measure soil color. Computers and Electronics in Agriculture. 121. 141–148.
31. Stiglitz, R., Mikhailova, E., Post, C., Schlautman, M. & Sharp, J. (2017). Using an inexpensive color sensor for rapid assessment of soil organic carbon. Geoderma. 286. 98–103.
32. Gómez-Robledo, L., López-Ruiz, N., Melgosa, M., Palma, A. J., Capitán-Vallvey, L. F. & Sánchez-Marañón, M. (2013). Using the mobile phone as Munsell soil-color sensor: An experiment under controlled illumination conditions. Computers and Electronics in Agriculture. 99. 200–208.
33. Stiglitz, R., Mikhailova, E., Post, C., Schlautman, M., Sharp, J., Pargas, R., Glover, B. & Mooney, J. (2017). Soil color sensor data collection using a GPS-enabled smartphone application. Geoderma. 296. 108–114.
34. Breul, P. & Gourves, R. (2006). In field soil characterization: Approach based on texture image analysis. Journal of Geotechnical and Geoenvironmental Engineering, 132(1), 102–107. doi:10.1061/(ASCE)1090-0241(2006)132:1(102)
35. Aziz, M. M., Ahmed, D. R. & Abraham, B. F. (2016). Determine the pH of soil by using neural network based on soil's colour. International Journal of Advanced Research in Computer Science and Software Engineering. 6, 11. 51–54.
36. Aditya, A., Chatterjee, N. & Pradhan, C. (2017). Computation and storage of possible pouvoir hydrogen level of soil using digital image processing. International Conference on Communication and Signal Processing, India. pp. 205–209.
37. Babu, C. S. M. & Pandian, M.A. (2016). Determination of chemical and physical characteristics of soil using digital image processing. International Journal of Emerging Technology in Computer Science & Electronics. 20, 2. 331–335.
38. Gurubasava & Mahantesh, S. D. (2018). Analysis of agricultural soil pH using digital image processing. International Journal of Research in Advent Technology. 6, 8. 1812–1816.
39. Kumar, V., Vimal, B., Kumar, R., Kumar, R. & Kumar, M. (2014). Determination of soil pH by using digital image processing technique. Journal of Applied and Natural Science. 6, 1. 14–18.
40. Mohan, R. R., Mridula, S. & Mohanan, P. (2015). Artificial neural network model for soil moisture estimation at microwave frequency. Progress in Electromagnetics Research M. 43. 175–181.
41. Abu, M. A., Nasir, E. M. M. & Bala, C. R. (2014). Simulation of soil pH control system using fuzzy logic method. International Journal of Emerging Trends in Computer Image & Processing. 3, 1. 15–19.
42. ROBERT. (2019). pH-recognition, Version 1, Retrieved November 23, 2022, from https://www.kaggle.com/datasets/robjan/ph-recognition.

Chapter 14

Marine soundscape source separation in the Indian Ocean Region (IOR) soundscape using unsupervised machine learning

Misha Chandar, Abirami Parthiban,
and Arunkumar Balakrishnan

14.1 INTRODUCTION

Assessing an ecosystem involves observing its biological, physical, and social changes [1]. Until the last decade, remote sensing techniques were widely used in the underwater domain to identify the biophysical activities of habitat and study the biodiversity changes caused due to ramping up of anthropogenic activities in the ocean [2]. However, limited visibility and assessment hindered visual inspection and monitoring. Ecoacoustics as an emerging field aids in studying the relationship between the sound-producing biophony (living organisms), its geophony (physical habitat of the biophony), and anthrophony (human activities) of an ecosystem [3]. Factors like geophysical events, biodiversity, and anthropogenic activities contribute largely to the soundscape of an ecosystem [4]. Changes that hinder visual monitoring can be efficiently tracked acoustically using soundscape analysis. Soundscape analysis aids biodiversity assessment by evaluating the biological and anthropogenic contributors to the soundscape dynamics. Studying the biotic sounds helps in assessing the wildlife biodiversity and the abiotic sounds, on the other hand, reveal the influence of geophysical activities and human-related activities on biological life. Followed by audio visualization, source separation forms the next step of soundscape analysis and it is performed using audio source separation. Audio source separation is an audio-based technique that helps in recovering the source-specific information from biophony, geophony, and anthrophony amidst the highly interfering sounds from the diverse noise sources of the ocean [5]. Unlike traditional denoising techniques, source separation aims at separating the sound sources as sounds rarely occur in isolation, and any disturbances as spectral masking or signal distortion may cause biased results, which in turn affects the overall assessment. In recent years, a lot of efforts have been put in designing recording devices to perform the selective recording of biotic sounds in an ecosystem. However, unlike passive acoustic monitoring (PAM) [6], techniques that require the cooperation of the marine life to record sounds like active acoustic monitoring (AAM) and sonars can do more harm than good. Hence, the idea of designing a non-invasive monitoring technique needs to be ensured when dealing with biological life.

DOI: 10.1201/9781003433941-14

Other than biodiversity assessment, investigating the sounds of geophony and anthrophony can help in evaluating the impacts caused by anthropogenic activities like shipping and dredging on aquatic life [7]. An increase in the sound level in the ocean which is perceived as noise not only has a negative influence on the ocean habitat but also alters the soundscape of the ocean. It affects the echolocation of cetaceans masking the received biological sounds. To date, most deep ocean data and the acoustic metrics used in soundscape generation have not been converted into tools for effective use by managers and stakeholders. On the whole, marine soundscapes contain valuable ecological information that when effectively retrieved can aid in studying the unexplored dynamics of the ocean.

14.2 MARINE SOUNDSCAPES OF THE INDIAN OCEAN REGION

The Indian Ocean Region (IOR) has significantly gained importance as a hub for maritime trade in the twenty-first century. It is viewed as a strategically powered sea region with political, economic, and military griping by the nations within this region. Increasing merchant shipping activities and naval vessel traffic has altered the marine soundscape of this region drastically [8]. Multiple sources contribute to the ocean ambient noise in the IOR region. From a broader categorization, the sources are mainly natural and anthropogenic. Natural sources are sounds produced by natural physical processes like rain, waves, underwater earthquakes, and biological sounds from vocalizations of marine mammals, fishes, and marine invertebrates. Natural sources occupy the mid-frequency range of the ocean noise frequency spectrum (Figure 14.1). Human-related activities like shipping, underwater excavation, sonars, and dredging constitute anthropogenic sources [9].

The altered soundscape has impacted the cetaceans largely leading to acoustic habitat degradation. With great geopolitical, socio-economical, acoustical significance, the IOR needs to be restored of its acoustic degradation to witness no mass stranding of whales in this region in the near future. Refer to Figure 14.2 for the distribution and composition of the marine soundscape represented as a spectrogram for the IOR.

14.3 APPLICATIONS

14.3.1 Diversity of biotic and abiotic sounds and their assessment

The underwater acoustic community consists of a wide range of biotic and abiotic contributors. Assessing the behavioural pattern of the biotic species in response to the abiotic sounds helps in understanding the general reflex pattern of a species as a defence response or a masking behaviour. Recent studies

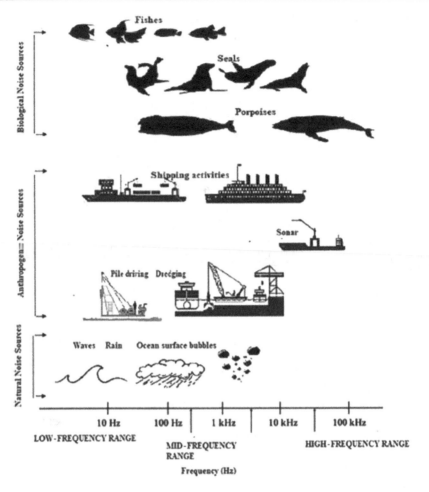

Figure 14.1 Frequency sharing illustration of various acoustic systems in the ocean [10].

have proved that Beluga whales have altered their echolocation pattern of too much higher frequencies in the presence of interfering noises [11]. Certain species are highly sensitive to the noise intervention by artificial sources that leads to changing their acoustic habitats, while few develop tolerance towards the condition. Acoustic habitat degradation is seen as a serious issue in recent times as its severe consequences break the normal behavioural pattern of biological life in the oceans.

14.3.2 Noise evaluation

The melting sounds of glaciers are recorded to access the rapid climate change of a region [12]. Similarly, noises from geophysical sources like underwater earthquakes, rain, and waves are assessed to understand the dynamic ocean

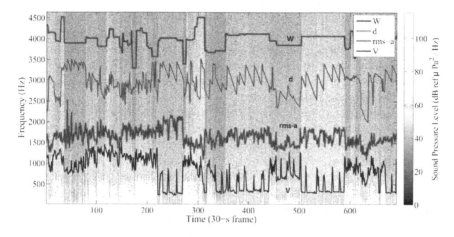

Figure 14.2 A sample of the marine soundscape of the IOR.

environment. The noise produced by anthropogenic activities in the ocean is recorded to investigate the influence of human-related activities on ocean life and to develop conservatory measures. Moreover, ocean noise evaluation helps in accessing the changing soundscape of oceans.

14.3.3 Temporal and spatial relationship

Changing seasons, climatic conditions, and day–night patterns influence the vocalizing behaviour of species [13]. Snapping shrimps showed high acoustic activity and sound production during dawn and dusk. Studying the temporal and spatial relationship of an ocean favours the innumerable lives that benefit from it.

14.4 RELATED WORKS AND LIMITATIONS

Recent research contributions in soundscape source separation are limited as identifying and separating the sources is quite challenging, especially for an ocean soundscape. In reference to the recent research publications in this regard, the emphasis is largely on separating high-frequency biological sounds produced by cetaceans from non-biological sounds. The camouflaging of low-frequency biological sounds from fishes and invertebrates in the background noise of the ocean hinders its precise separation. Hence, vocalizations of fishes and invertebrates are often neglected in a marine soundscape separation to avoid false separation results. Lin et al. [14] have investigated the application of deep-sea acoustic observation through a long-duration platform to observe and monitor the changing dynamics of the ecosystem using audio source separation. The long-term acoustic recording is visualized as long-duration false-colour spectrograms to aid in large-scale source separation. The clustering-based model with minimal supervision segregated the major sources of biotic and abiotic sources from a deep-water soundscape of Taiwan using the distinctive source-specific spectral features. The source separation results helped in studying the diurnal and seasonal interactions between the different biotic sources.

Biodiversity assessment is a vital application of soundscape source separation as the ecosystem and the dependent communities are changing at a faster phase. Tracking and accessing the biodiversity unwraps the hidden cause of the distressed habitat. In Reference [15], the authors have emphasized the use of acoustic indices to access the biodiversity changes of the deep sea. Acoustic indices aids in making biodiversity assessments from long-duration spectrograms in a rapid time frame. Few popular ones include the acoustic complexity index (ACI), acoustic entropy index (H), and many more. Each of the indices is adapted to highlight certain features of a signal. An appropriate combination of these indices in connection with the nature and type of the signal helps in reflecting predominant fluctuations of sounds across time. Data annotation is an important step in deciding the choice of model for deployment. Deep learning models require large volumes of annotated data for training the model. Having proven to be very effective in handling image data, deep learning is now becoming efficient in dealing with the image like audio-based signals called spectrograms. In Reference [16], the authors have applied deep learning for soundscape emotion recognition. Deep learning models like convolutional neural networks (CNN) with transfer learning and long short-term memory recurrent neural networks (LSTM-RNN) were applied to perceive the emotion of a soundscape recording. In terms of results, deep learning models outperform most machine learning models. Massive volumes of passive acoustic ocean noise recordings are recorded every year. If manually inspected and annotated, they would form a great source of data to develop efficient automated classification and detection systems in the future.

Owing to the biodiversity conservation application of soundscape source separation, many species with limited population size are being acoustically identified and monitored regularly. As one such effort, Znidersic et al. [17] have monitored the population of a bird species of conservation concern and small population by investigating its vocalization behaviour. Continuous long duration of acoustic recordings was recorded non-invasively and represented as long-duration false-colour spectrograms to aid visual inspection and annotation. The breeding behaviour of the species was confirmed with a typical sound pattern in the spectrogram. The detection was automated using a machine learning technique that was capable of identifying the bird call from a large audio dataset. Likewise, the information about a species of interest can be used to effectively optimize the existing monitoring methods and increase the probability of detecting of a species.

14.5 REGULATORY FRAMEWORK

In managing the adverse impact of underwater noise on the underwater habitat resulting in a drastic acoustic habitat degradation, a regulatory framework in this regard concerning the underwater domain awareness is the need of the hour. The approach to a full-fledged regulatory framework takes its attempt from the initial underwater noise assessment to the final acoustic sound source allocation. With the sources and the nature of the acoustic composition in a marine soundscape data to be erratic, a reasonably quantifiable soundscape source assessment technique is needed to assess the composition of the acoustic sources and to facilitate easier sources separation, but the frequent onset and offset of the sound sources makes their assessment very complicated. The low- to high-frequency sounds from anthrophony, geophony, and biophony spread highly, overlapping across the entire ocean spectrum; the mid-frequency bands also hinders its easier separation. The ocean noise regulatory framework is designed addressing every possible practical aspect of a real-time ocean soundscape. Figure 14.3 shows the proposed ASDCLA ocean acoustic spectrum utilization framework.

Ocean acoustics is becoming a growing field of research in the recent times as the scope of acoustics in studying the behaviour of sound in underwater is expanding. With the better applicability of sound as a medium of communication in water, the range of applications it can offer has sprung over the years with much emphasis on exploratory and conservatory applications. The increasing intervention of anthropogenic activities in the oceans has drastically impacted the natural functioning of the ocean habitat calling for better marine habitat monitoring approaches. Research efforts in this regard can envisage a healthy ocean environment in the future. Designing a marine habitat monitoring application of Underwater Acoustic Sensor Networks imposes major concerns like limited bandwidth, high propagation, resource utilization, and power constraint–related challenges, which are oft-addressed research challenges, whereas improper spectrum utilization in oceans is an underrated issue that poses serious threat to marine life. Most Underwater Acoustic Networks are designed as a single network neglecting the existence of natural acoustic systems in the ocean. The prevalence of diverse natural and artificial acoustic systems in an ocean environment overuses the mid-frequency bands of the ocean spectrum leading to a heavily shared scare ocean spectrum. Despite the oversharing, the underwater ocean spectrum is still temporarily and spatially underutilized leading to an inefficiently utilized ocean spectrum. As an effort to calm down these adverse impacts, a non-invasive end-to-end marine habitat–friendly acoustic frequency distribution framework is designed to efficiently utilize the ocean spectrum and avoid frequency clashes between acoustic sources. All marine species are considered in the spectrum utilization and just not limited to marine mammals. This chapter aims to improve the spectrum utilization while avoiding harmful interference with other acoustic systems and design a marine habitat–friendly

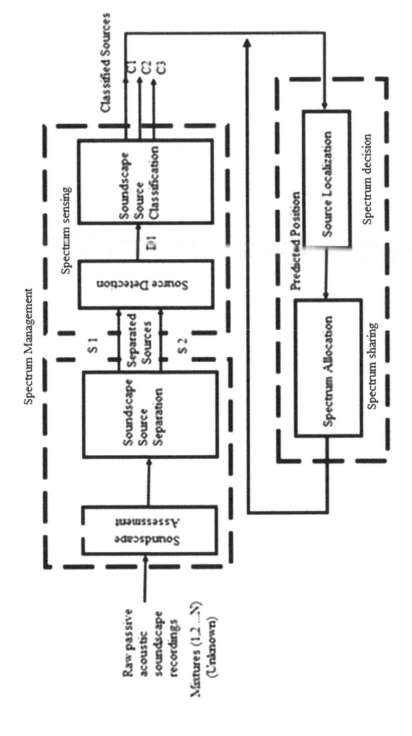

Figure 14.3 ASDCLA framework for effective ocean spectrum utilization.

acoustic frequency distribution framework for efficient spectrum utilization in oceans. An efficient end-to end acoustic ocean spectrum utilization framework is required to effectively utilize the scare ocean spectrum without frequency clashes between acoustic sources and the acoustic ocean spectrum addressing underutilization.

Existing regulatory frameworks are focused mainly on tackling noise in the ocean; however, identifying the anthropogenic stressors and limiting their prevalence on ocean grounds can only control the level of impact and serve as a temporary solution. The challenge of ocean conservation is to deal with the greater complexities of assessing, identifying, separating, and allocating the sources with relevance to their function rather than restricting their usage. The proposed framework is designed in this regard, touching on every small practical aspects of the ocean front from both time and size perspectives resulting in an effective solution as an ocean acoustic spectrum management framework.

14.6 METHODOLOGY

Supervised machine learning techniques are largely applied in data-deficient domains. The lack of availability of large-scale annotated audio data as passive acoustic ocean noise recording hinders the application of deep learning models for soundscape source separation. Deep learning–based source separation requires large volumes of annotated data for training and a set of clean signals to test the model. Data annotations are done manually by experts by visually inspecting the spectrograms (image representation of sound). Manual annotations are cost- and time-consuming leading to the limited availability of annotated data. In this case, machine learning algorithms find purpose in handling raw unannotated data and produces close results to deep learning models. Soundscape source separation is approached in the following three stages.

14.6.1 Audio visualization

Audio visualization refers to transforming an audio signal in its time domain to a time–frequency domain representation known as spectrograms [18]. A spectrogram is an image-like representation of an audio signal. Many authors use the audio signal as a raw waveform, but for a signal that constantly varies with time, spectrogram representation suits best. Feature extraction techniques that highlight prominent distinguishing characters in audio like timbre, soprano, alto, and tenor are adopted according to the nature of the data used.

14.6.2 Audio source separation

Supervised source separation techniques are capable of separating the components of a soundscape without any annotated training data. Blind source separation techniques are widely adopted to separate unknown sources mixed with unknown methodologies. Based on certain distinguishing factors like threshold or frequency range, similar sources are grouped and audio source identification techniques are applied to reveal the category of sources.

14.6.3 Audio source identification

Post the separation of the sources from the soundscape, the sources are identified adopting audio source identification techniques. Clustering-based techniques are widely used to group similar sources into clusters. Information about the exact source is still not achieved, rather the grouping is done based on the similarity of the extracted features.

14.7 CHALLENGES AND WAY FORWARD

The challenges associated with soundscape source separation, on the whole, is to be viewed from the following three main aspects.

14.7.1 Audio visualization

The acoustic indices have been widely adopted as acoustic indicators of biological activities [19]. A proper combination of acoustic indices offers better visualization of the acoustic communities in their soundscape. The choice of using the appropriate indices is done by studying the sound sources in a soundscape. Underwater recordings are often influenced by multiple stationary and non-stationary sound sources, hence a choice and combination of appropriate acoustics indices aid precise revealing of sound sources in their representation. Another important aspect of audio visualization is the choice of signal representation. Long-duration spectrogram representation is the most preferred choice of audio signal representation by the research community owing to its ease of visualizing a long-duration acoustic recording as a single spectrogram across large temporal and spatial scales. Similarly, hybridising of existing feature extraction is gaining importance amidst the audio community [20].

14.7.2 Choice of source separation technique

The choice of the source separation technique largely depends upon the acoustic scene. In a complicated soundscape like ocean soundscape, the source separation is often tedious as the sources that contribute to the noise are mostly unknown and highly interfering. In this case, a complete separation of the foreground from the background noise is highly challenging. Hence, the choice of technique depends on the nature of the soundscape (deep ocean or shallow water or freshwater), the contributing sources, the mode of recording, and the distribution of sound alone in the spectrogram. The performance of unsupervised source separation models is still not achievable by supervised models [21]. Hence, novel source separation algorithms need to be designed to build a completely supervised model with no need for training data that can produce results at par to unsupervised models.

14.7.3 Source identification and generalizability

Until now, efforts to identify the exact sound source in a soundscape are not to be achieved by the research community, rather similar sources are grouped and identified broadly [22]. The performance of a source separation model depends largely on its generalizability to other soundscapes of a different environment. Most source separation models designed for a particular soundscape are non-generalizable to other soundscapes with different sources. Therefore, generalizability aspect has to be considered every time a source separation algorithm is designed.

14.8 CONCLUSION

With the growing demand in audio-based applications, research on developing novel audio signal denoising and source separation techniques is gaining importance in extracting the pure form of signal from its noisy background. An efficient soundscape monitoring network can produce massive volumes of acoustic data in a single deployment that contains habitat-rich information about the ecosystem and the quality of its acoustic habitat, the sound-producing nature of the marine life, and the impacts caused due to human-based activities. Increasing underwater noise is risking the lives of aquatic life. In all cases, management approaches are needed to calm and achieve a "quiet ocean". This chapter serves as an introduction to soundscape source separation touching ocean noise contribution, spatiotemporal planning, and biodiversity monitoring for a more extensive assessment of the ocean's health. As part of the future research work, the insights discussed in this chapter will be developed as a supervised machine learning–based marine soundscape separation model capable of separating the highly overlapping sound sources of an ocean soundscape.

REFERENCES

1. I. L. Boyd *et al.*, "An international quiet ocean experiment," *Oceanography*, vol. 24, no. 2, pp. 174–181, 2011.
2. T. Lin, T. Akamatsu, F. Sinniger, and S. Harii, "Exploring coral reef biodiversity via underwater soundscapes," *Biological Conservation*, vol. 253, p. 108901, 2021.
3. A. Farina, "Ecoacoustics : A quantitative approach to investigate the ecological role of environmental sounds," *Mathematics*, vol. 7, no. 1, p. 21, 2019.
4. S. R. P. Ross, N. R. Friedman, M. Yoshimura, T. Yoshida, I. Donohue, and E. P. Economo, "Utility of acoustic indices for ecological monitoring in complex sonic environments," *Ecol. Indic.*, vol. 121, p. 107114, 2021.

5. T. Lin, Y. Tsao, Y. Wang, and S. Lu, "Computing biodiversity change via a soundscape monitoring network," PNC 2017 Annual Conference and Joint Meetings, 2017.

6. D. De Leon, "Passive acoustic monitoring of blue and fin whales through machine learning", MBARI, 2017.

7. J. Hildebrand, "Impacts of anthropogenic sound," *Marine Mammal Research Conservation beyond Crisis*, vol. 124, pp. 101–124, 2005.

8. A. Das, "Underwater radiated noise: A new perspective in the Indian ocean region," *Maritime Affairs: Journal of the National Maritime Foundation of India*, vol. 15, no. 1, pp. 65–77, 2019. doi: 10.1080/09733159.2019.1625225

9. K. M. Awan, P. A. Shah, K. Iqbal, S. Gillani, W. Ahmad, and Y. Nam, "Underwater wireless sensor networks: A review of recent issues and challenges," *Wireless Communications & Mobile Computing*, vol. 2019, p. 6470359, 2019.

10. B. Mishachandar and S. Vairamuthu, "An underwater cognitive acoustic network strategy for efficient spectrum utilization," *Applied Acoustics*, vol. 175, p. 107861, 2021.

11. L. Sayigh *et al.*, "The Watkins marine mammal sound database: An online freely accessible resource," Fourth International Conference on the Effects of Noise on Aquatic Life, 2016. doi: 10.1121/2.0000358

12. P. Subramanian, T. Nantha Kumar, and J. Jayashankar, "Underwater wireless sensor networks," *International Journal of Chemical Sciences*, vol. 14, pp. 809–811, 2016.

13. D. Stowell, M. D. Wood, H. Pamuła, Y. Stylianou, H. Glotin, and D. Stowell, "Automatic acoustic detection of birds through deep learning : The first bird audio detection challenge," *Methods in Ecology and Evolution*, vol. 2019, pp. 368–380, 2019.

14. T.-H. Lin, T. Akamatsu, and Y. Tsao, "Sensing ecosystem dynamics via audio source separation : A case study of marine soundscapes off northeastern Taiwan," *PLoS Computational Biology*, vol. 17, pp. 1–23, 2021.

15. L. P. Maia, A. Silva, and S. M. Jesus, "Environmental model-based time-reversal underwater communications," *IEEE Access*, vol. 6, pp. 10041–10051, 2017.

16. J. Fan, F. Tung, W. Li, and P. Pasquier, "Soundscape emotion recognition via deep learning," 15th Sound and Music Computing Conference, 2018.

17. E. Znidersic *et al.*, "Ecological informatics using visualization and machine learning methods to monitor low detectability species: The least Bittern as a case study," *Ecological Informatics*, vol. 55, p. 101014, 2020.

18. D. K. Mellinger and C. W. Clark, "Recognizing transient low-frequency whale sounds by spectrogram correlation," *Journal of the Acoustical Society of America*, vol. 107, no. 6, pp. 3518–3529, 2014.

19. M. Sankupellay, M. Towsey, A. Truskinger, and P. Roe, "The use of acoustic indices to characterise natural habitats," 2015 Big Data Visual Analytics (BDVA), 2015.

20. G. Sharma, K. Umapathy, and S. Krishnan, "Trends in audio signal feature extraction methods," *Applied Acoustics*, vol. 158, p. 107020, 2020.

21. B. Mishachandar and S. Vairamuthu, "An underwater cognitive acoustic network strategy for efficient spectrum utilization," *Applied Acoustics*, vol. 175, p. 107861, 2021.

22. B. Mishachandar and S. Vairamuthu, "A review on underwater acoustic sensor networks: Perspective of Internet of Things," *International Journal of Innovative Technology and Exploring Engineering*, vol. 8, no. 6, pp. 1603–1615, 2019.

Printed in the United States
by Baker & Taylor Publisher Services